SUBURBAN DOMESTIC ARCHITECTURE SERIES

HOUSES OF MISSOURI

1870–1940

Ravenswood, Bel Air, Cooper County, 1880

SUBURBAN DOMESTIC ARCHITECTURE SERIES

HOUSES OF MISSOURI

1870–1940

CYDNEY MILLSTEIN AND CAROL GROVE

FOREWORD BY
RICHARD LONGSTRETH

ACANTHUS PRESS
NEW YORK : 2008

Published by Acanthus Press LLC
54 West 21st Street
New York, New York 10010
800.827.7614
www.acanthuspress.com

Library of Congress Cataloging-in-Publication Data

Millstein, Cydney.
Houses of Missouri, 1870–1940 / by Cydney Millstein and Carol Grove; foreword by Richard Longstreth.
p. cm.
Includes bibliographical references and index.
ISBN 978-0-926494-54-1 (alk. paper)
1. Architecture, Domestic—Missouri. 2. Architecture—Missouri—19th century. 3. Architecture—Missouri—20th century. I. Grove, Carol. II. Title.

NA7235.M8M55 2008
728.09778—dc22
2008015358

Printed in China

SUBURBAN DOMESTIC ARCHITECTURE SERIES

FOR THREE HUNDRED YEARS, Americans have sought to fulfill the promise of a better life that a rich wilderness held out to the first settlers as they stepped onto the shores of the North Atlantic. The American engagement with a vast continent has been defined by the necessary development and expansion of cities and the simultaneous preservation and enjoyment of a bucolic countryside.

The Acanthus Press series, Suburban Domestic Architecture, presents landmark domestic buildings of the last two centuries that display the innovative housing solutions of Americans and their architects as they addressed their desires for the ideal domestic life.

Contents

APPENDICES

ACKNOWLEDGMENTS

Houses of Missouri 1870–1940 brings together hundreds of documents and photographs from public and private collections across the state and beyond. For helping gather these materials and making our work possible, the following research institutions and libraries and their staff have our sincere appreciation: Ellen Thomasson and Dwayne Sneadicker of the Missouri Historical Society Research Library; Christine Montgomery and Sara Przybylski of the State Historical Society of Missouri; Nancy Green at Linda Hall Library; Suzy Frechette and Tim Willman of the St. Louis Public Library; David Boutros, Melissa Slaton, and Cynthia Toliver of the Western Historical Manuscript Collection, WHMC-Kansas City; Peter McCarthy and Bill Stolz of WHMC-Columbia; and Zelli Fischetti of WHMC-St. Louis. Special thanks to the State Historical Society of Missouri, director Gary Kremer, and the Richard S. Brownlee fund.

We also wish to thank Sonya McDonald and Miranda Rectenwald of Washington University Archives; Adrienne Brennecke at the Washington University Art and Architecture Library; Bryan McDaniel of the Chicago History Museum; Rebecca Rich-Wulfmeyer of the Albany [New York] Institute of History & Art; Nathaniel Parks at the Ryerson & Burnham Archives (Art Institute of Chicago); Laura R. Jolley at the Missouri State Archives; Chris Ludwig and the staff of the St. Louis County Department of Parks & Recreation; and the staff of the Missouri Valley Special Collections at the Kansas City Public Library, especially Mary Beveridge, Sara Nyman, Sherrie Kline Smith, and Jeremy Drouin. Christopher Leitch and Denise Morrison at the Kansas City Museum and Brad Wolf and Heather Gilbride of the Kansas City Landmarks Commission also provided invaluable time and assistance.

In addition, many thanks to Marilyn Carbonell and Roberta Wagener of the Spencer Art Reference Library at the Nelson-Atkins Museum of Art; Kelly McEniry at the Kenneth J. LaBudde Department of Special Collections at the Miller-Nichols Library, University of Missouri-Kansas City; the reference department at Mid-Continent Public Library, Independence, Missouri; Michele Hansford at the Powers Museum, Carthage, Missouri; Joel Rhodes at Southeast Missouri State University; Patty Crane at the Joplin Public Library; Leslie Simpson of the Post Memorial Art Reference Library of Joplin and Linda Vorce, manager of the University of Missouri Digitizing Services; the reference staff at the Pusey Library, Harvard University; and Douglas Doe and Andrew Martinez at the Fleet Library, Rhode Island School of Design. We also appreciate the research and publications of the Landmarks Association of St. Louis under the directorship of Carolyn Hewes Toft. The authors are particularly grateful to Christopher Marsden for his critical assistance with the photographic collection of the Historic American Buildings Survey (HABS), which was invaluable.

Individuals affiliated with historical societies who assisted us include archivist Sue Rehkopf of the Historical Society of University City; Daffany Jefferies of the Camden County Historical Society; Donna Ayers and George Morgenweck of the Macon County Historical Society, with special thanks to Billy Franke and Merlyn Amidei; Frank Salter of the Friends of Historic Hannibal; and Donald Jackson of the Jackson County Historical Society.

At the State Historic Preservation Office of Missouri we thank director Mark Miles; historic preservation specialist Kris Zapalac; Kerry Nichols, cultural resource inventory coordinator; and especially Tiffany Patterson, National Register coordinator. Deserving special thanks to Bothwell Lodge State Historic site administrator Jill White, and Marissa Cowen and Charles Wise, who went out of their way to help with this project. We are grateful to the following preservation consultants, whose work has helped document so much of Missouri's important architecture: Karen Bode Baxter of St. Louis; Terry Foley and Jeanette Juden of Cape Girardeau; and Dr. Sherry Piland of Springfield, who for years expertly chronicled so many of the architectural landmarks and architects of Kansas City's past.

To the hundreds of individuals who passed along vital (and many times, obscure) information and photographs, to those who had us over for coffee and met us for lunch to talk about the why and how of the subject, we are in your debt. This group includes architectural historian, preservationist, and mentor Osmund Overby; Cole Woodcox of Truman State University; writer and architectural critic Bob Duffy; Barbara Fitzgerald, executive director of the Missouri Alliance for Historic Preservation; and Lake of the Ozarks historian Dwight Weaver. Also included here are Mary H. Gass, Chris Kirmaier, Mike Stephens, president of Parkview Agents, and especially Judy Little and Mrs. O. B. Hirsch of the Parkview neighborhood; Stockstrom house owner Shelley Donaho and assistant Ann Stanley; Jim Human, Barry Cervantes, and John and Robin Porta, all of Westmoreland Place; Beverly Bowman of County Blue Reprographics; St. Louis photographer Robert Pettus; Rick Rose and Heather Pfeifer of Rockcliffe Mansion; Wardwell Buckner of the Lafayette Park Conservancy; Greg Silkman and Melanie Peterson in campus facilities management at the University of Missouri-Kansas City; Meghan Nichols of the research library at the *Kansas City Star;* Doug Boe of River Bluff Architects, St. Joseph, Missouri; the staff and volunteers at the Vaile Mansion-DeWitt Museum, Independence, Missouri; Wendy Shay, historic preservation manager, City of Independence; and Scott DesPlanques, historic preservation planner with the City of St. Joseph. Thanks also to our project assistants Monica Anderson, Mary Ann Warfield, Soodie Beasley, and Len Fohn. A tip of the hat to Steve Bridgens, Mary Corneil, Elisabeth Kirsch, and Dorothy Slegman, listeners extraordinaire, day and night. And for John, always.

We are greatly indebted to Richard Longstreth for lending his authority to this project. We owe a special thanks to all at Acanthus Press, particularly Barry Cenower and Carla Sakamoto, for believing in us. Without the decades of research and the help of Esley Hamilton, preservation historian at the St. Louis County Department of Parks & Recreation, this book would be lacking. His contribution and participation were vital to the process.

Lastly, we are grateful to the Missourians whose homes are included here, particularly those who opened their houses and histories to us. Many of you handed over plans and photographs with the faith of a saint; we thank you sincerely. You are gentle reminders that the finest architecture is about not only brick and stone and wood, or the form and style these materials take, but about the people who envision and who live within it.

FOREWORD

I WAS INTRODUCED to some of the houses appearing in this volume more than 40 years ago when I was a freshman at the University of Pennsylvania. Nosing through the formidable collection of volumes in the university's architecture library, I discovered a substantial tome entitled *Missouri's Contribution to American Architecture*, published by the St. Louis Architectural Club in 1928. It was in part a vanity book depicting a generous selection of recent work, but a large portion of its content was devoted to presenting, for the first time, a historical record of building design in that state since the inception of white settlement.

That summer of 1965, I had the opportunity to drive through much of the Midwest and upland South to examine buildings in those regions firsthand. My journey extended to St. Louis, where the immense houses lining Portland, Westmoreland, and other private streets were a primary destination. Proceeding south along the Mississippi, I saw Selma Hall and Greystone, among other dwellings. The experience brought home the rich array of architecture the state has to offer. Since then, I have visited St. Louis, Kansas City, and many other Missouri communities on numerous occasions, and they have never disappointed me.

All too often, however, Missouri and other states in the American heartland are still cast in stereotypical terms that greatly oversimplify and in other ways distort the historical record. Missouri's architectural legacy seldom enters the larger arena of discussion, save a few landmarks, most notably Adler & Sullivan's Wainwright Building and Eero Saarinen's Gateway Arch in St. Louis, and recently, Steven Holl's additions to the Nelson-Atkins Museum of Art in Kansas City. Urban historians widely acknowledge as benchmarks in modern planning the extensive park system in Kansas City, whose development began at the turn of the 20th century, and J. C. Nichols' extraordinary Country Club District that developed over the succeeding 50 years. But for the most part, Missouri remains ignored by those outside the region who have an interest in the built environment, professional or otherwise.

Missouri was never, of course, on the cutting edge of architectural design in the residential or any other sphere, save the schools designed by William B. Ittner, which established new national standards in the early 20th century. There was no locally based Richard Morris Hunt or Stanford White, for example—no Charles Platt or Wilson Eyre, no Bernard Maybeck or Greene brothers, no Richard Neutra or Pietro Belluschi. If they wanted a house that was exceptional, some Missourians commissioned prominent architects from the East Coast or elsewhere, including Henry Hobson Richardson and Frank Lloyd Wright.

But such circumstances should not invite dismissal. Much can be learned from the houses built in Missouri over the past century and a half. For one thing, the record clearly demonstrates that the population of St. Louis was becoming sufficiently wealthy and sophisticated to attract architects of considerable ability by the 1850s. During the decades that followed, a high level of professional performance began to emerge in other urban centers, most notably St. Joseph and Kansas City. The decision by the distinguished Boston architect, Henry Van Brunt, to relocate in Kansas City during the early 1880s had a major impact on local architecture; it also reflected the rapid maturation of the state's urban centers. By the early 20th century, Barnett, Haynes & Barnett; Eames & Young; James Jamieson; and Mauran & Russell of St. Louis, as well as Henry F. Hoit, Edward W. Tanner, and Wight & Wight of Kansas City were all prominent figures in the dissemination of accomplished design. Documenting the extent of this accomplishment was a major objective of the St. Louis Architectural Club's lavish tome of the late 1920s. Missouri may never have been a crucible for major innovation, but it has long produced work that collectively affords an instructive representation of broad patterns in American architecture.

The state has also harbored strains of pronounced individualism. The highly pictorial style of Harvey Ellis, working for Eckel & Mann in St. Joseph during the late 19th century, gives evidence to that tendency, as do the personal interpretations of prevailing modes apparent in the work somewhat later of Kansas City architects Frederick Hill and John W. McKecknie. Louis Curtiss, also based in Kansas City, developed an unusually strong style of his own by 1910, idiosyncratically and engagingly drawing from both the examples of Wright and his followers and from the Jugendstil in central Europe. Beginning in the late 1930s, William Adair Bernoudy developed distinctive variations on Wright's Usonian houses for his work in suburban St. Louis. Clients could demand breaks from convention from architects otherwise disinclined to do so, as can be seen in the exhibitionistic display of Wrightian and Viennese Secession motifs in J. W. Thompson's St. Louis house or Walter Bixby's suave, streamlined residence in Kansas City.

With few exceptions, the authors have selected the work of Missouri architects rather than that of often more famous practitioners from elsewhere, so that readers can glean a clear sense of the local record from the pages that follow. They also reveal that even though the great majority of examples here were built in urban centers, few possess true urban character either in their imagery or settings. Architects tended to turn to country houses for models far more than to their counterparts in town—a preference that typified work through much of the Midwest and in a number of other parts of the nation as well. To enhance architectural form and character, many of these houses were developed as miniature rural estates even when situated within the city limits.

There is also illustration of the urge to build true country houses, not as part of an enclave, as on the North Shore of Long Island or along Philadelphia's Main Line, but in places quite isolated from any others of their ilk. Such landscape characteristics are likewise indicative of broader American preferences among those who could afford to pursue them. In several respects, then, the dwellings in this book represent more of an American mainstream than comparable examples in, say, New York, Boston, or San Francisco. Missouri deserves our attention.

—Richard Longstreth

INTRODUCTION

A VISITOR TO MISSOURI in the 19th century described it as "neither east nor west nor north nor south." For much of that century, it served chiefly as the gateway to somewhere else, funneling thousands of travelers to the western frontier. Before the Louisiana Purchase it was a territory under French, then Spanish, then French control again. Missouri was a border state during the Civil War, pulled in both directions over the issue of slavery, culminating in the Missouri Compromise.

Even today in politics the state defies a convincingly "red" or "blue" categorization. Missouri has been defined and redefined by its many inhabitants, who are likely to be German or French, black or white, Jewish or Catholic. It is home to anonymous farmers who till 30 million acres of land (two-thirds of the state) and has been home to well-known visionaries like William Rockhill Nelson, the legendary founder of *The Kansas City Star,* who championed civic beauty and bestowed that city its now famous Nelson-Atkins Museum of Art, and Robert S. Brookings, creator of the Brookings Institution, the political think tank in Washington, D.C. Inhabitants' contributions over time have engendered rich cultural patterns that overlap and sometimes mingle. Missouri, it seems, has no distinct provenance, but rather one woven together from many histories. This tug upon, and ever-changing nature of, what Missourians call home has without doubt contributed to the character of its residents and the built environment.

As director of the Missouri Historical Society in 1946, Charles van Ravenswaay wrote that it is harder to define Missourians than it is to define Missouri. Claiming that "attempts to sum Missouri up in one pat phrase have always failed," he described its people as a conservative bunch who live well and dislike ostentation.[1] Missourians believe in hard work, owning their own homes, and tolerating their neighbors. "They seldom lose their sense of humor or their sense of proportion, and are consequently slow to take up fads or to join radical movements." They are at once solid and traditional, eclectic and innovative. These observations reflect Congressman Willard Vandiver's speech of 50 years prior avowing that "frothy eloquence neither convinces nor satisfies" Missourians; they insist that "you have got to show me."

Missouri may be geographically and ideologically in the middle but, perhaps due to its history of flux, there is little consensus among its citizens; they are divided in their opinions. Its populace considered either fragmented or diverse, this contradictory characteristic is manifest in its architecture. As Van Ravenswaay notes, a Missourian's home may be functionally modern, a stately Greek-Revival mansion with a temple front, a French chateau, or a sturdy German brick building set "flush with the sidewalk." No single style dominated between 1870 and 1940, and no particular ideology inspired Missouri's architects and patrons.

Selma Hall, Jefferson County, ca. 1855 (renovated 1939)

Generally speaking, people on the east side of Missouri tended to build in brick and on the west, in limestone. Well-to-do Kansas Citians named their houses; their counterparts in St. Louis did not. Kansas City developed from a comprehensive and visionary master plan that gave order to its growth; St. Louis grew organically as a patchwork of discrete neighborhoods and "private places." Those in the southern regions and along the rivers situated their houses at the edges of bluffs in contrast to owners in Kansas City, who built on vast acreage not far from downtown. Those in the east preferred natural landscapes, whereas residents in the west commissioned formal grounds. Westerners made their money from infrastructure and materials, easterners from products that often became household names; in between, vernacular traditions persisted, and farming-related activities—corn and cattle—were key to the economy.

Characterizing the state by region, there are at least four. The eastern region, along the Mississippi River, was the first established, and many people still view it as southern in its tendencies. Fields and close-knit communities make up the central and northern parts of the state; the southwest borders on the Ozark Plateau and has a distinctly different geography. For many, Kansas City and St. Joseph evoke barbecue and the Pony Express and a lingering ideological link with the West. In St. Louis and its surrounding county, taste and expression vary by neighborhood; the city behaves more like a cluster of diverse, discrete communities lying in proximity rather than a civic whole. Straddling the state line and evolving from the strict grid pattern of its city core, Kansas City advanced east and south to become a metropolis of winding, tree-lined boulevards that follow the natural topography, where new and wide-ranging subdivisions intertwine.

Despite the differences within Missouri, architectural trends that were evolving on a national level around 1900 were evident in the state's architecture and planning. Missouri's buildings were often written about in *Western Architect, Inland Architect,* and *Brickbuilder.* In the first decade of the 20th century, *Architectural Record* had a regular report on Missouri projects, covering the community planning work of Henry Wright in St. Louis and J. C. Nichols in Kansas City, the increased interest in context on the part of architects and owners, and architecture's new freedom from constraint that created a wealth of styles in the early 20th century, some without precedent. Although Missouri architecture was at times innovative, the suburban ideal was highly regarded, and it persisted.

In general, Missourians who could afford to do so moved away from the civic hub to neighborhoods that were the visual manifestation of domestic pride and ownership. In 1903 *National Magazine* aptly recognized that certain neighborhoods were successful because the city "had *planned* for its homes," resulting in a worthy environment. One year later, in a January article for *Brickbuilder,* architect John Lawrence Mauran commented on the move toward suburban living, noting that:

> not far from the business center of St. Louis, in the rolling country to the west . . . at a point easily reached by both trains and trolley and intersected by one of the fine state roads . . . a goodly number of sensible moneyed men of the city have established their homes and settled down to enjoy the good and simple things of this life, away from the noise, dirt, and heat of the metropolis.

The houses they built represent a range of architectural styles as varied as their owners. The following pages illustrate the Flemish Queen Anne, French Eclectic, Italian Renaissance, and others, along with such unique styles as "Brewer's Baronial."

• • •

The suburban tradition that evolved in America in the 19th century had, at its core, the single family house. That tradition can be traced in part to A. J. Downing and his belief in the home as the anchor of human activity; Downing regarded the home as a symbol of one's character and pursuits. He believed that all individuals deserve a tasteful and appropriate house and grounds regardless of their status or wealth. Along the rivers and in wooded enclaves around St. Louis lie many such houses representing this suburban ideal. One 19th-century observer noted that "as the ridges rise from the river, so rise the grades of social status."[2] Ultimately those with the highest status would gravitate out beyond the ridges into the countryside. Wealthy families were the first St. Louisans to build homes there, embracing the pastoral surroundings for their second homes, often to escape the summer heat, in places such as Chouteau's Pond to the south and Florissant in North County. Among these prominent citizens were Louis Auguste Benoist and the Chambers family, who named their estates Oaklands and Taille de Noyer, respectively.

The city's population doubled between 1850 and 1860 to over 160,000—the city would remain the fourth largest in the country for many years—and inhabitants pressed to the outer reaches to escape the

East gate of Vandeventer Place, St. Louis, ca. 1880

consequent coal smoke, crime, and disease. To avoid these "nuisances" and to enjoy the civilizing effect of nature so crucial in the 19th century, the well-to-do, and later the middle class, demanded houses and grounds that would separate them from what was becoming a crowded urban core.

In fleeing encroachment and the city's other negative aspects, the wealthy led the way by moving to a series of "places," or private streets, each one a step further removed from the city than the one prior. Each move provided a temporary solution to the problem of maintaining a genteel way of life in a growing metropolis. Swallowed up fairly quickly by development were such early private places as Lucas Place (1851) and Benton Place (1866). Civil engineer Julius Pitzman, who worked on the plan for Forest Park with Maximillian G. Kern and Theodore Link (et al.) in 1876, is responsible for many of St. Louis's finest private places—he invented them and they are unique to the city—including Vandeventer Place (1870). Until about 1910, it was the grandest of the early examples, most of which were linear in arrangement, with houses lining long streets shaded by center parkways often ornamented with sculpture and fountains. Vandeventer Place had deed restrictions mandating that owners have basement kitchens and multiple curtains at the windows, and that they scrub the steps weekly. But even these covenants, coupled with the money and class that backed them, couldn't keep the noise, crime, and growth along the nearby commercial corridor from eroding living conditions. After only a few decades, with increased connectivity by means of the railroad and streetcars, the distance between the neighborhood's inhabitants and those less privileged was diminished, necessitating a move. As a result, a sort of elite caravan ensued, made up of the privileged families of St. Louis, including the Pierces, the Lionbergers, and the Mallinckrodts. All moved from one formerly great private place to the next. The wealthiest families would live in two or three of the best of such neighborhoods over a lifetime.[3] As the century progressed, this procession would become larger and more middle class, yet all were bound, in part, by their desire for the suburban ideal.

Lafayette Park, St. Louis, ca. 1872

Private places are unique in their organization, which is why some of the finest, such as Portland and Westmoreland Places (also planned by Julius Pitzman) continue to exist.[4] Closed to through traffic, these private streets are the property of the owners rather than the city; a board of trustees oversees them. Control lies in enforcing deed restrictions rather than municipal codes, and owners share responsibility for services and maintenance. In the early 20th century, new developments such as Carrswold and Brentmoor Park, employed a variety of approaches to organization and upkeep. However, covenants and restrictions continued to dictate the size and type of structure (Carrswold allowed no California bungalows, for instance), the construction materials used, and the landscaping. In Carrswold, landscape architect Jens Jensen dictated using native plants and shrouding the main drive with trees to ensure a sense of privacy. Other remarkable projects in the county followed, such as University Hills and Parkview, both near Washington University; the latter is an upper-middle-class neighborhood smaller in scale than Carrswold and so well planned it remains a highly desirable place to live today. The exodus that began in the mid-19th century was perhaps complete with the construction of Pasadena Hills northwest of the city. The last of the private place models, Pasadena Hills was built in 1929 as an automobile suburb. Its planning emulated the countryside and offered residents their choice of Revival-style architecture and a garden spot amid rolling grounds graced by cool breezes.[5]

There were a number of adaptations of the private street that advanced the concept of suburban living in St. Louis, the county, and beyond. Although not strictly private, the neighborhood bordering Lafayette Park (1832) was an early example of living outside the city proper and adjacent to art and nature, promoting the idea that "life toward the flowers is pleasanter than toward the dust," and by association communicating a more refined sensibility on the part of its owners. The later West Cabanne Place (1888) embodied an East Coast idiom that combined the informality of Shingle-style houses on large lots with deep setbacks that created great green sweeps of lawn in front. An advertisement for West Cabanne Place circa 1887 touted it as the ideal suburban home—a private street without dust or heavy traffic. The corner Henry S. Potter house, designed by H. H. Richardson in 1886, with its sheathing of wood shingles, was the model for all building in the neighborhood (the house would later be lived in by architect Ernest J Russell, of the firm Mauran, Russell & Garden, before being demolished in 1958). West Cabanne Place was confirmation that not only was the trend to move out into the country, but that both architects and a new group of clients, no longer only the very wealthy, were taking part. This drift toward suburban living made possible by the railroad also produced the commuter suburbs of Kirkwood and Webster Groves, advertised as "Queen of the Suburbs" in 1892, in South County.

Compton Heights in St. Louis may be the best example of a neighborhood shaped by a full understanding of the suburban ideal. Although announcement of an 1854 land auction heralded plans for this "suburb . . . adorned with beautiful cottages, ornamental grounds, gardens, and fine avenues," it would be more than 30 years before real growth—and true appreciation for what constituted the suburban ideal—came about. Julius Pitzman (who happened to live there) made improvements to the project in 1888, reflecting contemporary currents in landscaping and community planning on a national level by weaving park spaces and curving roads ("two gigantic outlines of the letter S") into the existing tract of land, creating a picturesque effect that complemented the view of the remaining prairie to the west and the city to the north. The following year, a St. Louis *Globe-Democrat* article on Compton Heights entitled,"The Suburban Ideal: How It Is Improving and Beautifying the City," commented on progress there.

Compton Heights was only one of some 40 projects in which Julius Pitzman was involved. Representative of the civil engineers, planners, and landscape architects who shaped city and county, Pitzman is a key figure in transforming the original common fields and prairies that spread from the river and platting them into neighborhoods. Others who contributed to the process during this period include Henry Shaw, Almerin Hotchkiss, Ernest Bowditch, Warren Manning, Frederick Law Olmsted, Henry Wright, Jens Jensen, and John Noyes. Collectively, their designs and plantings shaped the landscape, first into linear plans with shaded boulevards, and later into sophisticated arrangements of green space and vistas, with houses relating to one another and to the general context. Their history and contributions deserve further attention.

• • •

Kansas City, like St. Louis, experienced a drastic increase in population beginning in 1870, after the Civil War; by 1880, Kansas City's population had risen from 25,000 to 55,000. In just another five years, the population swelled to 100,000. Housing, of course, was an immediate concern, and the preference was for detached single-family residences. Even before the Civil War, Kansas City's elite chose to reside on some of the highest elevated terrain above the Missouri River—Quality Hill—where the landscape consisted of elegant mansions, wide lawns, and pastures for grazing cattle.

Unlike the private places of St. Louis, Quality Hill was not a gated community. It developed quickly nonetheless as a prestigious suburb, a haven for the wealthy, by dint of its proximity to Kansas City's commercial and business district and its natural seclusion. The influx of railroad, meatpacking, and merchant money contributed to the quiet elegance of life on Quality Hill, which was distinguished by brick arches leading to private places *and* ways with names like Tullis, Aldine, and Hasbrook (named for Charles Hasbrook, the editor of *The Kansas City Times*). One of the first to build an elaborate mansion here was Dr. Johnston Lykins, a staunch Unionist and former mayor of Kansas City, who in 1856 chose the plot at the corner of Ottawa (now 12th) Street and Washington Avenue.

Other first-generation residents included meatpacking mogul Kirkland B Armour and Kersey Coates, who saw the area's potential for development and platted Coates's Addition, centered around 10th and Pennsylvania. By placing a restriction in his deeds to build exclusively in brick, Coates was successful in shunning modestly constructed homes built of inferior materials.[6] His own residence, located at the heart of Coates's Addition, was "a showplace, distinctively ornate with its captain's walk atop its flat roof, wide chimneys, and shaded piazza on the northeast corner."[7] During the real estate boom of the 1880s, Quality Hill reached its pinnacle of social dominance, but by the first years of the 20th century, the "last of the distinguished original residents left," making their way south to the more fashionable neighborhood of Hyde Park and later, the Country Club District. One provoking factor was the considerable stench wafting up from the ever-expanding stockyards. Coates's vision, if indeed he had one, did not sustain, for Quality Hill's original architectural and social aura was lost.

Outside the Kansas City city limits when it was developed in 1886, Hyde Park was a ravine within the Town of Westport. George Edward Kessler, the landscape architect hired by Samuel Jarvis and C. C. Conklin, financial backers of this new suburb, later transformed it into an exclusive locale to draw new homeowners. Kessler's attraction, which embraced the natural topography, was coveted; "residents became so obsessed with privacy that they put up an iron fence with locked gates, to which only subscribing residents could obtain keys."[8] Wealthy Kansas Citians, several of whom had moved from Quality Hill, chose prominent architects, most of local renown, to design their mansions here. Former Bostonian Henry van Brunt and his partner Frank Maynard Howe, fostered the area's prestige with their plans for the Armour and Smith family residences, as did Stanford White's plan for T. H. Mastin's. Even van Brunt himself chose to live in this elite neighborhood.[9]

The sole private residential plan within Kansas City was that for Janssen Place. Arthur Stilwell, who had made his home in the Hyde Park area, envisioned a restricted, controlled development to be modeled after Pitzman's Vandeventer, Portland, and Westmoreland Places in St. Louis. Unlike its St. Louis prototypes, Janssen Place was slow to catch on, possibly because of its imposed limitations and Stilwell's financial problems. Within nine years of its inception in 1897, the remaining lots in Janssen Place were titled to W. P. Patton, and by 1917, architecturally significant homes, most of masonry in revival idioms, filled the two-block neighborhood.[10]

Kansas City's leaders also claimed stretches of Independence and Troost avenues and McKinney Heights, high on the bluffs overlooking the Missouri River Valley. With the exception of McKinney Heights, the grand estates in these locations—some designed by nationally known architects like Burnham & Root in the Romanesque Revival style—no longer exist, and portions of these major early thoroughfares have been transformed into a rambling mash of residential husks and commercial boxes.

The insights of William Rockhill Nelson, George Edward Kessler, and J. C. Nichols produced the most important innovations in Kansas City's planning. Collectively these dynamic individuals imparted a remarkable consistency to the city, a framework for development that preserved and enhanced the natural beauty of the landscape and coordinated urban growth. Nelson, publisher of *The Kansas City Star,* not only single-handedly developed the Rockhill District (another fashionable neighborhood not far from his residence, Oak Hall), but through his incessant editorializing, promoted the idea of a comprehensive parks and boulevard system. Kessler, acquainted with Nelson and August R. Meyer (Nelson's neighbor) through his work in Hyde Park, was eventually appointed by the Kansas City park board to prepare perhaps the "most complete example [ever] of a comprehensive city plan."[11] Kessler's assessment of Kansas City, published in 1893 as the first parks board report, "appeared at what is generally considered the beginning of the City Beautiful Movement,"[12] and his plan anticipated the city's growth south of 31st Street and east of Cleveland Avenue, then the city limits.

Inspired by the work of Nelson and Kessler, Nichols began acquiring property for his large-scale residential and commercial development—the Country Club District—in 1907, with financial backing from friends. It was apparent that Nichols got his cue from Nelson's Rockhill development; he took advantage of the route of Rockhill Road leading into the eastern section of his initial land purchase. Almost concurrently, Kessler recommended that a parkway be established in the southern portion of Kansas City, along the western side (near the state line). Named Ward Parkway after Hugh Ward, this thoroughfare is divided by an expansive green median strip embellished with a wide variety of flowers and trees and fountains, mirror pools, and European objets d'art that Nichols donated to the city. It is along the northern end of Ward Parkway, aptly called the Gold Coast, where we find several examples of the *Houses of Missouri*.

Janssen Place, Kansas City

At the time Kessler commenced his planning in cooperation with Ward and Nichols, the entire area that would become known as the Country Club District, served by Ward Parkway, was south of the city limits. Comprising mostly unimproved land, the area appeared to the Kansas City real estate profession on the whole to have little potential. It was Nichols' imagination, supported by Ward's financial backing and Kessler's design expertise, that transformed these farmlands and hillsides into the most desirable residential section in the city.[13]

By 1908, in just one year, Nichols had gained control of a thousand acres, (including a portion in neighboring Mission Hills, Kansas), solely for residential purposes. Like Baltimore's Roland Park, developed by Edward Bouton and planned by Frederick Law Olmsted, the Country Club District carried deed restrictions, including that of race; Nichols believed this would ensure stability and an air of quality to his enterprise. To his credit, Nichols had the foresight to hire the landscape architecture firm of Hare & Hare in 1913 for subdivision planning, and many of the individual homeowners hired the father and son team to design their spacious grounds. It was for this excellent choice, among others, that the Country Club District has been recognized as "one of the finest residential sections in the United States."[14]

Unlike Kansas City, St. Joseph did not experience continued economic and population expansion throughout the early decades of the 20th century; the city's greatest prosperity occurred from the 1880s through 1900, when the population rose from approximately 32,400 to 52,320. Elaborate single-family residences like those of Hall Street and the Harris Addition reflect St. Joseph's heyday, the golden age fueled by the city's river trade, banking and wholesaling interests, and meatpacking houses. And, as in Kansas City, there was strong momentum for the upper class to relocate to the hilly terrain surrounding the central business district in the city's original location. Promoters claimed that the "hills rising behind

Advertisement for J. C. Nichols' Country Club District, Kansas City

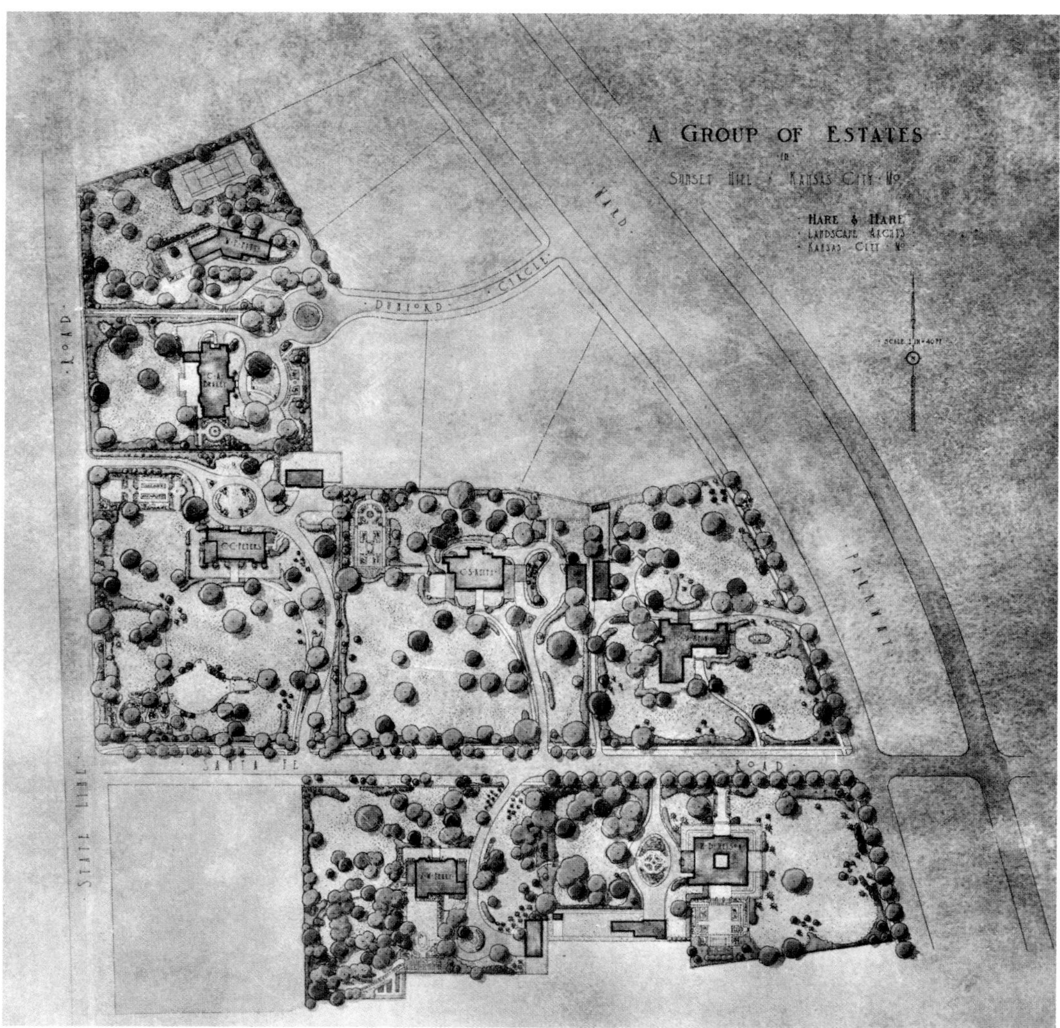

Sunset Hill site plan for a group of estates by Hare & Hare, Kansas City

the business portion of the city offered admirable sites for the location of private residences, with tasteful grounds overlooking the beautiful and broad river, with the hills of Kansas beyond, over all of which the glow of the Western sun casts a halo of almost matchless magnificence and glory."[15]

In the Harris Addition, now listed in the National Register of Historic Places, stately homes had frontages greater than 50 feet. The H. E. Barnard house, built in 1878 in the Italianate tradition, the Queen Anne–style R. T. Davis house, designed in 1890 by Joseph Bennett, and six properties by the nationally recognized architect Edmond J. Eckel and his various partners demonstrate the strong impulse to build imposing expressions of wealth. This is likewise true of the late 19th-century houses ranging along the 600–800 blocks of Hall Street, high on the crest of the bluffs. Flamboyant houses built of opulent materials, such as the Italianate Farber-Schuster-Farrish house by L. S. Stigers and the Romanesque Revival A. Smith house by Eckel & Mann are also listed in the National Register for their historic and architectural significance.

Undoubtedly influenced by Kessler's work in Kansas City, civic leaders in St. Joseph saw the benefit of developing a parks and boulevard system that would limit idle growth and lend cohesiveness to the outlying neighborhoods. Springing initially from a small but persistent grassroots effort that lead to the hiring of city planner and journalist Charles Mulford Robinson, followed by Kessler, Percival Gallagher of the Olmsted Brothers firm, George Burnap, and others, St. Joseph implemented a comprehensive system of parks and boulevards, a plan that took more than 14 years to initiate.[16] While a far-reaching scheme, it differed greatly from Kansas City's in that subsequent development did not occur until the plan was completed during the close of the 1920s. Furthermore, the architecture born of the suburban growth stimulated by establishing the system provides a distinct contrast to that of Kansas City, where elaborate residences were set in formal grounds.

With few exceptions, residential architecture in Independence, the seat of Jackson County, is not typically the grand, imposing designs of leading architects, nor was it built in outlying areas to create a distinct suburban tradition. In this place, there was not a deliberate, collective effort to escape the city and build lasting registers of lives of opulence. Most of what we see is allied with the modest local tastes and entrenched conservative socioeconomic outlook.

Once a starting point for the Santa Fe, Oregon, and California trails, the pattern of residential development in Independence is most closely associated with that in the immediate vicinity of the Harry S. Truman residence, which remains "one of the earlier and architecturally more substantial [residences] in the area."[17] Other standout examples include the Queen Anne–style Hughes Childers house designed by the local firm of Gibbs & Parker, the Porter Chiles house designed in the Second Empire tradition in 1860, and the Bingham Waggoner estate, an Italianate residence originally constructed in 1855 on 19 acres. Artist George Caleb Bingham owned the property from 1864 to 1870. While residing here, Bingham painted *Order Number Eleven,* one of his most controversial works.

Lee's Summit, located southeast of Kansas City and 14 miles south of Independence, had a deeply agrarian foundation. Poultry, dairy, cattle, crop, and orchard farms proliferated in the landscape, while single-family residences in and around the original town plat were slow to materialize. Owing to sluggish population growth (between 1880 and 1940 the town grew from 900 to just over 2,200 residences), "early additions remained available for new houses for decades, not just a few years."[18] From the late 1800s through the early decades of the 20th century, architecture in Lee's Summit remained modest in scale and design. The majority of late 19th-century residences, placed parallel with the railroad line that slices through the center of downtown, were styled in the National Folk tradition, followed by moderately scaled and appointed vernacular variations of more sophisticated designs. It wasn't until the close of World War II that the outer fringes of Lee's Summit saw the construction of new residential neighborhoods.

• • •

In 1875 visitor Edward King observed that "the passion for suburban residences is fast taking possession of the citizens of St. Louis,"[19] but his comment could in truth have described the enthusiasm evident all over the state. For example, the Harris house, a "suburban villa" illustrated in a circa-1876 state atlas, represents just such a place at the edge of the small town of Kirksville, a farming community in the north central part of the state. Around the town of Eolia, near Hannibal, off the Great River Road that winds along the Mississippi, one can find a number of such houses in a landscape once covered with apple orchards and described as "a haze of pale pink" in spring. In Carthage, a town in the far southwest corner of the state known for marble mining, Cassill Park provided a remarkably refined sweep of green space as

Dunford Way—a secluded pedestrian walkway, Kansas City

the setting for a number of its fine houses. Still other examples can be found across the state, some near small towns and others now in the middle of the large cities that have grown up around them.

The suburban ideal is a fluid concept, at once broad and specific. Encompassing a boundless range of architectural styles, the choice communicates the owner's personality and concept of home. The ideal reflects changes in taste and style over time and by region, and its definition has been worked and reworked. When the palatial houses of the 19th century seemed too large and ostentatious for early 20th-century sensibilities, the concept was assessed once again. As the ideal has changed, so have the spaces themselves; what once lay on the edge of a city is now more likely in the very midst, as seen, for example, at Marburg, August Meyer's house, once adrift on vast acreage, is now the nucleus of the Kansas City Art Institute campus. In Missouri, suburban residences run the gamut: one finds traditional neoclassical architecture that appeals to many and the occasional idiosyncratic fantasy that, it seems, could fit only the taste of a particular individual.

Our goal is to document here some of the best examples of Missouri's historic suburban architecture and to shed light on the families who resided there. We also look at the architects and designers who planned these stately country houses in cooperation with an array of personalities who, for the most part, shaped their communities as much as did the houses they built. Our choices were dictated by the limits of available archival material and, as such, reveal the architectural history of the state within these parameters.

NOTES

1 Charles van Ravenswaay, *Missouri: Heart of a Nation*, exhibition catalog of the Scruggs-Vandervoort-Barney Department Store collection (1946), 9.

2 Edward King, *The Great South: A Record of Journeys in Louisiana, Texas, the Indian Territory, Missouri, Arkansas, Mississippi, Alabama, Georgia, Florida, South Carolina, North Carolina, Kentucky, Tennessee, Virginia, West Virginia, and Maryland*. Reprint. (New York: Burt Franklin, 1969), 1:217. Hereafter cited as King, *The Great South*.

3 Isaac Lionberger's comment that "progress has been accompanied by horrid waste," implies his understanding that the move onward and upward left huge houses to languish, unsuitable for people with smaller purses. As quoted in James Neal Primm, *Lion of the Valley: St. Louis, Missouri, 1764–1980*. 3rd ed. (St. Louis: Missouri Historical Society Press, 1998), 345.

4 The definitive work on the subject is Julius Hunter and Esley Hamilton, *Westmoreland and Portland Places: The History and Architecture of America's Premier Private Streets, 1888–1988*. (Columbia, MO: University of Missouri Press, 1988).

5 Karen Bode Baxter, Pasadena Hills National Register of Historic Places Nomination, Sept. 2004.

6 William S. Worley. *J. C. Nichols and the Shaping of Kansas City*. (Columbia, MO: University of Missouri Press, 1990), 43.

7 Henry Van Brunt. "Eastern Culture at Home on Quality Hill." *The Kansas City Star*, June 4, 1950. *See also* Clifford Naysmith, "Quality Hill: The History of a Neighborhood." Kansas City, MO, 1962, 1. Paper at WHMC. Naysmith states that Van Brunt "relied heavily on the research and recollections of Pierre R. Porter."

8 Worley: 53. *See also* Joan Michalak, Hyde Park Historic District National Register of Historic Places Nomination, Nov. 1980.

9 Frank Maynard Howe, "The Development of Architecture in Kansas City, Missouri." *The Architectural Record* 15 (February 1904), 153.

10 Victoria Karel and Edward J. Miszczuk. Janssen Place National Register of Historic Places Nomination, Sept. 1975. Landmarks Commission, City Hall, Kansas City, MO.

11 Tourbier & Walmsley Inc., Architectural & Historical Research, LLC, and Theis Doolittle Associates. Landscape Architectural/Historic Survey of Parks and Boulevards, 1893–1940. Kansas City, MO. Prepared for the Board of Parks and Recreation Commissioners, Kansas City, and the Missouri Division of Natural Resources, Division of Parks, Recreation and Historic Preservation, Jefferson City, MO. 1990, Vol. 1, 31.

12 William H. Wilson, *The City Beautiful Movement in Kansas City*. (Kansas City: The Lowell Press, 1964, 1990), 45. *See also* Kurt Culbertson, "George Edward Kessler," in Charles A. Birnbaum and Robin Karson. *Pioneers of American Landscape Design*. (New York: McGraw Hill, 2000), 212–215.

13 William S. Worley. "Ward Parkway," in *The Grand American Avenue, 1850–1920*, ed. Jan Cigliano and Sarah Bradford Landau. (San Francisco: Pomegranate Artbooks, 1994), 284. *See also* Tourbier & Walmsley, et. al. Landscape Survey Parks and Boulevards, Vol. 1, 897–906.

14 Norman T. Newton. *Design on the Land: The Development of Landscape Architecture*. (Cambridge: The Belknap Press of Harvard University Press, 1971), 474.

15 As quoted in John Linn Hopkins and Marsha R. Oates. "Historic Resources of St. Joseph, Buchanan County, Missouri." Multiple Property Form, National Register of Historic Places Nomination, Sept. 1999, E8.

16 Deon Wolfenbarger. "Historic Resources of St. Joseph, Buchanan County, Missouri. The Jewels of St. Joseph: The Parks and Parkways System, 1910–1943." National Register of Historic Places Nomination, Nov. 1994, E.

17 Robert S. Gamble and Frank B. Sarles Jr. Division of History, National Park Service, "Harry S. Truman Historic District,' National Historic Landmark Nomination, Sept. 1971.

18 Historic Preservation Services, LLC, "Historic Preservation Plan, City of Lee's Summit, Missouri." September 1, 2002, 81. Until the 1905 annexation, there were sparsely populated residential neighborhoods beyond the city limits. After World War I, farmlands were converted into subdivisions.

Houses of Missouri

1870–1940

GREYSTONE

MAJOR EMORY S. FOSTER HOUSE

Pevely, Jefferson County (c. 1870)

THE INFLUENCE of A. J. Downing arrived late to Missouri—some might argue never—but his teachings were clearly the model for the charming Gothic cottage that has come to be known as Greystone, near Pevely, in Jefferson County. Downing's endorsement of taste and propriety in architecture were lessons not lost on the owner, Major Emory S. Foster, who had fought for Union forces in the Civil War, and ultimately became the editor of the *St. Louis Journal.*

Foster intended to retire to this river town and cultivate fruit on his approximately 180 acres but it was the following owner, Isidor Bush (1822–1898), a Jewish emigrant from Austria-Hungary, who had

Entrance facade

Front and side view, 1940

North facade, 1940

Living room mantel

Second floor bedroom, 1940

horticultural success there. Bush developed the largest grape propagating nursery in the United States; his Bushberg Vineyards produced 60,000 gallons of wine annually. The firm's 1868 publication on American grapes, *The Bushberg Manual,* remained the standard for generations and Bush, with business partner Gustave Meissner, sent vines to France to help control the phylloxera virus devastating European vineyards.

High bluffs overlooking the Mississippi River are favored residential sites and Greystone is perched at a bend in the river on the edge of such a bluff. As if drawn from Downing's *Cottage Residences,* the house and grounds create the kind of picturesque vignette proposed by that arbiter of taste. The house is constructed of "fawn-colored" rusticated masonry—grey limestone with honey-colored quoins and trim. Its varied fenestration includes lancet and rectangular windows with stone lintels, all with Gothic tracery. Highly decorative bargeboards, clustered chimneys, and an assortment of finials and pendants

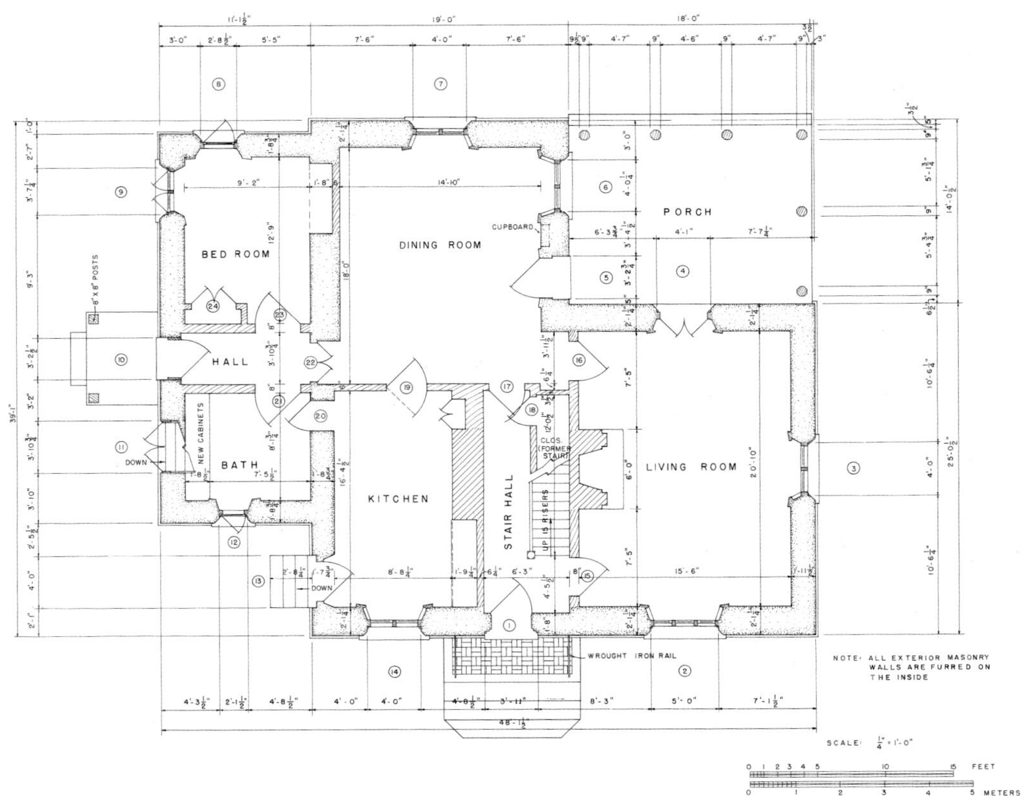

First floor plan

ornament the exterior. The general asymmetry of the nine-room plan is heightened by the veranda, an element that Downing promoted as essential to outdoor living. Gothic details continue throughout the interior, particularly with the built-in shutters in the window treatment and the complex intersection of doors and ceilings.

Greystone has not served as a primary residence since 1918. However, the cottage has been owned since the 1960s by a family known for their commitment to preservation and who enjoy it on holidays and weekends. It is the only residence of its style and caliber in the state.

Seth E. Ward Residence

Kansas City (c. 1871, with additions)

PROBABLY no other property in Kansas City has as rich and varied a history as the Seth E. Ward residence—a two-story vernacular Greek Revival farmhouse designed by local architect Asa Beebe Cross (c.1871) and originally located in the Town of Westport. "The site of the Ward homestead has been associated with several prominent [episodes] in the exploration, conquest, and settlement of the American West," from the contentious Indian Removal Act, to Joseph Smith and the Latter Day Saints immigration, settlement, and expulsion, to the Battle of Westport, one of the fiercest combats in the Civil War.

Individuals who had an early foothold on the property include Dr. Johnston Lykins, the first mayor of the Town of Kansas (now Kansas City), and William Bent, a prominent St. Louisan turned frontiersman, trapper, trader, and early Colorado explorer.

View from southwest, c. 1920

Detail of main facade, 1977

Entrance facade

North and east facades, 1977

Virginia-born Seth Edmund Ward moved to Westport from Colorado, where he'd befriended William Bent in the course of making his fortune in trading and fur trapping; he left behind a Native American wife and four children.

With his new wife, Mary Frances McCarty Harris, Ward purchased Bent's farm, totaling 212 acres, at auction in August 1871, and in subsequent years, they acquired an additional 228 acres to the south and west. After a brief failed banking venture, Ward retired, already a millionaire from his trading, and spent the remainder of his life on the land he homesteaded.

Dating Ward's house derived from the trans-Appalachian region is somewhat difficult. Over the years, widespread conjecture was that there had been antebellum buildings on the property prior to Ward's purchase and that Ward modified the existing structures. However, architects specializing in historic properties who have examined the Ward house suggest that Asa Beebe Cross designed the irregularly shaped residence with its main unit on an east-west axis and a smaller north extension immediately after the August 1871 auction, their findings based on "similarity of structural systems" and use.

Features of the Ward residence, including the delicately framed main entrance with slender sidelights held in the front gabled bay, the two-over-two, double-hung, pedimented fenestration (averaging 9 feet in height) placed at regular intervals, the side gable roof, and boxed cornice sound the Greek Revival.

Parlor, 1977

The intricately composed wooden Italianate veranda running partially across the south facade is a late 1870s addition. Built without wood framing, the Ward house has 20-inch-thick brick walls mostly set in stretcher bond.

Typical of the period, there are several parlors, all with fireplaces, at the first floor of the 14-room residence—two located on opposite sides of the hallway in the main block, and a third placed at the west, L-shaped wing. Open string staircases with turned and planed balusters and newels and wainscoting in Lincrusta dress the hallways. Most of the rooms at the main unit and west wing have floors of 5-inch-wide pine, and window sills rest level with the floor. Milled tongue-and-groove flooring, wood wainscoting, and plaster walls finish the north extension.

During Ward's later years, he leased the northeast pasture of his property to Kansas City's first golf course and country club. After a subsequent annexation, the Ward family began selling their land for development. In 1926 after Congress declined to turn the site of the Battle of Westport into a national military park, Ella Loose bought 80 acres of Ward's holdings and donated the land to the city for a park in memory of her husband, Jacob Loose.

Today, the greater part of Ward's original 440 acres lies within the Country Club District's Sunset Hill Subdivision, a decidedly fashionable and highly restricted residential neighborhood that includes a number of Missouri's great houses. The Ward house remains in private hands and is listed in the National Register of Historic Places.

Ravenswood

Captain Charles Edward Leonard House

Bell Air, Cooper County, (1880)

Nathaniel Leonard came to central Missouri from Woodstock, Vermont, and started a 1,932-acre farm near Bell Air that his family continued to work for generations. It was Nathaniel's son, Captain Charles Edward Leonard, who hired St. Joseph architect W. Angelo Powell in 1880 to design a fashionable Italianate residence on the property and named it Ravenswood. Nathaniel's grandson, Nelson, made additions to the house between 1907 and 1914, including a portico with monumental columns, a crenellated tower, and a conservatory. A new French Second Empire mansard roof contributed yet another

View of farmstead

Entrance facade, later-day view

period reference to the classical and medieval elements that first accrued to the original Italianate core. The result is an eclectic architectural statement that remains firmly grounded in the 19th century.

Ravenswood is the second house on the site. The original frame house, built with slave labor, burned in 1850. The extant 1880 building is three stories high and 125 feet deep, with a 54-foot facade that faces west toward grounds that slope past the circle drive down to the Petite Saline Creek. The house is built of red brick fired on the property, with a rubble stone foundation faced with ashlar limestone; five fireplaces provide the heating. Anchored by the original central hall, off which the main staircase winds to the attic, its rambling additions give it an irregularity that suits its eclectic interior.

The music room and dining room suggest generations of collecting. Heavy dark furnishings, Turkish carpets, Japanese screens, fringed lamps and bibelots contrast with severe ancestral portraits reminiscent of Missouri artist George Caleb Bingham. Floor-to-ceiling bookshelves with handsome carved Corinthian columns flank the fireplace in the library. The 1907 additions include a morning "withdrawing room" and breakfast room attached to the rear of the house. A charming conservatory was part of a 1913–14 expansion, as were a playroom and a summer kitchen, connected to the main house by an arched link.

Cooper County is farm country and the Leonards not only farmed, they raised purebred shorthorn cattle imported from England. They were the first breeders west of the Mississippi River to specialize in

Southeast (rear) corner of house and conservatory

Sitting room

Dining room

Library

shorthorns. An operation the size of Ravenswood required a good number of outbuildings, including servants' quarters, a manager's house, a carriage house, and four large barns. Two of the barns had fairly elaborate decoration; the Tally-Ho Barn and the mule barn, for example, had fan lights, finials, scalloped roof ornamentation, and a glazed cupola.

The Leonard family still owns and runs Ravenswood and the public may visit by appointment. It has suffered losses in recent years, particularly its barns, which have been damaged by fire and lightning.

MAISON D'OR

HARVEY MERRICK VAILE HOUSE

Independence (1881)

STANDING as an anomaly in the midst of modestly proportioned 20th-century frame houses is the towering Maison d'Or, a 31-room mansion completed for Harvey Merrick Vaile and his wife, Sophia Cecelia Graham, in 1881. Trained as a lawyer, Vaile became involved with two of his lifetime devotions during his early career in Indianapolis—antislavery issues and organizing the Republican Party. History claims him a "strong supporter of Abraham Lincoln, whose name was anathema in pro-South Missouri." His home and personal life were the makings of a Gothic novel.

General view, 1898

Vaile, with two partners, was most noted for establishing the Old Star Mail Route, a mail delivery service in contract with the U.S. government. Using stagecoach, wagon, and rail, the Star Route eventually covered mail routes in five states and two Indian territories. When reform of the route was established in 1880, Vaile was one of several individuals charged with defrauding the government in questionable contractual activities. Subsequently, Vaile attracted national attention in the "Star Route Scandals." Vaile was acquitted after a second trial in 1883, but during the trial, Vaile's wife, who had been ill, died from an overdose of morphine.

Vaile amassed a fortune from the Star Route enterprise and from cattle ranches he controlled in the Dakota Territory during this period. After the trial, Vaile sold his holdings in the route and moved back to his mansion in Independence, where he concentrated on crossbreeding imported English Herefords with longhorn cattle and expanding his cattle ranch ventures throughout the Southwest.

Vaile's arresting Second Empire house, designed by Kansas City architect Asa Beebe Cross, bears a strong resemblance to William Boyington's Terrace Hill (1867–69), now the Governor's Mansion, in Des Moines, Iowa. Its comparison to the Governor's Mansion in Jefferson City, Missouri (1871; George Barnett), is surprisingly less pronounced.

Extravagant in character, the hand-pressed red brick and limestone-trimmed house abounds with exterior detail; it features an intricately carved full-width porch, heavy bracketed cornices, multiple finials, and an iron-crested, diamond-patterned slate mansard roof. A profusion of long, narrow fenestration further accentuates the verticality of the double-mansard central tower. It is a vastly complex and distinctive expression, not unlike the apparent nature of Vaile himself.

South facade, later-day view

Detail of the main entrance, later-day view

Detail of east parlor, later-day view

The interior is likewise overly ornate. From the main vestibule floored with Dutch and Stoke-on-Trent tile, one reaches the 40-foot-long center hall. A parlor and drawing and sitting rooms lie on both sides of the hall. The main parlor, to the right of the grand hall, features a white Carrara marble fireplace with onyx insets; there are eight other fireplaces similarly finished with exotic stone throughout the first and second floors. Interior walls, trimmed in faux-grained pine, are painted vivid hues and selected ceilings are embellished with frescoes and hand-painted murals of botanicals and grapevines, reflecting some of Vaile's passions. Most scandalous in its time was the master bedroom's ceiling mural of a recumbent female, nude from the waist up; the bared breasts were later covered with a painted lace veil.

Spread over the grounds of Vaile's estate was a cherrywood-lined stable, a spring-fed lake, fountains, pergolas, and a boathouse. A 45,000-gallon capacity wine cellar, vineyards, and a greenhouse gave Vaile further enjoyment.

After Vaile's death in 1894, the house was used as an inn, a sanitarium, and a home for the aged. Rescued from demolition in the 1960s by the DeWitt family, the Vaile Mansion-DeWitt Museum is owned now by the City of Independence and operated by the Vaile Victorian Society.

Henry Clay Pierce Residence

St. Louis (1886)

Considered one of the most spacious and extravagant residences in the Midwest when it was completed in 1889, the 26-room Pierce mansion was the ultimate suburban residence in one of the city's earliest and most prestigious private places. Laid out in 1870 by surveyor and civil engineer Julius Pitzman, Vandeventer Place, with its broad tree-lined boulevard, was home to leading St. Louis

Main facade

Detail of loggia

businessmen and civic leaders. Henry Clay Pierce had come to St. Louis from New York after the Civil War and had risen from a factory worker to an oil magnate and financier of international stature. It is fitting that Pierce chose to build such a strikingly powerful architectural statement for his residence at Vandeventer Place.

Rather than hire one of several competent local architects for his project, Pierce returned to New York to find the appropriate firm, choosing Fuller & Wheeler of Albany. In addition to residential architecture, the firm executed public buildings in Albany and YMCAs as far away as Oakland, California, and Paris, France, working most often in the Richardsonian mode. Construction of the Pierce project took three years and a purported investment of $800,000, resulting in a mansion with a rather severe exterior at odds with the richly exuberant, typically High Victorian interior.

An assortment of turrets, dormers, and gables and a variety of fenestration punctuated the planar facade, all anchored by a rusticated ground floor. Stained glass and leaded glass ornamented the windows and vines softened the porte cochere. The 26 rooms included a huge reception hall, music

Entrance hall

rooms, a rococo sitting room, library, a Moorish nook, billiard room, men's smoking room, dining and breakfast rooms, and a kitchen "equal in size to that of a small hotel." Gun and trophy rooms and a large wine cellar were located in the lower level, and the 15 bedrooms (including the master) were located on the second and third floors. All were accessible by both the sweeping staircase and the elevator. The interior exhibited Pierce's appreciation of late 19th-century ornament and eclecticism as is apparent in the overlaying of patterns and prints, tiles, throws, and fur. Works of art, including portraits of Pierce and his wife by Swedish artist Anders Zorn and a bas-relief of his father over the fireplace, were set against rich walnut and mahogany paneling and silk-tapestry-lined walls, lit by chandeliers and chinoiserie floor lamps. Outbuildings included a richly carved stable (with tack room and carriage house) for Pierce's three white horses and a separate "dormitory" for the 26 servants employed in the residence.

Breakfast room

Pierce returned to New York in 1910 after living at Vandeventer Place for 20 years. Local newspapers reported that he was living on Fifth Avenue in New York City when he died, without a will, in 1927. His St. Louis property was valued at $48,565 at his death and remained vacant for the following decade. It was torn down in 1938 at the cost of $500. Just as the residence had set the bar for opulence when it was built, it foretold the neighborhood's gloomy fate when it was demolished, as half of Vandeventer Place was razed by 1950.

Oak Hall

William Rockhill Nelson House

Kansas City (1887, with additions)

In a eulogy for William Rockhill Nelson published in *Collier's*, William Allan White reminisced the titan who moved to Kansas City from Ft. Wayne, Indiana, in 1880: "He was 39 years old, with better than a fair education and with more of the air of a man of the world than most men about him . . . he looked different than the ordinary run of men . . . he was big—monumental, with a general Himalayan effect . . . He had a great voice [that] rattled like artillery." He was pedigreed yet rebellious, intelligent yet rabid, boisterous yet introverted. Nelson made a fortune as a newspaper publisher and real estate developer and brought culture to the city he prized.

General view

Original view, rear of house, 1890

Rear of house after 1890s expansion

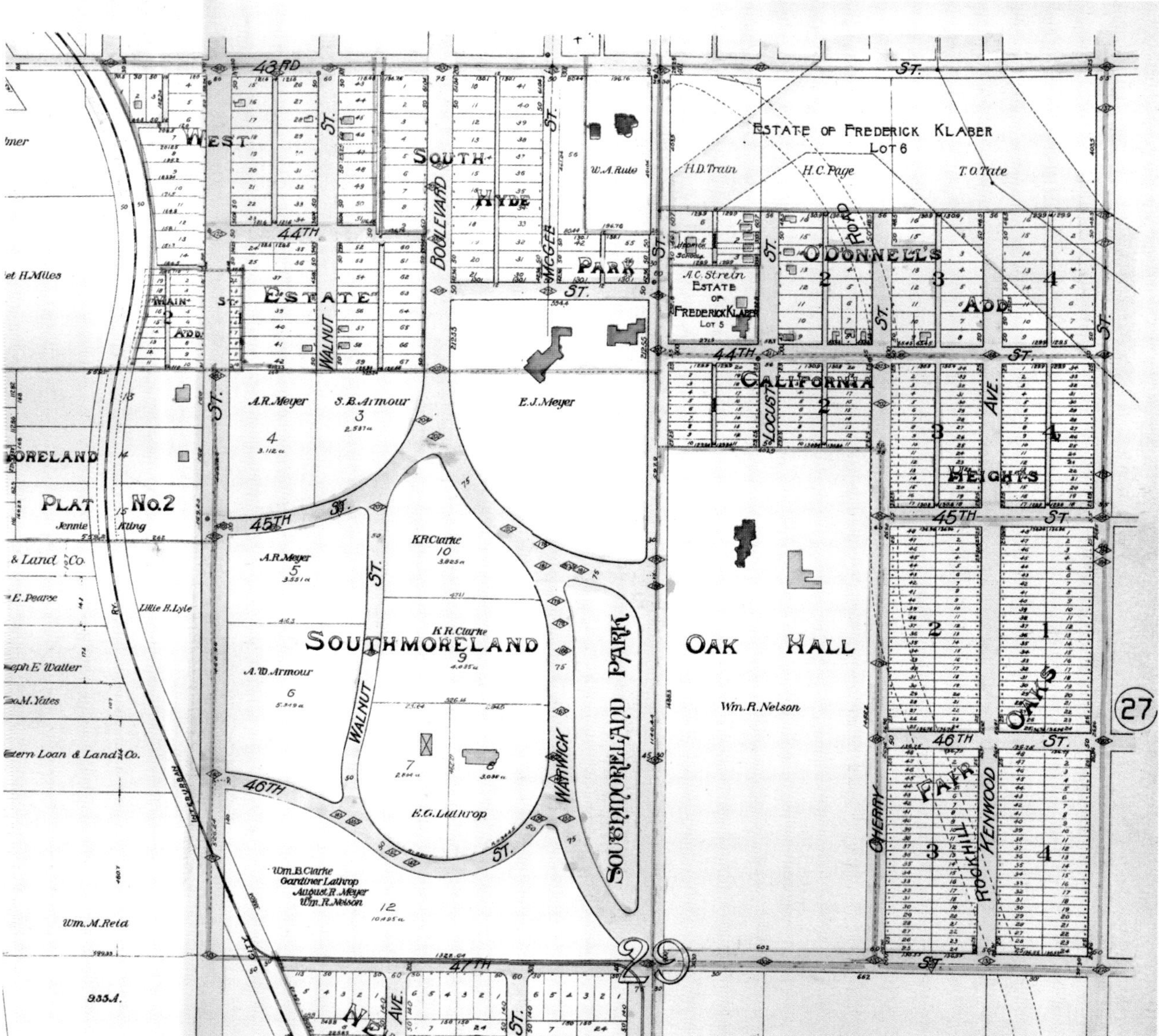

Atlas illustrating Nelson's house and surroundings, 1900

Founder and editor of *The Kansas City Star,* Nelson was ensconced in public affairs; he was one of the most aggressive leaders to fortify the decade-long struggle for a comprehensive park and boulevard system to beautify and define the burgeoning city. Abetting his fierce campaign to transform the "rugged, precipitous, and uninviting" Kansas City into a metropolis of national rank, Nelson plunged into urban planning and real estate.

Nelson built Oak Hall on 20 acres bordered on the east by his Rockhill District, a picturesque, fashionable residential neighborhood defined by curvilinear tree-lined streets and native limestone walls studded with roses and honeysuckle. To the south, he constructed rental houses modest in scale, but with the same devotion to an expression of beauty and class. In order to provide access to the neighborhood, he personally financed Rockhill Road, which originally featured a stone arched bridge over Brush Creek,

Salon

Living room

Interior hall

Grand stairway

Bedroom

designed by the enigmatic architect Louis S. Curtiss, who was in part responsible for the dual architectural expressions of Nelson's baronial mansion.

Nelson tore down a farmhouse located on his vast landholdings before building his residence in 1887. Working initially on the massive limestone structure with architect Frederick E. Hill, and over the ensuing six years with Frederick C. Gunn and Curtiss, Nelson integrated two distinct architectural idioms in his fabled house. Hill's original design, with its asymmetrical arrangements and bulging towers, was Shingle style, while the subsequent modifications, employing multiple front-facing gables of varying heights, affirmed the Tudor tradition at the rear facade.

An explosion of rich tapestries, furnishings, crystal chandeliers, and valuable artwork amplified the opulent eclectic interior (a choice portion of which Nelson willed to the Nelson-Atkins Museum of Art, the Kansas City museum that bears his name and that of the reclusive Mary McAfee Atkins). Nelson had collected works by Jan Steen, David Teniers, Constant Troyon, Sir Joshua Reynolds, Monet, and Pissarro, among others.

Colonel Nelson, as he was often called, died in 1915, leaving his house to Ida Houston Nelson, his widow, and their daughter, Laura, while the remainder of his $15 million estate was put in trust only for their lifetime. Ida instructed in her will that a great museum be built in Kansas City to include works of art purchased with the proceeds from their vast fortune. Laura Kirkwood, who died at the age of 43, left

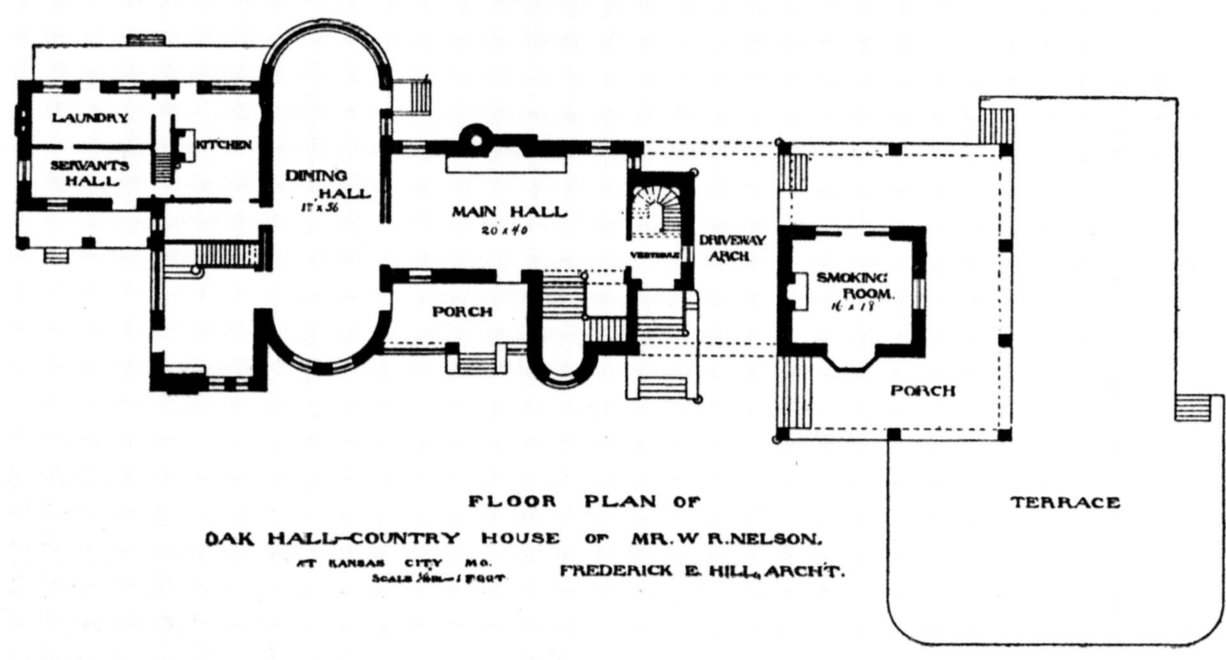

First floor plan

Oak Hall and the combination stable/ballroom to her husband, Irwin, with the mysterious provision that the house and outbuildings be razed at his death. The Kirkwoods left no heirs and Oak Hall was eventually dismantled in 1928. Much of the exterior materials were recycled in the construction of houses in neighboring subdivisions on both sides of the state line, while vestiges of the residence were burned at the site. In 1930, the Nelson-Atkins Museum of Art was built upon the rolling site of Nelson's house.

Marburg

August Robert Meyer House

Kansas City (1895–1896)

THERE ARE but a handful of salient individuals who helped shape Kansas City's famed parks and boulevard system, and August Robert Meyer, as the city's first parks board president, is one of them. Meyer often enjoyed riding horseback through the town of Westport, a richly forested and rugged suburban area yet to be annexed to the city. His love of the natural landscape in Kansas City led him, along with William R. Nelson and Gardiner Lathrop, to crusade successfully for civic improvement in a reluctant city.

Meyer, born in St. Louis in 1851, was educated at the Polytechnic School in Zurich, and at mining schools in Freiburg and Berlin. He began his remarkable career as a mining engineer in the United States when he was appointed government assayer of Fairplay, Colorado, in 1874; one year later, he established A. R. Meyer & Company, an ore-crushing mill in Alma, Colorado. The pinnacle of his career in the Rockies was helping found and develop the town of Leadville, where he also established his first smelting works.

Meyer moved to Kansas City in 1881 and purchased a smelting plant in nearby Argentine, Kansas. Meyer's Kansas City Smelting & Refining Company owned mines throughout the New Mexico Territory and the state of Coahuila, Mexico. Eighteen years later, the Guggenheim family purchased Meyer's controlling interest in the company.

Garden facade (south)

Entrance facade (north)

Northeast view

Designed by Van Brunt & Howe, Meyer's 35-room mansion located northwest of Colonel Nelson's Oak Hall, is one of the few extant examples of the firm's work in Kansas City. The three-story Queen Anne brick and stone residence was originally sited on 8½ acres landscaped by George E. Kessler, who designed Kansas City's park and boulevard plan when Meyer was board president.

This high-style, irregularly shaped residence features an unrestrained and exuberant exterior, highlighted by multiple shaped parapets, varied massing, and molded and contrasting brickwork throughout its

Dining room

three main rectangular blocks. Van Brunt & Howe responded to the sprawling site by employing balloon framing, a progressive building technique that allowed them to maneuver the continuity of the wall plane, which resulted in a work of elegance and complexity, yet steeped in academic tradition. It is no coincidence that Marburg's design follows the general scheme for Harvard's Well Hall, an early work by Van Brunt while he was affiliated with William Ware.

The interior of Marburg exhibited a neutrality of spatial relationships, certainly common of many 19th-century country residences. The drawing room, reached from the main hall, was simply crafted but lavishly adorned. Except for the denticulated cornice and a classically detailed, mirrored hearth, the room was the setting for the Meyers' rich display of period furniture, which continued throughout.

From the drawing room, one entered the dining room, where the mantel combined a system of arched niches and shelving with extensive classical and Adamesque detailing that overshadowed the fireplace below. A curved and mirrored breakfront, richly stained, was set in a delicately detailed plaster surround flanked by fluted pilasters. In direct contrast to the lightnenss and minimalism of the dining room, the library was densely filled with built-in bookcases doubling as pedestals for pottery and sculpture.

In 1908, three years after Meyer died at the age of 54, Marburg was acknowledged as the most beautiful house in Kansas City. Meyer's widow, Emma J. Hixson Meyer, sold Marburg to Howard Vanderslice, a Kansas City grain dealer and art collector, who in 1928 donated the house and grounds to the Kansas City Art Institute (KCAI) for its permanent home. Listed in the National Register of Historic Places in 1983, Marburg is now part of the larger KCAI campus.

LODGE AT STONEY RIDGE FARM

JOHN HOMER BOTHWELL HOUSE

Sedalia, Pettis County (1897; additions through 1928)

"THE ORNAMENT of a house is the guest who doth frequent it," reads the carving above the music room doorway at the John Homer Bothwell residence. The attorney and politician who built the Lodge at Stoney Ridge Farm may have been without a family—his wife having died in childbirth a short three years after their marriage—but he was certainly not without friends. He built Bothwell Lodge (as it is now known) as a 55-acre recreational retreat for his friends and extended family. When he died in 1929, Bothwell left the property to a group of 38 friends and relatives whom he had dubbed the "Bothwell Lodge Club."

Aerial view of house, ca. 1930

View of house and bluff

Built in three successive phases between 1897 and 1928, Bothwell Lodge reflects its owner's careful supervision in an ongoing collaboration with three architectural firms. Local builder Thomas N. Bast was responsible for the cubic first section, which ultimately became the east wing. Henry Wright, an urban planner with a keen sensitivity to landscape, proposed additions to the lodge that Bothwell to some extent employed. The St. Louis firm of Eames & Young made the last additions.

Bothwell's grand lodge at Stoney Ridge Farm recalls the medieval castle of the same name on the River Clyde in South Lanarkshire, Scotland, that inspired him (two evocative prints of the Scottish castle remain at the lodge), but it also suggests a purely vernacular approach to building that persisted in Missouri. The plan evolved organically in exchanges between the designers and client rather than from a single master plan. A kind of gloried camping, the rustic experience at the lodge was tempered by Bothwell's interest in modern conveniences: A powerful Delco light system provided electricity; steam radiators warmed the rooms in winter; and a boiler room was nestled into the bluff on the lowest level. A cave buried deep in the hillside provided cool air in stifling summer months through shafts that accessed upper rooms.

The lodge appears to cling to the bluff, rambling over four levels and three caves. Three quarries on the property provided the limestone for the project. Grapevines draped pergolas, labyrinthine passageways

Side porch

linked rooms of the tower section to adjacent wings, and the 31 rooms (occupying 12,000 square feet) provided ample, although sparely-decorated, space for living. A tiny reading nook with a giant window overlooking the valley was tucked beneath a sharply vaulted roofline at one end of a long narrow corridor. The library was lined to the ceiling with first editions of George Eliot, Charles Dickens, and references (with Bothwell's notes intact) on landscape and nature. The off.ce was in the tip of the attic,

Library, present-day view

where the owner could access the tower roof—the highest point on the property—and take in a sweep of oak and maple forest below.

In the house, 5½ baths accompanied the 11 bedrooms. Outbuildings included a bungalow called the Cliff House; a masterful Stick-style garage (later enlarged to accommodate four cars and sleeping quarters for their drivers) that housed the owner's Chandler Roadster; and two rustic pavilions—the Gypsy Camp and a stone gazebo—built on the trail looping along the edge of the bluff. After Bothwell's death, a farmhouse on the property became the caretaker's cottage.

When the last surviving member of the Bothwell Lodge Club passed away, the property was given to the state of Missouri, as dictated in Bothwell's will. Today it is a state historic site.

JUDGE EDWARD L. SCARRITT RESIDENCE

Kansas City (1898–1899)

JACKSON COUNTY native Edward "Lucky" Scarritt, a distinguished attorney and circuit court judge in Missouri, is well rooted in early Kansas City history. Edward was the son of Rev. Nathan Scarritt and Martha Matilda Chick, both descended from pioneering local families. A dedicated missionary, Rev. Scarritt was also astute at buying property. During the Civil War, he purchased hundreds of acres of wooded land in northeast Kansas City, from which he platted the Melrose Addition. He later divvied up these holdings among his children, and Edward built his Colonial Revival residence here, on high ground overlooking the Missouri River.

The site on which Edward Scarritt built was aptly described in an early history of the county: "Nature has formed and fashioned these grounds especially for the erection of elegant houses where a

Southwest view of main facade

Main facade

grand panorama of beauty can be viewed from every doorway." Frederick E. Hill, the architect for the Scarritt residence, took full advantage of the site, working closely with his client. Chicago designers Alice E. Neale and Edith Sheridan had charge of the interior finishes, and like Hill, cooperated diligently with the family.

In completing his drawings for the 2½-story house, Hill had to contend with Scarritt's exacting requirements, apparently stated somewhat strongly in correspondence. In a letter to Scarritt dated April 17, 1897, Hill responds, " . . . I can understand now what I have often heard about the power of an eloquent lawyer to lead a conscientious jury to render a decision in his favor regardless of the main facts in the case. But the 'logic of events' is no more 'irresistible' than the forces we have to contend with in laying out a plan to a scale."

The result of the collaboration is a plan fully appropriate for the site. Using uncoursed native limestone for the foundation, the first story, and throughout the centered, gabled entry bay, the dignified Colonial Revival-style house reflects the dominance of the Scarritt family in Kansas City and deftly complements the craggy landscape surrounding the estate.

Classical elements delineate doorways, fenestration, and the two-story verandas at the east and west facades. Multiple slender Ionic columns, pilasters, and dentils define the main entrance porch; verandas feature thicker Tuscan columns and pilasters. Window type and configuration and overall symmetry of

Stair hall, present-day view

design is typical of the style, yet the heavy arch above the main entry formed by large stone voussoirs surrounding a fanlight evokes the Romanesque Revival.

A central hall running the full length of the house ends at an inglenook with upholstered seats. Large mahogany pocket doors in the main hall lead to the living and dining rooms, dressed in mahogany and Flemish oak wainscoting, respectively; the mantels in both rooms are of matching wood and faced with glazed ceramic tile. The first-floor ceilings are beamed. Set around a U shape at the second floor, each of the four bedrooms has an individually designed fireplace. The rooms open onto the full-height verandas and connect to each other by paneled doors.

The Scarritt house initially occupied one entire city block; over the years, portions of the property were sold. In the late 1890s, members of the Scarritt family donated and sold some of their landholdings to the city for parkland development. Cliff Drive, the winding road through the center of what is now called Kessler Park, follows the cow path that the Scarritt brothers used to access water for their cattle. Today, this tree- and rock-lined drive is among America's Scenic Byways.

Standing for more than 100 years with little modification, the Scarritt residence may be the oldest house in the state of Missouri that has been continuously owned and occupied by descendents of the original family. It is listed in the National Register of Historic Places.

Living room, present-day view

Dining room, present-day view

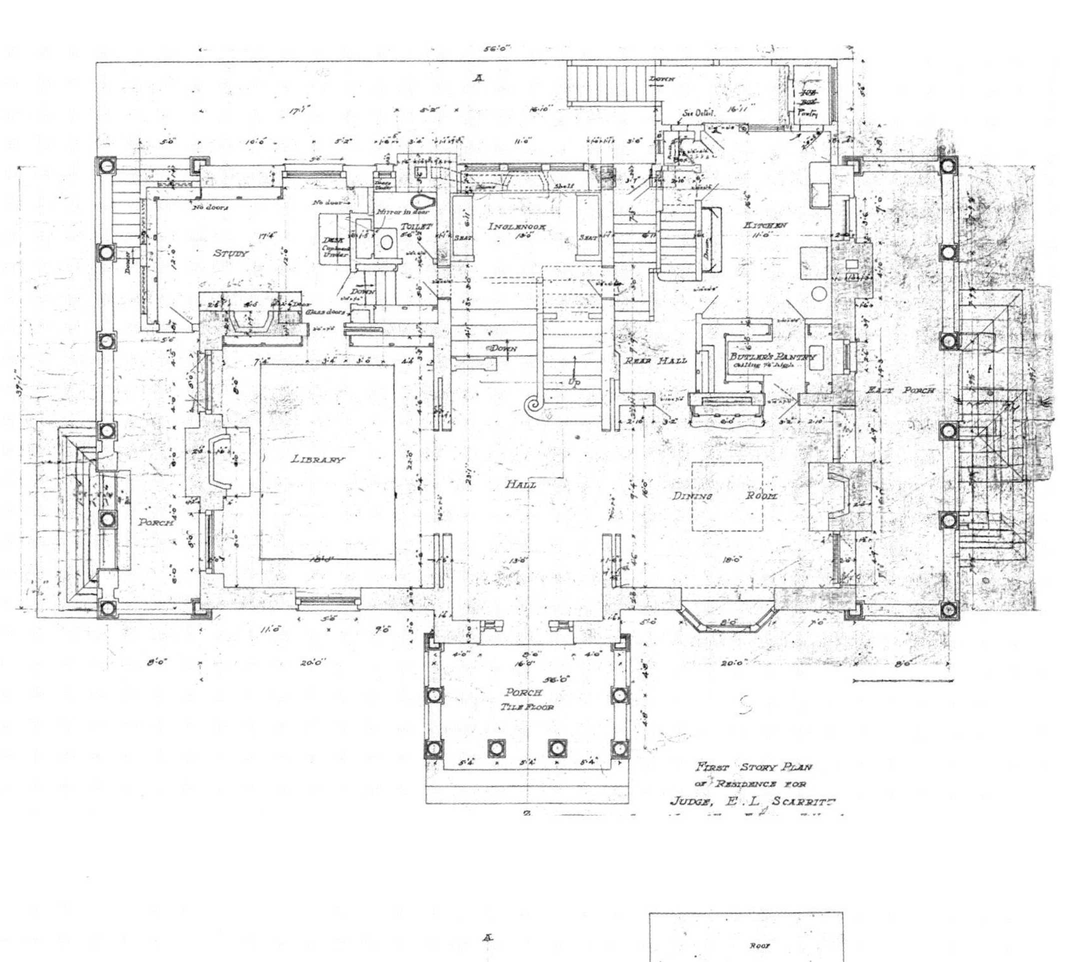

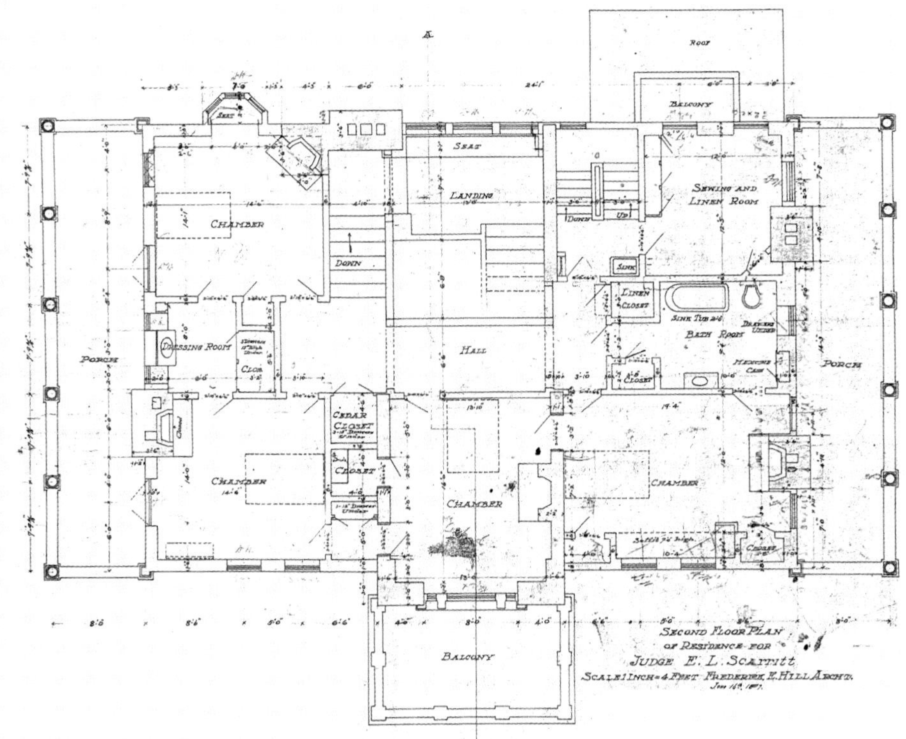

Original plans, Frederick Hill

ROCKCLIFFE

JOHN J. CRUIKSHANK HOUSE

Hannibal (1898)

JOHN J. CRUIKSHANK'S fortune was founded on lumber and he fittingly chose a high spot overlooking his logging operations on the Mississippi River on which to set his massive Colonial Revival residence. After moving the existing family home from the site, he employed the St. Louis firm of Barnett, Haynes & Barnett to design a much grander house that he appropriately named Rockcliffe.

The staid exterior featuring a monumental double-height portico with Corinthian columns gives no hint of the richness within—an interior embellished with exotic woods, South African pink marble, and Tiffany stained glass. The owner's business connections in lumber and construction presumably helped control building costs, which are nevertheless reported to have been $125,000. A St. Louis newspaper cited it as the finest residence in the state soon after the family moved into the house in 1900.

Main facade, ca. 1928

Side view with porte cochere and new plantings

Front porch

Parlor

When the family moved out in 1924 after Cruikshank's death, no one else ever moved in; the house sat empty for 43 years.

Arranged around the central hall are grand public rooms meant for entertaining. To one side is the reception room, with gilded wallpaper, quarter-sawn oak paneling, and Tiffany fixtures, furnished with a lemonwood sideboard and olivewood reception table commissioned in Florence. The pink and green music room is anchored at each end by a grand piano; the Green Room reflects the sensibilities of Mrs. Cruikshank in its gold leaf and garlands, lace and velvet drapes, and white onyx fireplace. Friend and writer Mark Twain addressed 300 guests and Hannibal citizens from the double staircase on the second floor during his visit in 1902. The Moorish Room provides the de rigueur eclecticism embraced by the period.

The house has 125 windows and 10 fireplaces. Cruikshank prided himself on the structural and decorative uses of wood on the property, and employed mahogany, oak, and walnut throughout the house. Greek Revival and Art Nouveau decorative motifs recur in various rooms.

Moorish room

Rockcliffe was purchased by private individuals in 1967 and preempted its being razed. During the house's four-decade vacancy it had settled less than half of an inch. After the restoration, a Cruikshank daughter returned to the property some of the original furnishings, linens, and lace, which she had carefully stored for decades. Rockcliffe is in the National Register of Historic Places and is open to the public for tours and special events.

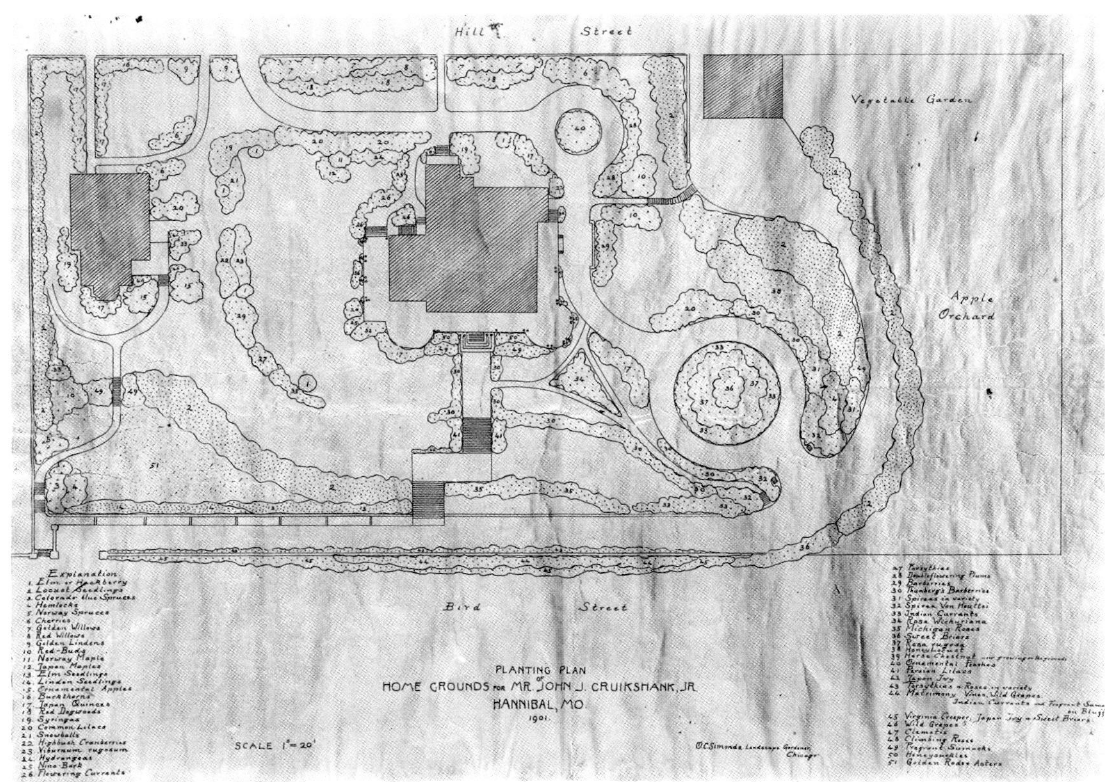

Planting plan for grounds, Ossian C. Simonds, 1901

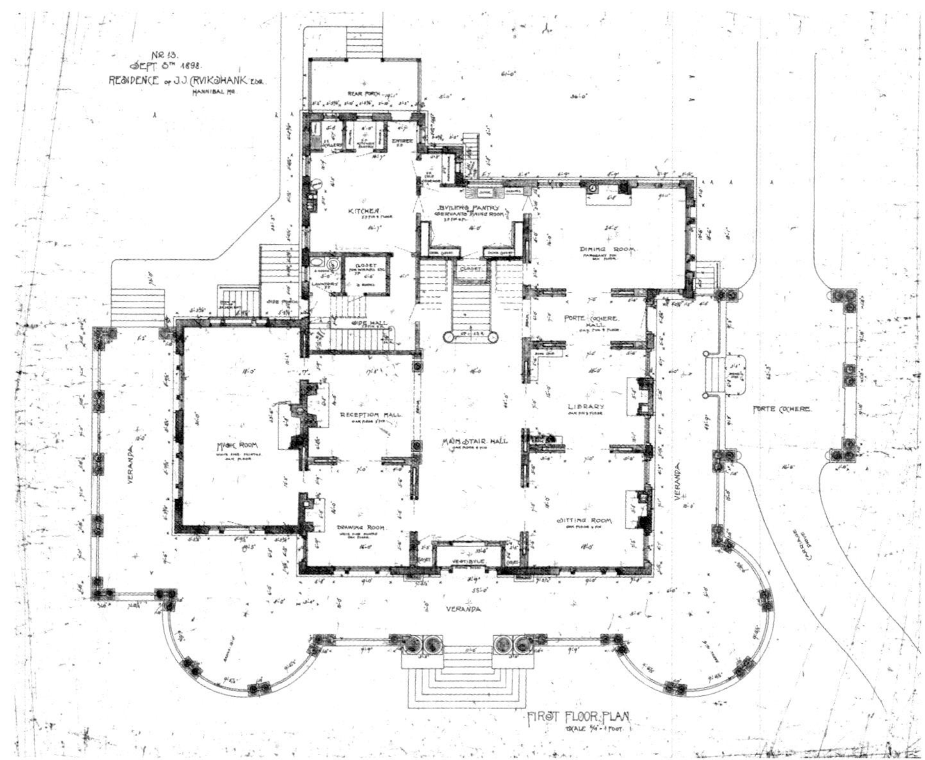

First floor plan

Edward Gardner Lewis Residence

University City, St. Louis County (1904)

In 1902, entrepreneur Edward Gardner Lewis purchased 85 acres just west of the St. Louis city limits, in a rapidly growing region near Forest Park, an area later incorporated, with his help, as University City. Over the following decade, Lewis began many business ventures there, among them a successful publishing company that specialized in women's magazines, two banks, and a subscription-gathering organization called the American Women's League. He also began the development of University Heights Number One.

Borrowing from the private place concept originated by engineer and planner Julius Pitzman, Lewis envisioned University Heights Number One as a fashionable suburban address, affordable all the same to a range of middle-class families. Now known as "U City," the neighborhood still prides itself on the socioeconomic mix of its population. Lewis's purchase of this hilly acreage may have stemmed from his belief that great cities rise from hilltops—perhaps likening his University Heights dream to Rome; in any case, the undulating terrain influenced his layout of the suburb and his personal property. Boston landscape architect Ernest W. Bowditch oversaw the planning and planting of University Heights in 1903, and Lewis's 15-room Tudor Revival house at 2 Yale Avenue sprawled down one of its many hillsides. His was the first house to be built in the neighborhood.

Main facade and grounds

Side view and grounds

Rear view with double pergola

Living room

Breakfast room

Edward Gardner Lewis in the President's office of Women's National Daily building, designed by Herbert C. Chivers

Early photographs show the house adrift in a yard not yet planted, but the grounds were soon ornamented with twin pergolas, a Chinese bridge, a serpentine body of water, and fences laden with grapes. Photographs record his nieces, his wife, Mabel, and the family dogs enjoying the idyllic suburban life. The house's interior blended Arts and Crafts with elaborate turn-of-the-century ornamentation and German coziness, harkening back to the Brewer's Baronial examples on the city's South Side.

The rooms reflected the couple's interests: Edward Lewis's Art Academy offered basic classes in art, as well as ceramics, china painting, and textile arts; Mabel, an accomplished ceramic artist, later oversaw the University City Porcelain Works. Deer and elk trophy heads, art pottery, velvet couches, and evocative murals ornamented the Tudor Revival residence; a view of the Parthenon overlooked the billiard table. In contrast, the drawing room was a rococo delight showcasing delicate carved wooden boiseries framing floral wallpaper, a white marble fireplace with a curvaceous mantle, and furnishings worthy of Marie Antoinette. Elsewhere, a fern nook provided a tranquil spot for pets to nap. Like several others in the neighborhood, the house is attributed to architect Herbert C. Chivers, who also designed the buildings for Lewis's businesses.

The Lewis family's genteel life at University Heights did not last. Edward Gardner Lewis suffered repeatedly from financial mismanagement: In 1911 he was forced into bankruptcy, and in 1928 he went to prison for mail fraud. In the interim, the Lewises moved to Atascadero, California, to establish an agrarian community. There Lewis began another publishing company, built a vegetation-dehydration plant, and took a short, controversial part in the early development of Palos Verdes, now an upscale community in Southern California. The house at 2 Yale Avenue burned in the late 1940s, and the site is now Lewis Park.

Ha Ha Tonka

Robert McClure Snyder House

Camden County (1905)

Robert McClure Snyder, a grocer-turned-banker and utilities executive, kept his primary residence on Kansas City's Independence Avenue. When he sought less citified surroundings, he retired to an opulent "castle" 130 miles southeast that had a sweeping panorama of the Niangua River valley and the northern edge of the Ozarks. Ha Ha Tonka, so named after a Native American reference to its "laughing waters," is set at the edge of a 250-foot bluff overlooking the bubbling, luminous water of the spring below and the estate's 5,400 acres. Snyder was not the first to appreciate the wild beauty of the place: the Osage Indians were notified of the Louisiana Purchase while assembled there, and Daniel and Nathan Boone trapped beaver on the upper lake. The remarkable collection of natural wonders that ultimately became part of the estate includes stalagmite-filled caves and formations, such as Balanced Rock, the Devil's Promenade, and a natural bridge.

Aerial view

View of porch with water tower in the distance

Bluff view of Ha Ha Tonka

Center hall, ca. 1940

West lounge, ca. 1940

Drawing of Ha Ha Tonka and grounds

Adriance Van Brunt, a member of the first official Kansas City parks board, trumped the site's wild nature with an equally rugged architectural style that evoked the baronial castles of Europe. Thirty master stonemasons were brought from Scotland to quarry stone on the site and begin construction of his house in 1905. When completed Ha Ha Tonka had 37 rooms and cost nearly $300,000. The interior was spare but comfortable (yet lacked the elder Snyder's personal touch). Outbuildings on the estate included a carriage house large enough to house 100 horses (and later, 30 automobiles), an 80-foot stone water tower, and multiple greenhouses with limestone foundations.

The project came to a halt in 1906 when Snyder was killed in one of the state's first automobile accidents. His sons inherited the estate but not their father's passion for the project. Nevertheless, when Union Electric built Bagnell Dam in 1931, creating the Lake of the Ozarks, the integrity (and privacy) of the estate was threatened. The Snyder brothers sued the builders, charging damage to Ha Ha Tonka's scenic beauty. Sculptor Gutzon Borglum was called away from his Mt. Rushmore project in the Black Hills to testify; the Snyder family attorney collapsed in his hotel room after a dramatic defense at the condemnation proceedings. The trial and appeals process drew out until 1938, when the Snyders won a $200,000 judgment.

Meanwhile, the brothers had converted the estate in 1935 into a lake resort. On October 21, 1942, the castle and carriage house burned to the ground, leaving only the stone walls standing.

Today Ha Ha Tonka is a state park, and its savanna—fields of sparse forest and native grasses—still evoke the presettlement landscape. Also an example of karst topography, a landscape characterized by caves, underground streams, and sinkholes, the site is still crowned with the picturesque ruins of Snyder's castle walls.

IDLEWILD

COLONEL DANIEL BURNS DYER HOUSE

Kansas City (1906–1907)

NEITHER IDLEWILD nor Colonel Daniel Burns Dyer, its builder, was of ordinary dimension. Both were conspicuously outrageous. Born out of the mere fabric of the World's Columbian Exposition of 1893, Idlewild was the very essence of the fair's architectural directive, as it was built almost entirely of rescued pavilion parts that formed its monumental neoclassical facade. Dyer was equally as audacious in his work and his appetite for art treasures from around the world—there was nothing idle about his chosen pursuits.

Although Dyer maintained a residence in Augusta, Georgia, he always considered Kansas City his home, perhaps because a good deal of his wealth derived from the city's boom years—the mid- to late-1880s.

Main facade

Drive and grounds

Originally from Illinois, Dyer claims to have enlisted in the Union army at the age of 15, along with his father and brother. His astonishing, multifaceted career thereafter ranged from banking to real estate, to railroads and utilities, to publishing. It even included a stint as an Indian agent, providing the means for him to befriend W. F. "Buffalo Bill" Cody.

While visiting the 1893 Chicago World's Fair, Dyer was smitten with the Victoria House. Following Queen Victoria's request, the structure was a montage of reproductions of some of her favorite palaces. Dyer had always envisioned building a residence in Kansas City, and he became fixated on incorporating the interior design of that exhibit into his new house. In 1898 Dyer purchased the Victoria House, which had been dismantled and lying in pieces in a Kansas City warehouse.

At the St. Louis World's Fair of 1904, Dyer admired the embellishments of the Alaska, Iowa, and Indian Territory pavilions. He instructed James Oliver Hogg, the architect for his Kansas City summer house, to buy the materials from those buildings. It took about 50 railcars to ship all this accumulated architectural salvage to Kansas City.

Beginning in 1906, Hogg worked to integrate these bits and pieces into his design for Idlewild, a mansion that overlooked the Missouri River from a 40-acre site near Beaumont Station on the Independence Electric line. The core of the irregularly shaped, 112- by 69-foot, three-story house was concrete. Multiple, colossal concrete Corinthian columns running along the south, east, and west facades dominated an 18-foot-wide veranda that bowed out to 26 feet at the main entrance.

From the front entrance, a wide vestibule led to a 70- by 23-foot-long reception hall flanked by a music room and parlor. The modeled plaster ceiling of the parlor and hall was copied from Plas Mawr in Conwy,

Reception hall looking towards grand staircase

Music room

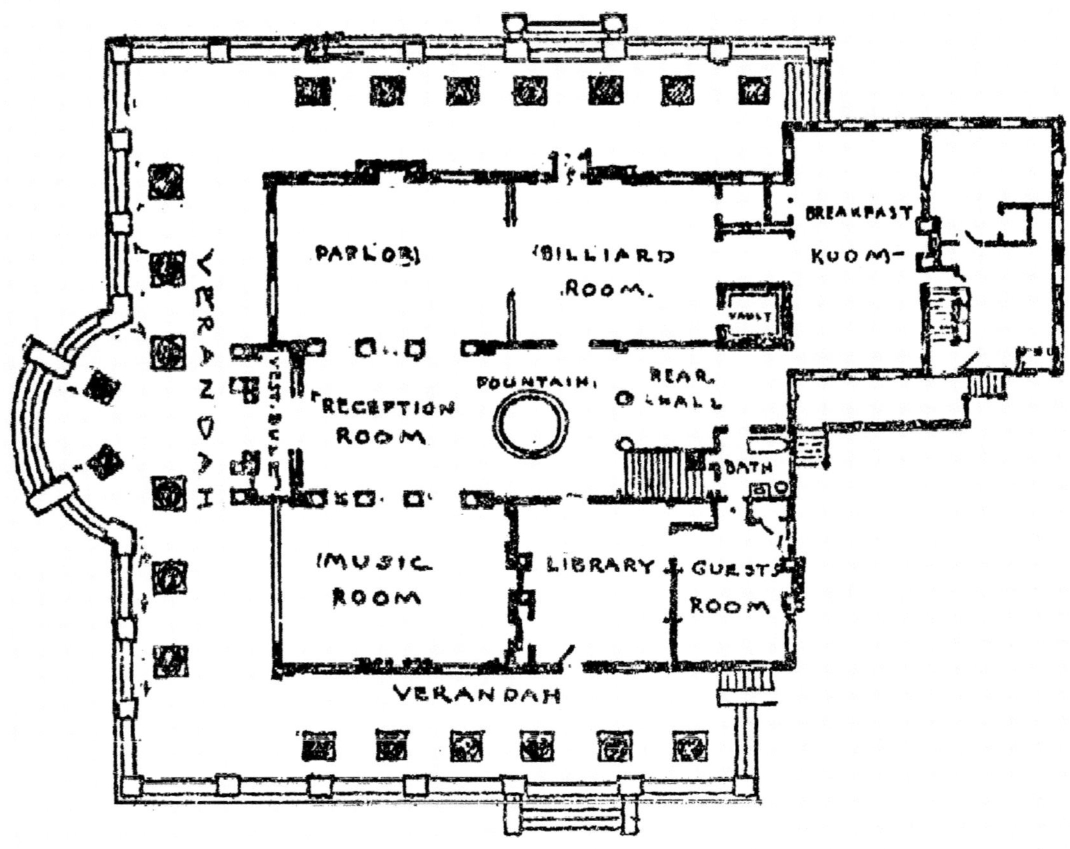

First floor plan

North Wales. Leading from the reception hall was a walnut staircase taken from Victoria House, with carved grotesques on the newel posts. Facing the landing, a 15-foot square window, originally from the Indian Territory exhibit, featured glass plate images of Native Americans. A 15-foot terra cotta fireplace, also from Victoria House, highlighted a billiard room off the parlor. The second story comprised eight bedrooms, each with access to the veranda.

Adjoining the rear of the main residence was a three-story addition; on its first floor were the dining room, kitchen, and pantries, with bedrooms for the servants above. The third floor held a large ballroom; in the basement was a bowling alley.

Surrounding himself with magnificence, Dyer was obsessed with filling Idlewild's every corner with furniture and objets d'art in scale with the house's immense interior. An antiquary of distinction, he collected nothing but the best, and only that with impeccable provenance. His collection included a six-foot-tall candelabra once belonging to Charles Tyson Yerkes (the Chicago streetcar magnate), a mirror from the home of James Buchanan Eads (the famous bridge engineer), and a Venetian chair once in the collection of New York architect Stanford White.

Dyer died in 1912, bequeathing his extensive collection of artifacts to the Kansas City Museum. In 1940 Idlewild was demolished.

Charles A. Stockstrom Residence

St. Louis (1907)

THE FALL of 1907 saw members of the Liederkranz Society, an organization focused on German culture, music, and family, celebrating the formal dedication of their new performance hall. At the same time, German-American architect Ernest C. Janssen was finishing the design for the most lavish residence on the city's south side, for Liederkranz member Charles A. Stockstrom.

With the help of his brothers, Charles Stockstrom had invented the gas cooking stove in 1902. He started the Quick Meal Company, which later became the Magic Chef Stove Company, for many years the largest of its kind in the world. This improved method of cooking, "releasing women from drudgery" in the kitchen, was a huge success, enabling Stockstrom to build this grand residence far beyond the scale of any others nearby.

Main facade

Entrance detail

The residence was in Compton Heights, a picturesque neighborhood on high ground known for its "pure air and healthy living" some 15 minutes from downtown and adjacent to the 40-acre Reservoir Park, the site of the Compton Hill Water Tower. Designed by Harvey Ellis, this decorative edifice concealed standpipes that assured area residents consistent water pressure.

Comprised predominantly of first- and second-generation Germans—leaders in medicine, law, and business—Compton Heights had an impressive collection of Queen Anne, Chateauesque, and Romanesque houses. Still, the 30-room Stockstrom residence, set on the brow of two landscaped acres, was in a category of its own.

The rosy glow of the buff-beige brick, crisp salmon-colored terra cotta ornament (a Janssen specialty), and red tile roof at 3400 Russell Boulevard are a mighty contrast to the rich dark reception hall and grand staircase just inside the main entrance. The hall features quarter-sawn oak panels (nearly 8 feet in length and from floor to ceiling), stenciling, pocket doors, and tapestries; portieres drape the doorways.

The Strockstrom house is considered Chateauesque in style; locally it is likened to the "Brewer's Baronial" residences Janssen designed in Portland Place and elsewhere in Compton Heights. Here he

Dining room

Salon

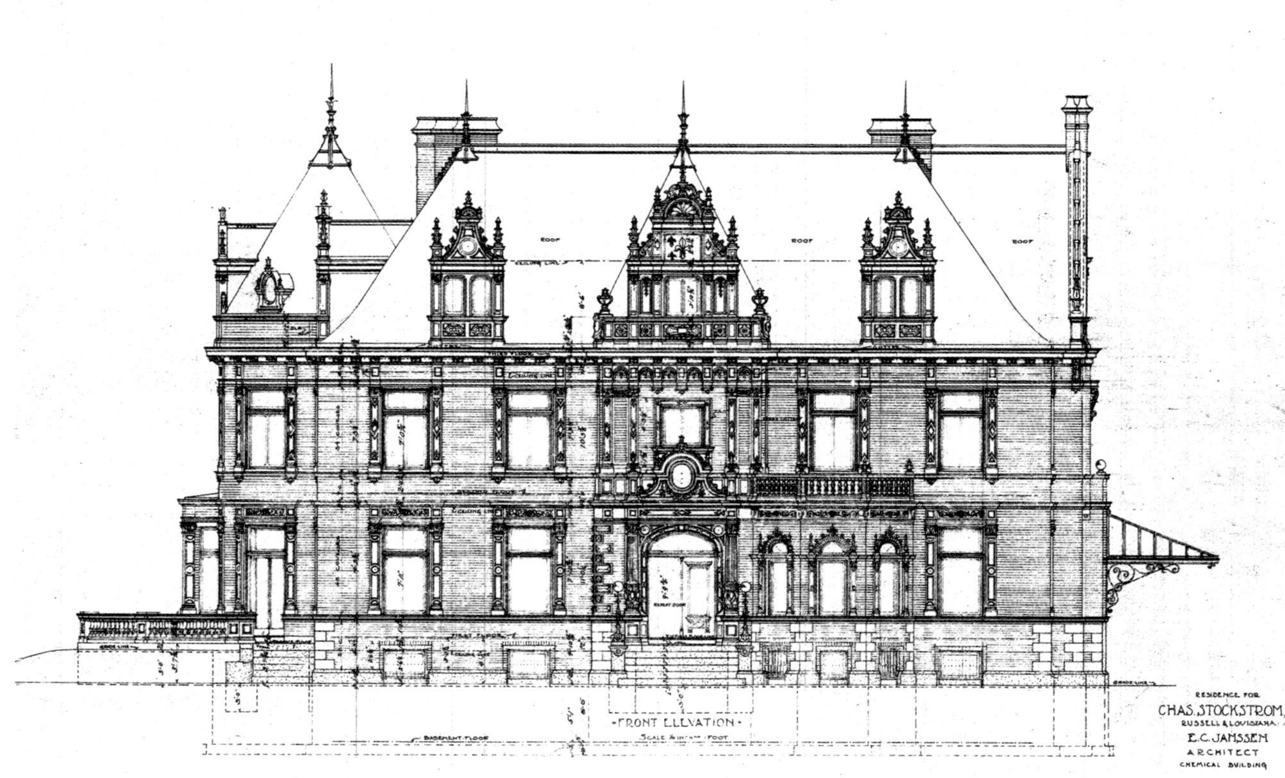

Architect's elevation drawing

synthesized Rococo ornament in public rooms—the music salon and delicately frescoed main parlor—with robust German sensibilities to provide *gemütlich* (comfortable and relaxed) spaces for family living, such as the library, hung with caribou and elk hunting trophies. Delicately patterned and leaded glass—clear and pale turquoise—is repeated throughout the house. Tucked beneath the main staircase is a circular "retiring room" for guests, hung with a multitude of hooks to accommodate coats; embroidery on the receiving room portieres repeats the pattern of the plaster ornament; cherubs playfully mimic the five senses in the gilded lavender rococo drawing room. The house had a phone booth and there was a bowling alley in the basement. The Magic Chef stove in the glazed tile kitchen is still in use today.

Stockstrom's daughter, Adda Ohmeyer, lived at the residence until 1990 (she was 93), when the present owners bought it. Their commitment to historic preservation in restoring this property helped save the landmark from demolition.

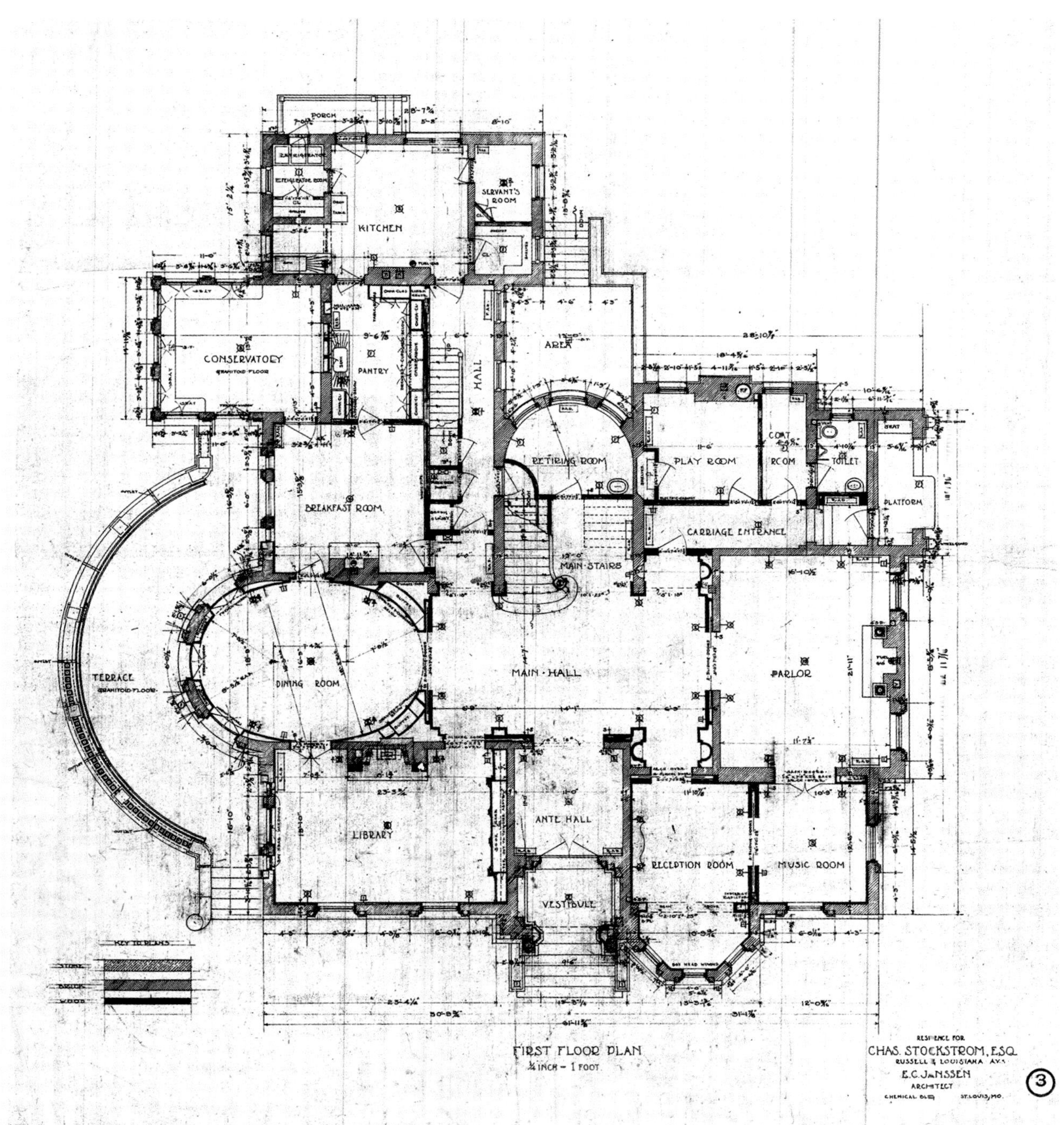

First floor plan

William Albert Hirsch Residence

St. Louis (1908)

On its inception in 1905, the unique suburban enclave of Parkview was quaintly touted as "artistic homes in artistic surroundings." Within earshot of downtown University City, northwest of Forest Park and directly adjacent to Washington University, Parkview is another of the distinctive neighborhoods planned by Julius Pitzman. Neither palatial nor elite, the houses in Parkview were originally built for a

Main facade

Stair hall

View to reception room

more middle-class clientele and they represent the move toward home ownership at a time when three-quarters of the city's households still rented. The majority of the neighborhood was built between 1906 and 1914 and is characterized by a rich mix of Craftsman, Tudor, and Colonial Revival styles.

The Pitzman plan represents his last and most sophisticated solution to creating an enclosed and private neighborhood, one able to hold its own against increased commercial growth north along

Dining room

Delmar Avenue and buffered from the Rock Island line railroad that ran directly to the south. Within the nearly square plan, Pitzman created dramatically curved (nearly horseshoe-shaped) streets interspersed with triangular pockets of green. Deep, narrow lots that are more characteristically urban than suburban combine with picturesque mature plantings to create the unique feel of the neighborhood. In Parkview, one's neighbors may be close but the bustle of the city is far removed.

Architect William A. Hirsch and his wife, Georgia, who "immediately fell in love" with the charm of the place, chose to build at 6236 Waterman Avenue. His design is a fine example of the Arts and Crafts aesthetic that still exists in Parkview: a spare facade of brown brick with matching mortar is subtly ornamented on the ground floor with decorative patterns created by alternating headers and stretchers; a broad arched cornice covers the oak entrance and glazed green tile caps the roof. Hirsch hired a professional landscape architect (to date unknown) to create a planting plan that included catalpa trees to shade the front and a more formal garden in the rear (later replaced by a garage).

Living room

In photographs, the interior's human scale belies the house's size. There are front and back stair halls and a first-floor sewing room, five bedrooms on the second floor, a billiard room and maid's room on the third. The interior is pure Arts and Crafts, evident especially in the living and reception rooms: built-ins (in one case, an alcove-like seat doubles as a room divider); the use of quarter-sawn red oak (stained to match the dark faux half-timbering and ceiling beams); Stickley and Mission-style furnishings (leather Morris chairs, the dining table, and umbrella stand); and the glazed tile of the hearth all speak to the Craftsman sensibility. The living room features an Art Nouveau carpet imported from Austria and the stylized ornament of the stained glass, light fixtures, and fabric window treatments echo the Art Nouveau aesthetic. Twin bearskin rugs add a final dramatic flourish.

Even today Parkview is referred to as an "urban oasis." The neighborhood remains highly desirable and residences are often handed down within families. In fact, members of the Hirsch family still reside at 6236 Waterman.

J. W. THOMPSON RESIDENCE

St. Louis (1908)

THE J. W. THOMPSON residence was designed by Thomas P. Barnett of Barnett, Haynes & Barnett, a second generation of St. Louis architects related to George I. Barnett (designer of Selma Hall and important country estates) The house is an eclectic addition to Hortense Place, another of the private places created near Forest Park, this one established in 1900 by cotton manufacturer Jacob Goldman.

Main facade and side drive

Entrance detail

Reflecting the taste of its owner, John W. Thompson, a railroad contractor whose offices were downtown in Louis Sullivan's then new Wainwright Building, the house represents an experimental departure for the architecture firm, whose work was grounded in classicism.

Barnett found inspiration in the Austrian art and architecture he saw at the 1904 World's Fair in St. Louis, including Josef Maria Olbrich's exhibition of arts and crafts, Peter Behrens' reading room and, in particular, the Austrian pavilion by Ludwig Baumann. Cofounder of the Architects' Central Association and architect of the 1904 Ministry of War building on the Ringstrasse in Vienna and a 1909 addition to the Austrian Museum of Art and Industry, Ludwig Baumann took a "neobaroque" approach to design that was favored by Archduke Ferdinand. Furthermore, Baumann's style more often coincided

Staircase

with the official preference for tradition in architecture, in contrast to the modernism of contemporaries Behrens, Otto Wagner, and Adolf Loos.

During a trip to Europe in 1907, Barnett was emphatically influenced by Secessionist architecture and the German Art Nouveau style of Otto Wagner's newly completed Kirche am Steinhof (1905). The Thompson residence is ultimately an expression of the cubic format and stylized ornament of the Secessionist Building in Vienna (1898).

The polychrome effect of pale buff brick and verde marble revetment and an encyclopedic array of ornament contributed to the drama of the Thompson residence. Strong vertical and horizontal elements, such as the freestanding pillars that punctuated the cornice and balconies suspended from bold decorative chains, enhanced the facade's play of light and dark. The cubic format successfully addressed the corner site (just inside the west gateway of Hortense Place) and was used again by Barnett at his own

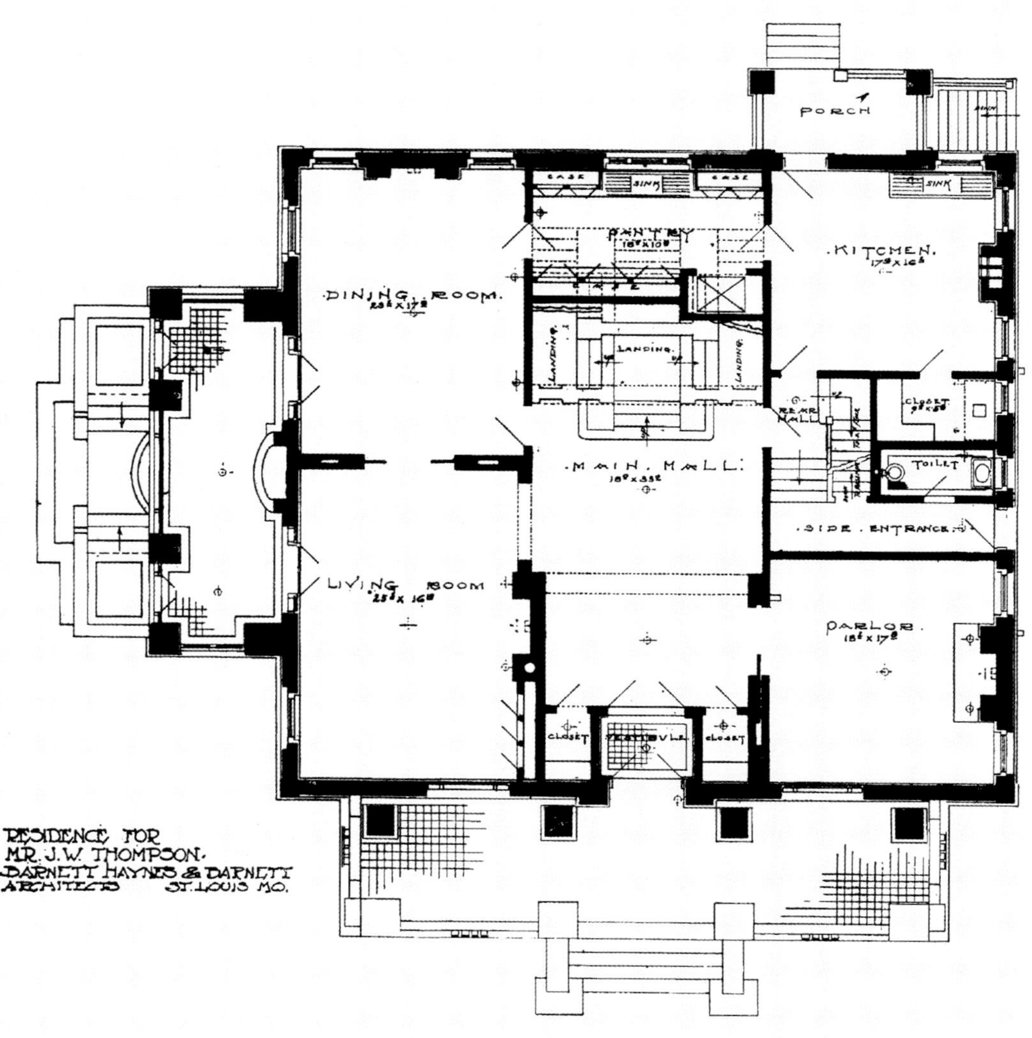

First floor plan

house built nearby in the same year. The sophisticated ornament, an aspect of particular interest to the architect, included broad terra cotta urns, weblike iron railings, and willow motifs. The stained glass entry was screened by a graphic pattern and flanked by twin busts of Minerva, goddess of wisdom, commerce, and crafts (and a favorite Secessionist motif).

The interior's foursquare plan, typical of Barnett, was mirrored on the main and upper floors, which shared the double-height main hall. The extensive use of rich materials like marble and stained glass and such details as mosaic on the staircase and a pinecone cornice in the dining room made for an interior as elaborate as the exterior. Subsequent owners removed much of the facade's ornament and stripped away the monumental pillars in an attempt to classicize the house, but in recent years it as been restored to a more accurate version of Barnett's original design.

Oaklands

Edwin Willis Shields House

Kansas City (1909–1910)

Wilder & Wight, the architects for Oaklands, were customarily engaged in the design of monumental neoclassical stone institutional and civic buildings throughout Kansas City, but early in their practice, they embraced other traditional forms of expression. One such commission was a house built in the Tudor Revival style for Edwin Willis and Martha Deardorff Shields. With its emphasis on solid brick masonry, it may appear restrained, but it is not the Americanized version of later counterparts.

Edwin Shields, a grain merchant and financier in association with Kansas City developer J. C. Nichols, filed the plat for Southwood Park, where he built his 2½-story house on a 10-acre tract. Wilder & Wight chose a three-part cadence for the house in form and detailing, as the main tripartite unit is echoed in the arrangement of the fenestration and south-facing entry. A pair of front-facing gabled wings flanks the main entrance, originally sheltered by a Tudor and Gothic arched entry porch with a balustrade of cut stone posts and strapwork. Recessed double-hung windows typically occur in groups of three, set in thick, cut-stone surrounds. Even the massive brick chimneys repeat the triad in their grouping of flues and pots. Finally, the rhythm is reaffirmed in the front-facing three-hipped dormers.

Main facade, east view

Rear facade

Main entrance detail

Main hall

Drawing room

The interior of Oaklands reiterates the Tudor Revival style throughout, drawing heavily on its historic precedent, with few exceptions. In the beamed and plastered great hall, Wilder & Wight deliberately replicated the carved oak staircase at Rothamsted. The dining room, living room and library, reached off the great hall, all feature paneled oak walls and parged ceilings of elaborate strapwork. Directly contrasting the style of the majority of the first-floor rooms, a Louis XVI drawing room had paneled white walls and a parquet floor. A total of 10 bedrooms were originally designed for the second floor and the attic housed drapery storage and Mrs. Shields' closet and sewing room.

While the interior of Oaklands was extraordinary in its materials and craftsmanship, it was most distinguished by Martha Shields' impressive, wide-ranging art collection. The daughter of Louis Deardorff, a pioneer lumberman, Martha was a well-known art connoisseur, amassing rare furniture, paintings, and decorative art for her residence. She fundamentally rejected modern tastes in favor of 17th-century Flemish tapestries and paintings by Sir Peter Lely, Sir Joshua Reynolds, William Gainsborough, and Thomas Lawrence. A large music cabinet in the drawing room featured Sevres plaques with ormolu mountings on its doors; in 1850 it won first place in a London furniture exhibition.

Edwin Shields died in 1920; Martha, in 1954. During her lifetime, Mrs. Shields gave the former University of Kansas City several gifts of land acquired by her husband in the original platting. Upon her death Martha left her remaining property to her daughter and son. As with the nearby estates of Walter Dickey and U. S. Epperson, Oaklands was deeded to the now University of Missouri–Kansas City. The Bloch School of Business at UMKC now occupies the house.

Library

Charles A. Stix Residence

St. Louis County (1909)

The 1909 Tudor Revival residence at 26 Portland Place was the design of Mauran & Russell. The third and most decorative of their Tudor works along the street, it added a new idiom to the neighborhood and provided a departure from the Richardsonian, Chateauesque, and Georgian Revival styles of houses nearby. Its picturesque massing contrasted with that of its neighbors, as did the crenellations,

Main facade and side view

Side view

clustered chimneys, quatrefoil balustrade, and great yawning entrance portico that evoked medieval gatehouses. Fenestration irregular in both size and type—leaded glass windows framed in stone, the oriel, arched, casement, and bay windows—and a mix of brick, half-timbering, and stone formed a composite as distinctive as its owner, or in this case, successive owners.

The residence was built for Charles A. Stix, the founder and president of Stix, Baer & Fuller department stores. Stix began his career as a stock boy for a Cincinnati dry goods store and ended it as a respected community leader at age 56, when he died of stomach cancer. Grieving crowds filled the streets during his funeral service; competitors closed their doors in his honor. Six years after Stix's death, in 1922, his widow sold the property to William K. Bixby, whose dedication to the city would match that of the previous owner.

Bixby had moved just down the street from 13 Portland Place, a quite different French Renaissance residence designed by architect W. Albert Swasey. His interest in staying in the neighborhood reflected the close social and business ties that bound the families who lived there. Bixby was chairman of the American Car & Foundry Company (a railroad business) and served on the boards of the St. Louis Union

Side view with sunroom

Trust and Boatman's Bank. Besides exclusive local private clubs, he was a member of New York's Grolier Club; in the summer, his family vacationed at Lake George, New York. His far-reaching patronage encompassed major civic institutions from the Missouri Historical Society to the Mercantile Library (his library included Shakespeare, Tennyson, Dickens, and the "children's poet" from St. Louis, Eugene Field) to the St. Louis Symphony Orchestra, the second oldest in the country. His appreciation and support of the arts set him apart; after his death in 1931, *The New York Times* eulogized him as "the ideal collector" of fine art.

Regardless of its exterior, there was little Tudor inside 26 Portland Place, save a few pieces of furniture. The interior was light and spacious—evoking Robert Adam more than medieval precedent—and filled with paintings and sculpture. The public rooms on the main floor, arranged around the reception hall, were oriented toward the south and east (with the front terrace and sunroom balancing each end);

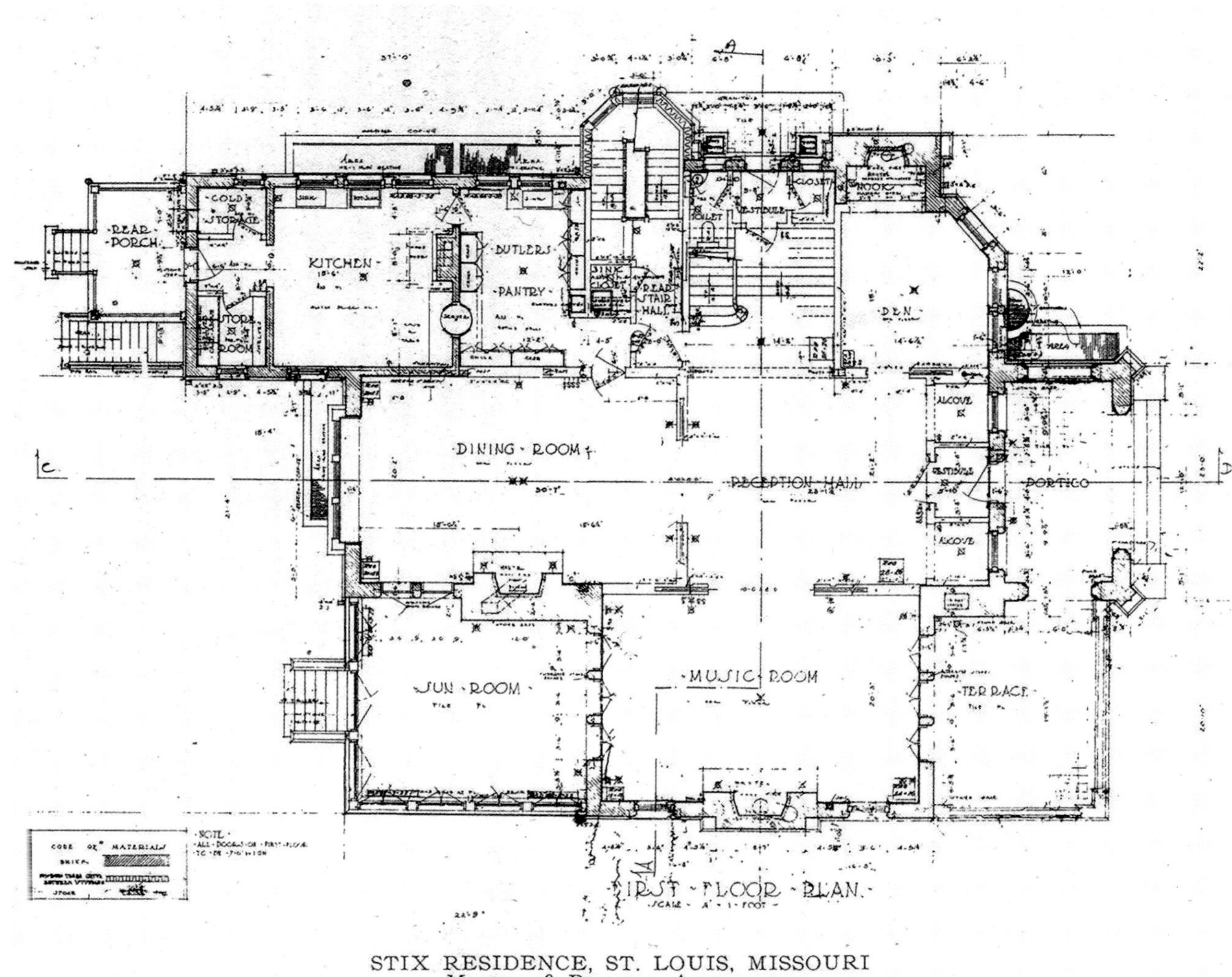

First floor plan

a den and a library (both with nooks) balanced the northwest side of the first and second floors, respectively. Upstairs there were four bedrooms, two with separate dressing rooms, and all with private baths.

Bixby lived at 26 Portland Place for only nine years. His private funeral service was held there; 180 honorary pallbearers, many of them neighbors, were named official mourners. As is the rule with the residences along Portland Place, the property remains in private hands.

CORINTHIAN HALL

ROBERT ALEXANDER LONG HOUSE

Kansas City (1909–1910)

RIVALING any Kansas City residence in scope, materials, design, and site is Corinthian Hall, a Beaux-Arts mansion built of buff Bedford limestone at a cost of $600,000. Located in the Melrose Addition subdivision at the crest of Kessler Park's forested terrain, the 72-room mansion was designed by Henry Ford Hoit, one of the top architects working in Kansas City in the first half of the 20th century.

Kentucky-born and hardworking from youth, Robert Alexander Long, in 1875, started a lumber business, R. A. Long & Company, with Robert White and Victor B. Bell, selling the wood from his dismantled hay sheds. The Long-Bell Lumber Company, as it later came to be, had a capital stock of $300,000 in 1884, and by 1910, the firm was the country's largest manufacturer of southern pine, with lumber yards throughout the Southwest.

In time, the understated yet worldly and vastly accomplished Long controlled interests in steamship and railroad lines, coal mines, and supply houses, and built the first all-steel skyscraper in Kansas City.

Main facade

View from southwest corner of grounds

Collaborating with J. C. Nichols and landscape architects George E. Kessler and Hare & Hare, Long developed the industrial town of Longview, Washington, to house and service the employees of his lumber mill; at the time, Longview was second only to Washington, D.C., as the nation's largest preplanned city.

Hoit's original plan for Corinthian Hall called for a three-story residence with a central portico supported by six Bedford limestone columns, each 25 feet high and 2½ feet in diameter, leading to bronze entry doors. Symmetry prevails in the placement of fenestration and multiple chimneys; the whole is balanced to the east and west by a one-story sunroom and a porte cochere, respectively.

True to Beaux Arts philosophy, the outbuildings, also constructed of limestone and detailed similarly to the main residence, sit on a biaxial plane. The two-story carriage house and adjoining stable (at one time boarding some of the nation's finest Hackney horses) are "aligned with the axis of the Great Hall of the main residence," while the "greenhouse and conservatory flank the long colonnaded pergola and form an east-west minor axis."

The interior of Corinthian Hall exhibits elaborate finish materials throughout: vestibules in pink Skyros and Siena marble, walls of Caen stone, and coffered plaster ceilings. The marble-floored entrance hall, measuring 50 feet by 26 feet, leads to the white marble and bronze staircase, the design of which is based on the Petit Trianon.

Hoit chose an interpretation of period styles in the individual rooms. The Adamesque breakfast room, Francis I living room, Louis XIV dining room, Elizabethan library, and Jacobethan living room reflect a flamboyant aspect of the otherwise subdued lumber baron. The most elaborate of the interior spaces, the Louis XVI grand salon, originally displayed a Gobelin tapestry and a Savonnerie carpet

Grand hall

Main stair at mezzanine

Louis XVI salon

purchased through William Baumgartner & Co., a New York firm that counted the Vanderbilts and Astors among its clients.

As president of the Liberty Memorial Association, Long led the campaign to build the Liberty Memorial commemorating World War I, now listed as a National Historic Landmark. When this Kansas City monument was dedicated in 1921, Admiral Earl Beatty, commander of the British navy, and Admiral R. E. Coontz, chief of U.S. naval operations, were guests of the Longs at Corinthian Hall.

Surrounded by the original stone and wrought-iron fence, Corinthian Hall is now the Kansas City Museum, with displays of regional and natural history (including dioramas) and a 50-seat planetarium. While most of the interiors serve as exhibit rooms and storage, the historic integrity of the exterior, interior, setting, and associated outbuildings remains intact.

Sun porch

Pergola and conservatory

Carriage house and adjoining stable

Conservatory

~N~
~CONSERVATORY~
~PERGOLA~
~GREEN-HOUSE~
~PERGOLA~
~WORK-RM~
~PLANTS~
~PADDOCK~
~STALLS~
~CARRIAGE-RM~
~STALLS~
~LIVING RM~
~PORCH~
~PORCH~
KITCHEN
~LIBRARY~
~ELIZABETHAN~
~MALL~
~RENAISSANCE~
(FRENCH)
~SALON~
~LOUIS XVI~
~LIVING-ROOM~
~FRANCIS 1ST~
~DINING-ROOM~
~LOUIS XIV~
~SUN-PARLOR~
~TERRACE~
~PORTICO~
~TERRACE~
VESTIBULE
SCALE

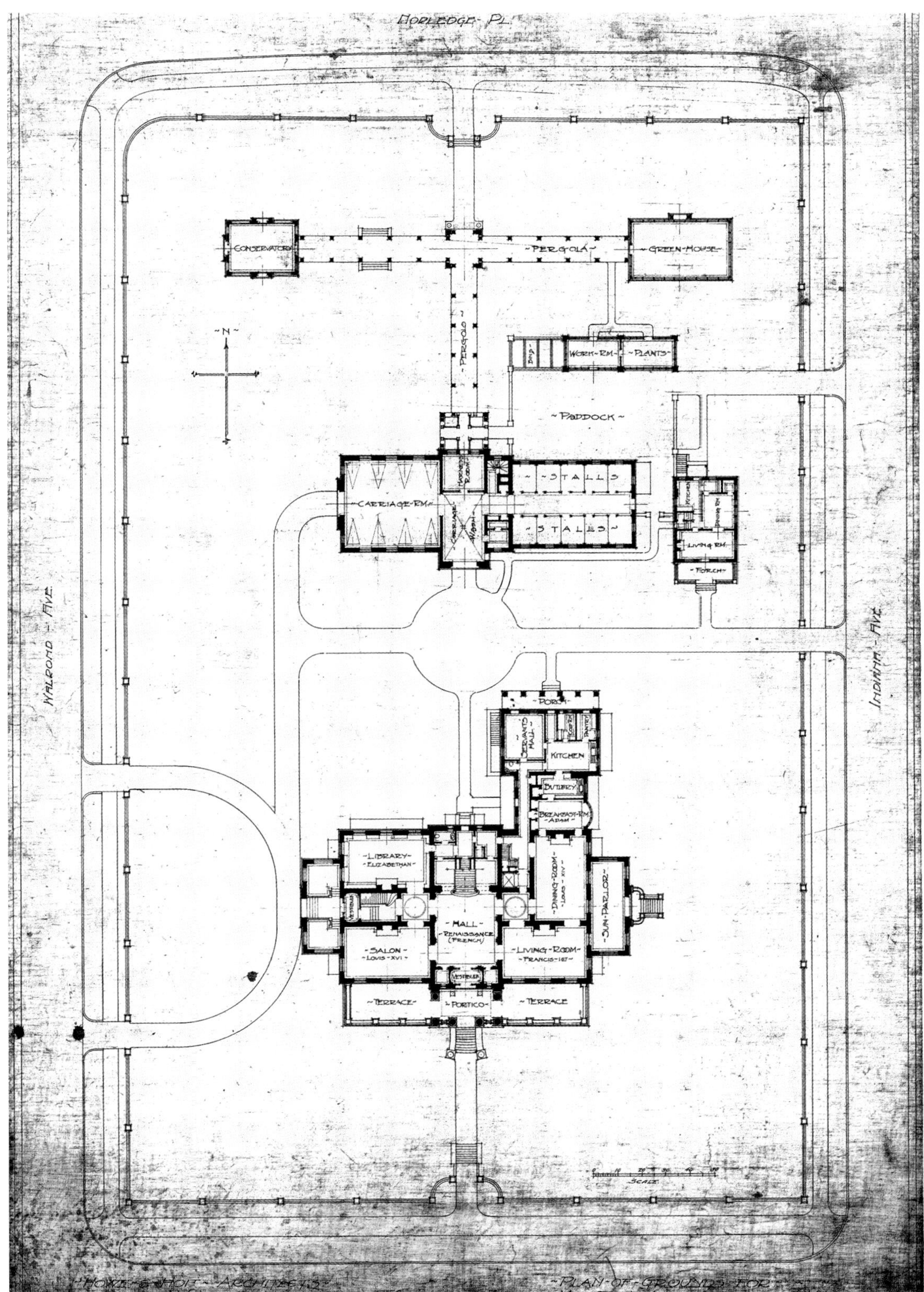

Site plan

CECILWOOD

ROBERT SOMERS BROOKINGS HOUSE

Clayton, St. Louis County (1911)

ROBERT SOMERS BROOKINGS conceived his Georgian Revival residence at 6510 Ellenwood Avenue as the place in which he would retire. It happened, however, that the 20 years he lived there were his most productive in the public sphere. He had shaped much of St. Louis at the turn of the century: as president of Washington University, he increased the institution's enrollment and status and worked to develop neighborhoods near the campus, in particular, Brentmoor Park. Under his leadership, Washington University relocated from 18th Street and Washington Avenue downtown to its present Hilltop Campus west of Forest Park, planned by Olmsted Associates circa 1895. Following World War I, in the early 1920s, he established a number of organizations that evolved into the Brookings Institution in Washington, D.C., a respected nonprofit with a mission to research current and emerging issues and propose solutions.

The Ellenwood house, located in what is now the Wydown-Forsyth District, is credited to Cope & Stewardson, the official architects of the new university campus. Both principals of the firm having passed away by 1902, it was James Jamieson, an architect prolific in St. Louis at that time, who planned the sophisticated Georgian Revival house that so suited Brookings' genteel personality, his collection of art, and his frequent entertaining. It was, in fact, Jamieson's professional connection to Brookings through which he received a good many commissions from prestigious and influential St. Louisans.

Private drive and grounds to Cecilwood

Entrance facade

Garden facade

Built from Flemish bond brick with white trim, the house's main block is capped with a gambrel roof of slate; it has east and west wings set at oblique angles. The five-bay entrance porch, evoking an 18th-century orangery, extends beyond the main block; it is ornamented by a Doric colonnade and fanlight over the door and topped by a flat roof with a Chippendale balustrade. The vocabulary of classical forms deftly repeated in Jamieson's design reinforces the harmony of parts to the whole: the rhythm of round-headed and segmental-arched windows, keystones that detail both doors and windows, and the Palladian-inspired window above the entrance are mirrored in the garden facade. Lattice and stick work ornament the garden side as well. Archival sources indicate that landscape architect George Kessler met with Brookings the year the house was built to advise on plans for the grounds.

Front hall

Parlor

Picture gallery

The plan skillfully addresses Brookings' specification to accommodate large groups for entertaining yet provide comfortable space for everyday living. The main hall, accessed through one of three near room-size alcoves off the entrance, is almost equal in size to the adjacent living room. The wings embrace the grounds to the south—the west wing accommodating service areas and the garage, the east wing housing a long vaulted corridor for Brookings's paintings. Bedrooms and servants' quarters occupied the second story.

In 1923 Brookings donated his residence and possessions (including his art collection and furnishings, "down to the silver") to Washington University. Today Brookings' long private drive is a public street and its ornamental iron gate is closed. The house serves as a gracious alumni center, with the dorms and parking lots of the burgeoning campus perhaps encroaching far closer than Brookings would have approved.

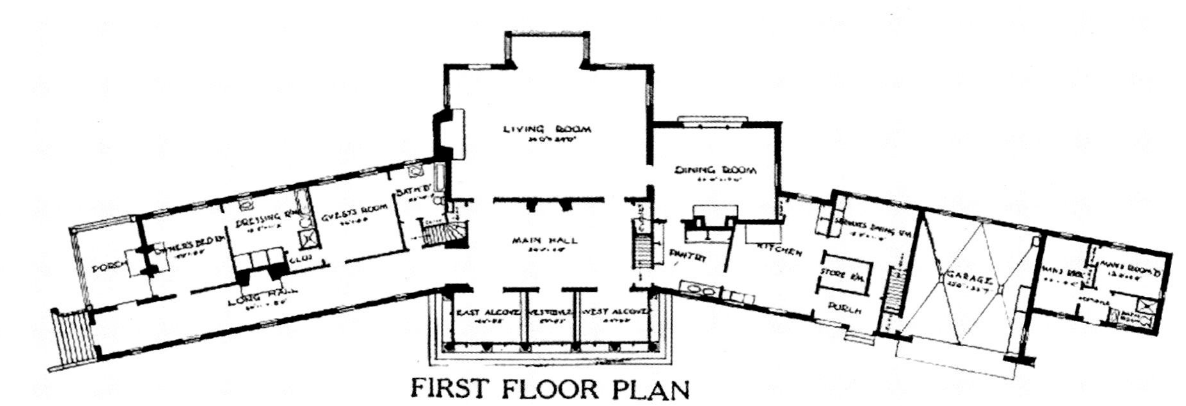

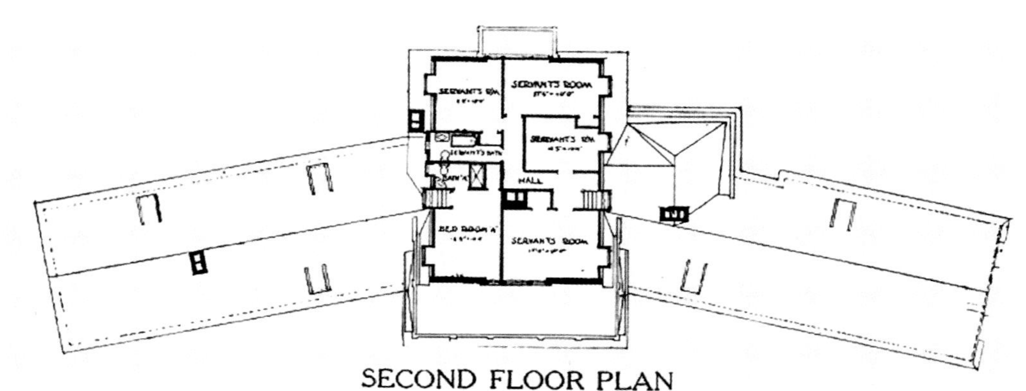

First and second floor plans

Robert S. Brookings at the parlor fireplace

WALTER SIMPSON DICKEY RESIDENCE

Kansas City (1911–1912)

BORN in Toronto in 1862, Walter Simpson Dickey set off for Kansas City in 1885 to revive a defunct glazed-clay-pipe manufacturing plant located in the East Bottoms, an industrial area nestled between the bluffs and the Missouri River. A descendant of *Mayflower* passengers and of combatants in the American Revolution, Dickey was a cunning profiteer who snatched up failed competitors and

Main facade, later-day view

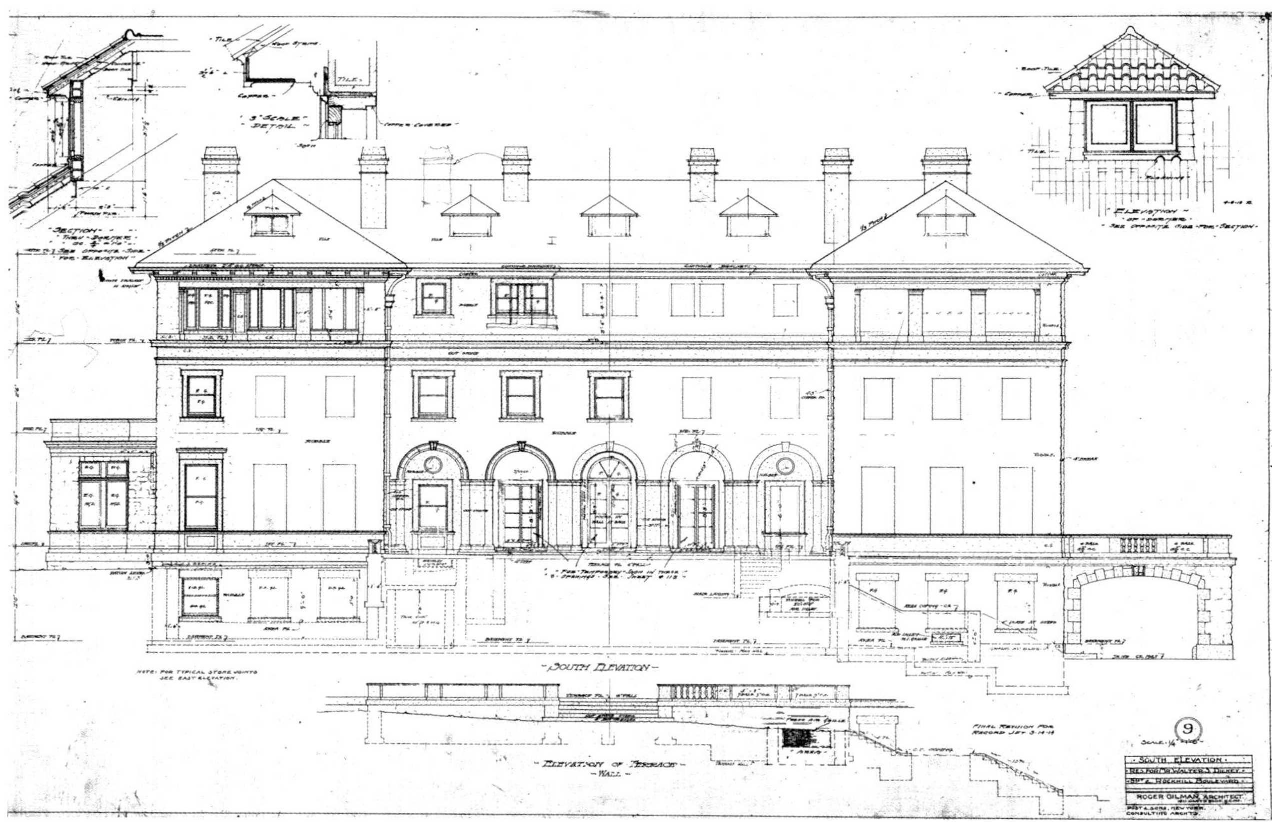

South elevation drawing

exploited cheap rail shipping for his product that formed the infrastructure for cities burgeoning across the United States. Dickey's unbridled spirit led him to shape an empire: not only was his "burnt-clay" business the largest in the world, he was the publisher and principal stockholder of two Kansas City newspapers (the *Post* and the *Journal*, which later consolidated), a pacesetter in raising thoroughbred cattle, and a figure well established in the national political arena.

Dickey was also a pioneer of inland waterways navigation in the Kansas City, Missouri River Navigation Company, a barge line between Kansas City and St. Louis established in 1909 with William Rockhill Nelson. In 1916, Dickey, an ardent leader of the Missouri Republican party, received the Republican nomination for United States Senator, an election he lost to James A. Reed.

During his rise to business, social, and political prominence, Dickey purchased a 10-acre site, for $10,000 an acre, in the Resurvey of Mulkey Park subdivision, included in the annexation of 1911. It was probably no coincidence that Dickey invested that year in freshly appropriated acreage that was lacking a modern sewer system: Until the annexation, Kansas City was not legally forced to lay costly sewer connections. This was the case not only with Dickey's property; it applied as well to the subdivisions owned by J. C. Nichols, directly to the south and west.

On the other hand, major business tycoons like Dickey helped to anchor Nichols' developments by constructing architecturally significant mansions, thereby setting a commensurate trend in the more expensive parcels of the protected land, especially that of the Sunset Hill district.

Living room converted to the University library

Dickey chose Kansas City architect Roger Gilman—assisted by George B. Post, of New York—to design his native limestone, three-story Italian Renaissance–neoclassical residence. Gilman's work in Kansas City is somewhat rare; Post, the architect of the New York Stock Exchange and the residence of Cornelius Vanderbilt, is the more recognized of the two.

For the 27-room Dickey mansion, Gilman and Post placed a broad, neoclassical portico supported by four slender stone Doric columns as a preface to the otherwise Italian Renaissance–style house, displaying the universal vocabulary of that idiom. The native limestone for the facade was quarried at the site, and upon the completion of the residence, it was converted into a pond at the northeast corner of the property.

The layout of the U-shaped interior was peculiar to the time: a two-story marble great hall and loggia are flanked by formal quartered-oak and beamed-ceiling drawing rooms, in which Dickey and his wife, Katherine, often entertained dignitaries, such as Vice President Calvin Coolidge.

Mcin staircase and foyer, later-day view

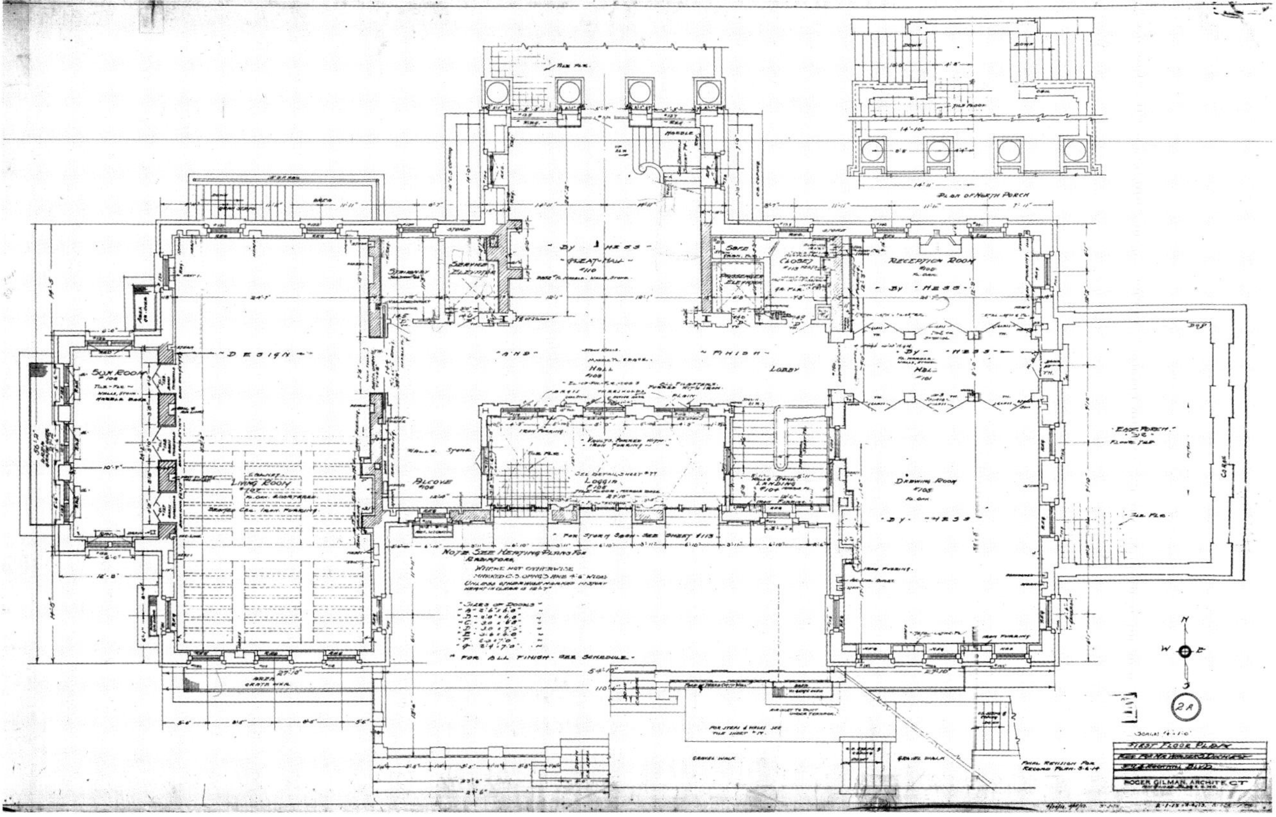

First floor plan

The second story was planned as the family's living quarters, with a large "dormitory" placed adjacent to the son's room and six bedrooms. A banquet-size dining room and kitchen, servants' bedrooms, "family bedroom," and library filled the third floor. The basement of the Dickey mansion, comprising a 25- by 15-foot tiled pool, a billiard room, dressing rooms, and ample space for storage and a houseman's workroom, was in part a recreation suite for the family and a separate workspace for their hired help. Two passenger elevators connected the basement to the upper floors.

After Walter Dickey passed away unexpectedly in January 1931 (he had lived alone in the mansion after the death of his wife, Katherine), philanthropist William Volker acquired the mansion and grounds for $75,000; it was included in the 40-acre site he donated for the campus of the former University of Kansas City, where it served as the initial building. Known today as Scofield Hall, it houses the administrative offices for the University of Missouri–Kansas City.

Brentmoor Park

Stanley Stoner House (1911)
C. H. Duncker House (1916)

Clayton, St. Louis County

ALTHOUGH the Stoner and Duncker residences were truly suburban when they were built—a streetcar line was their link to the city—they are now in the heart of Clayton. The neighborhood in which they sit, Brentmoor Park, retains the pastoral quality that characterized it in 1910, the year it was platted, due in part to the visionary plan devised by Henry Wright. While in St. Louis, Wright worked as a planner, architect, and landscape architect, perfecting techniques for which he became known at Radburn, New Jersey, and Sunnyside Gardens in Queens, New York. At Brentmoor Park, and

Side view of Stoner house

Duncker house, architect's rendering

its adjacent sister subdivisions, Brentmoor and Forest Ridge, Wright defined the elements that constitute a successful neighborhood, one of which is the belief that beauty is a vital component of the well-planned environment.

Over half the houses in Brentmoor Park, including the Stoner and Duncker houses, were built between 1910 and 1920. The cream of St. Louis society was represented in the neighborhood, as were the best local architectural firms—Cann & Corrubia, James Jamieson (for Cope & Stewardson of Philadelphia), Maritz & Young, and Henry Wright himself, as well as Chicagoan Howard Van Doren Shaw. The enclave's range of architectural styles includes Tudor and Georgian Revival, Mediterranean, and eclectic designs that defy categorization, such as that by Howard Van Doren Shaw for Stanley Stoner.

The Stoner house is a spare, vaguely French design, with restrained but highly original ornament in the form of trellises and shallow niches. It has a somewhat cruciform plan, entered from the west with its primary facade to the south, and is effective, according to a contemporary source, for its intimate relationship of interior and exterior space.

Cann & Corrubia's Duncker house in contrast has a Jacobethan flavor. Its H-shaped plan incorporates Flemish-bond and herringbone brickwork trimmed with carved vergeboards and stone balustrades, all originally enlivened with striped awnings that added to the variety of silhouette.

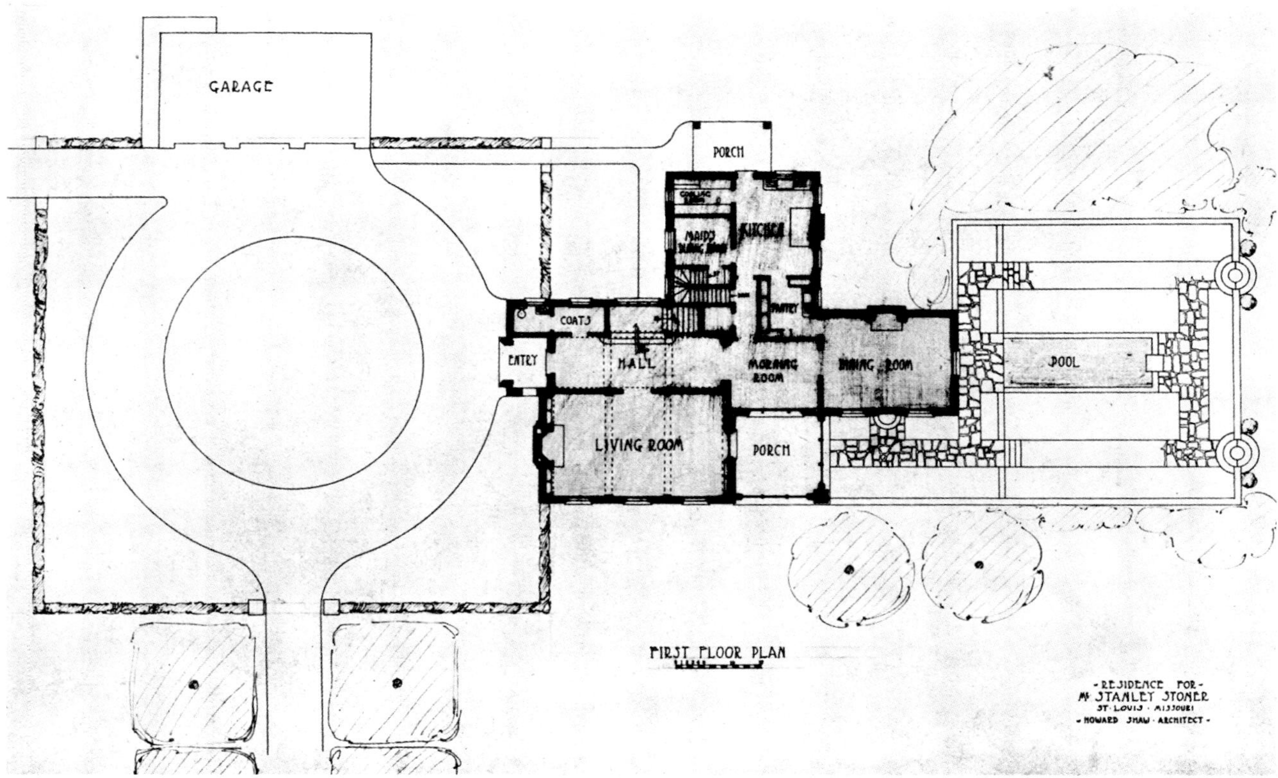

Howard Van Doren Shaw's plan of Stoner house

The integral relationship of architecture and landscape is evident in Wright's approach to planning the 34-acre tract. His comprehensive plan orients each residence inward toward the common and buried underground utilities. Working with the existing landscape—in this case, designating a swampy low spot (or "draw" as Wright described it) as common space, and ringing its periphery with drives while delegating service roads to the far edges of the plan—reflects an approach Wright may have acquired in working with Midwest landscape architect George E. Kessler. The creative use of such problematic landscape features as rocky outcroppings and irregular topography—capitalizing on them rather than considering them detriments—was a Kessler trademark that Wright may have picked up while working in Kessler's St. Louis office. Individual properties reveal the skill of other industry professionals, for example, local landscape architect John Noyes on the grounds of the Duncker property and Jens Jensen's collaboration with Cecil Gregg at 11 Brentmoor Park.

Charming stone gates (that originally provided protection for streetcar riders) still announce the entrance of Brentmoor Park and Forest Ridge. The landscape remains pastoral, and the houses highly prized, private properties.

Brentmoor Park streetcar pavilion

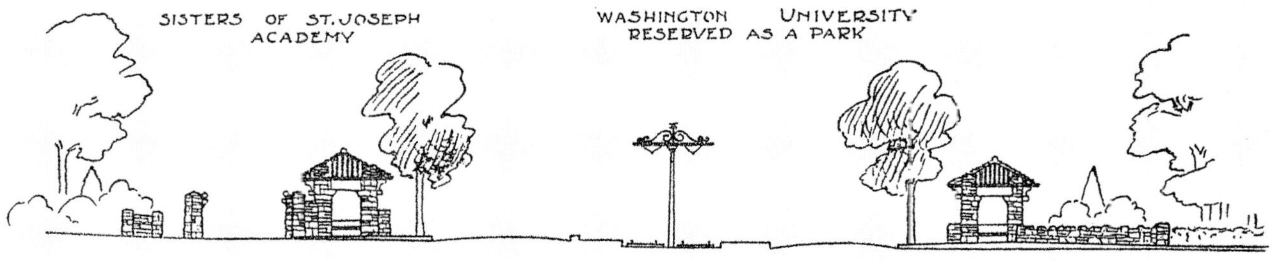

Drawing of Wydown Boulevard entrance

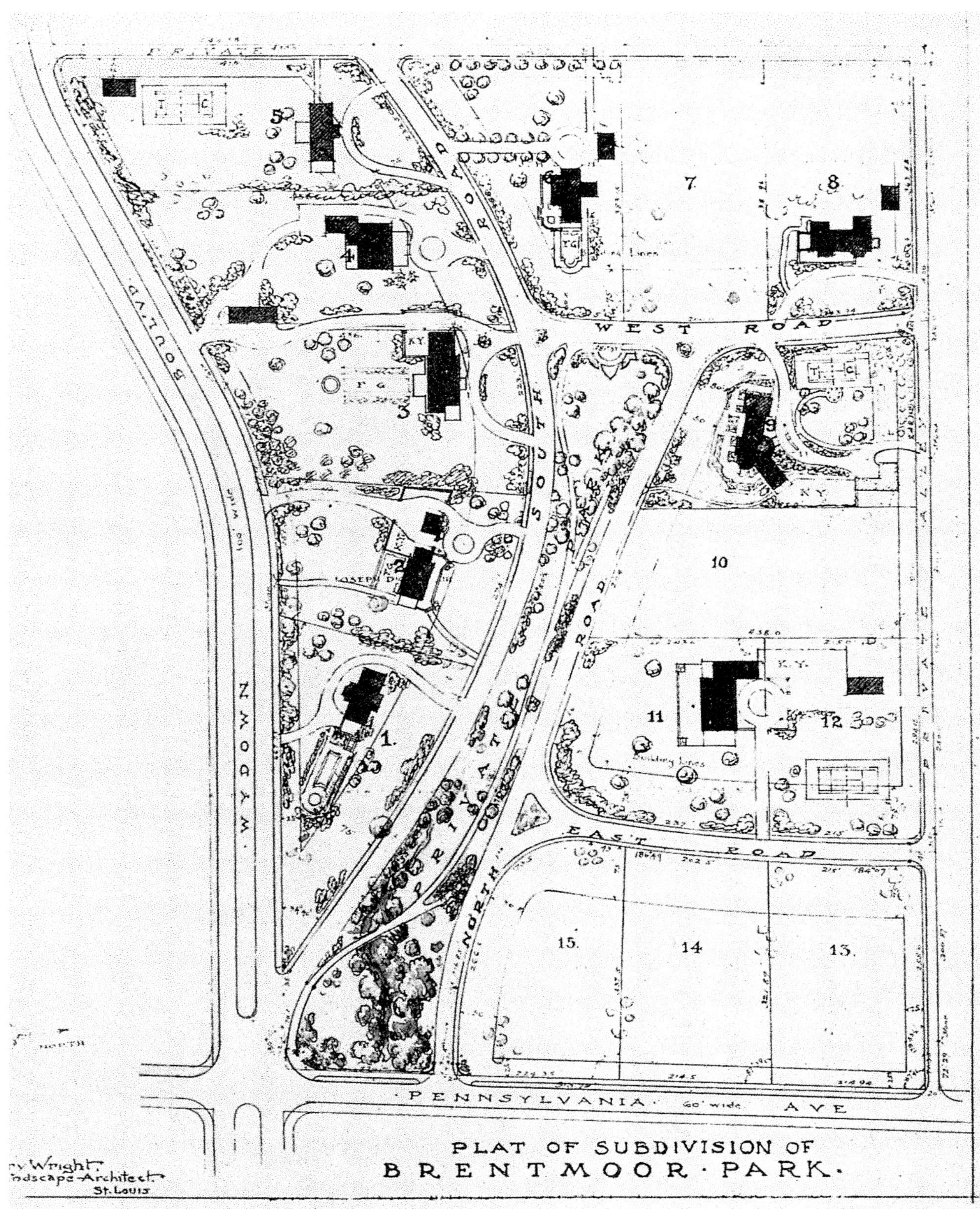

Brentmoor Park subdivision plat, Henry Wright

SUNVILLA

JAMES F. HALPIN HOUSE

Kansas City (1912–1913)

JAMES F. HALPIN was a Kansas City contractor and real estate broker whose lengthy business career involved him in some of the city's historic projects: He had a hand in developing the Intercity Viaduct, a 3,775-foot span connecting Kansas City, Missouri, and Kansas City, Kansas, along the Missouri River. He also laid the tracks for the Metropolitan Street Railway, a megaconglomerate that came by 1905 to monopolize the entire Kansas City metropolitan area.

Main facade from the southeast

Rear facade from the garden

In designing Sunvilla for James Halpin, John W. McKecknie may have been inspired by McKim, Mead & White's Villard Houses in Manhattan and Richard Morris Hunt's The Breakers, the Vanderbilt "summer house" in Newport, Rhode Island. McKecknie, one of Kansas City's most inspired architects at the turn of the 19th century, was not only a graduate of Princeton (in classical studies) and the Columbia School of Mines (in architecture), but a fervent professional in art and photography who taught at the Brooklyn Institute of Arts and Sciences. Assisting William H. Goodyear, then curator of the Metropolitan Museum of Art in New York City, McKecknie studied historic architecture in Italy for seven months, testing Goodyear's hypothesis that "mathematical regularity . . . was an exception rather than the rule." He published his findings and photographs in *Architectural Record* in 1896 and 1897.

Alain de Botton maintains, in *The Architecture of Happiness,* that "Palladio's laws were not to prove as enduring as the reputations of his houses." McKecknie played with variants on logical order and proportional relationships in the design of Sunvilla, a U-shaped, 2½-story concrete residence clad in ashlar.

Certainly there are parallels to Palladian principles, yet McKecknie circumvented any strict codes of cinquecento beauty and, instead, marked Sunvilla with strong elements derived from other architectural idioms.

The triadic composition of Sunvilla, with its central *corps de logis* and tightly hugging, flanking wings, was borne out of classic Palladianism. But McKecknie disrupts his rather loose avowal of Palladian values here. He places the loggia not at the center, but at the second floor of the wings; and the oversize tiled roof with expansive dormers suggests a feature more typical of McKecknie's Arts and Crafts–inspired designs from the same era.

The interior of Sunvilla proves more conventional, with a central hallway, measuring approximately 14 feet by 12 feet, bordered by a 46- by 17-foot living room to the east and a 17- by 20-foot dining room to the west. The front vestibule displays Arts and Crafts glazed tile and an intricate mosaic floor. The second floor has four chambers, as illustrated in the original plans, with a modestly scaled ballroom, servants' quarters, and a trunk closet placed at the attic level. A 12½-by 40-foot porch lines the eastern facade of the house.

The finishes at Sunvilla reflect McKecknie's knowledge of the Second Renaissance Revival. On the first floor, swags and strapwork of delicate light-colored plaster and Wedgwood lighting sconces contrast with thick Honduran mahogany and oak paneling and solid oak doors. Fireplace mantels on the first and second floors feature 7/8-inch white Colorado Yule marble and paired, composite fluted columns.

The Sunderland family installed an elaborate landscape planned by Hare & Hare on the 2-acre site, expressing the agrarian hobbies of Sunvilla's second owners. Among the planned features was a chicken coop at the east side of the garage, next to an elaborate rose bed and vegetable garden.

After sitting vacant in foreclosure for approximately six years, Sunvilla was purchased in 1956 by the current owner. It is one of the few residences designed by John McKecknie that remains extant.

BERNARD CORRIGAN RESIDENCE

Kansas City (1912–1913)

THE INITIAL Sunset Hill subdivision used lavish advertisements in the *Kansas City Star* and *Kansas City Times* to attract prominent individuals wanting to stake their claim; the ads plugged the names of property owners and featured their imposing residential plans on outsize lots, touting the development's charm and social climate. The subdivision's centerpiece was Ward Parkway, the dual boulevard designed by George E. Kessler that stretches through the exclusive area past Ward's original holdings, once referred to as the "Thousand Acres Restricted."

One of the first houses to be constructed adjacent to the thoroughfare remains an example of Kansas City's best architecture in every respect. Ironically, its design is the most progressive of all the houses in the subdivision, as subsequent plans fell back on somewhat restrained academic revival styles.

Main facade from the south

East facade and grounds

Designed by Louis Singleton Curtiss for Bernard Corrigan, his friend and most valued client, the three-story Prairie School house reflects the influence of Frank Lloyd Wright and his followers with its emphasis on horizontality, low-hanging wide eaves, and ribboned fenestration set in stone surrounds. Curtiss created a masterful geometric arrangement of form and massing with reinforced concrete clad in gray ashlars of shot-sawn limestone from Carthage, Missouri.

Curtiss broke the overall expansive planar exterior with a variety of ornamentation, some deriving from traditional Japanese motifs and overall Art Nouveau expressions, and others marking his interest in the work of Secessionist artists such as Josef Hoffmann and Koloman Moser. The Japanese Temple at the 1893 World's Columbian Exposition, for which Curtiss designed the Missouri State Building with his partner Frederick Gunn, undoubtedly made a lasting impression.

Designs in rolled opalescent art glass relieve the concrete and stone walls of the house's overall exterior, enhanced with gracefully drooping wisteria vines at the main entry door and sidelights, and bands carrying clusters of violet blossoms and arabesque traceries of leaves. Even the stone window surrounds feature foliated ornamentation. As Wright did with the Ward Willits house, Curtiss further broke the house's geometry with the application of traditional Japanese-inspired architectural elements. The most obvious of these are the pergola-style components at the east wing, reminiscent of the torii, or gates, of a Shinto shrine.

Entrance hall

Window detail

The prevailing interplay of dominant forms seen on the exterior is broken in the 15-room interior, which at the first floor is radically free flowing. Vast expanses of art glass in the double-height entrance hall, living room, and conservatory allow for multiple outdoor views. Hare & Hare envisioned the landscaping for the Corrigan's wedged-shaped 2½-acre lot, which included a tea garden and chicken house.

Corrigan, along with his brother, amassed a fortune by establishing the Corrigan Consolidated Street Railway Company, later bought out by the Metropolitan Street Railway Company for $1,250,000. With Corrigan as president, Metropolitan came to monopolize the entire area by 1905 by assuming control of 15 local mass transit companies. During his tenure, his interests included railroad and other construction.

It is no coincidence that Bernard Corrigan hired Curtiss to design the Prairie-style house for himself and his large family. Curtiss had designed the Baltimore Hotel for the Corrigan Realty Company in 1898 and from that time on, "Corrigan became the architect's great patron."

On the way to inspect building progress on the house in Sunset Hill one day, Corrigan fell ill; he died in January 1913, two months prior to the scheduled completion. Hattie, Corrigan's widow, chose not to live in the house and sold it for $101,370. Corrigan's death also affected Curtiss; it seems that subsequently his architectural practice all but came to a close. The house is currently listed in the National Register of Historic Places.

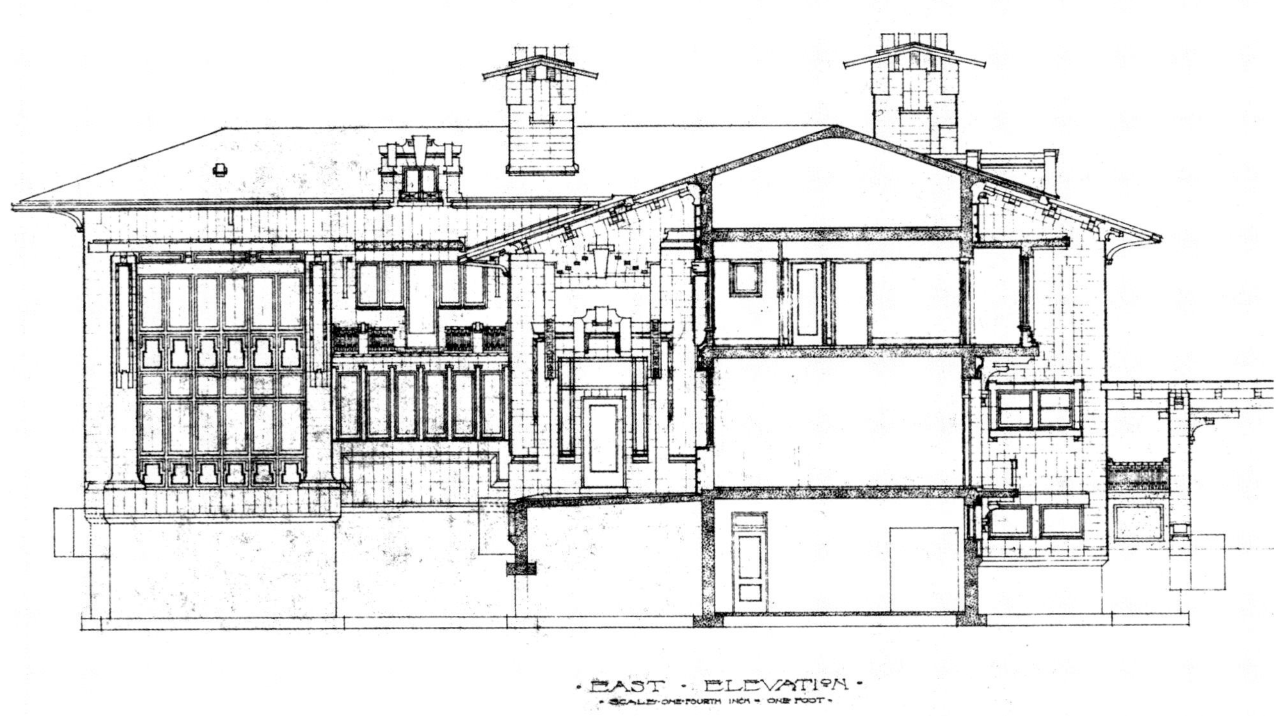

Elevation drawing, original front

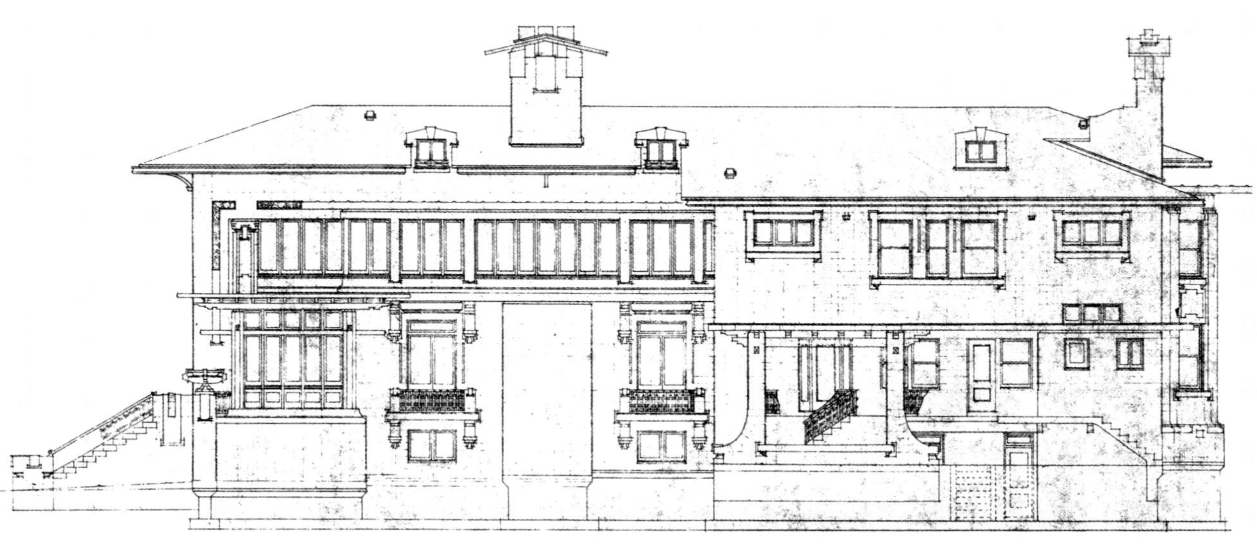

Elevation drawing, original side

Preliminary site plan

Ridgewood

Charles S. Keith House

Kansas City (1914)

Designed in 1913 and constructed in 1914, the Charles S. Keith house is one of the most successful examples of the classic residential work of the Kansas City architectural firm, Shepard, Farrar & Wiser. Located in the once highly restricted Sunset Hill subdivision in the famed Country Club district, the imposing 22-room Georgian Revival–style mansion was originally the home of Fordham University graduate Charles Keith, a rugged-individualist lumber baron, and president and general manger of the Central Coal & Coke Company, founded by his father. It was later the $75,000 home of Jesse Clyde Nichols, a mogul in Kansas City real estate development.

Main facade and drive

Main facade

View of garden facade towards the pergola

Preliminary site plan, Hare & Hare

A temperate interpretation of Georgian Revival, the Keith residence overall exhibits the characteristic symmetrical massing and form of that architectural style popularized by McKim, Mead & White in the mid-1880s. Setting this house apart from previous designs by Shepard, Farrar & Wiser are the elaborate cut-stone trim used everywhere on the exterior, the flanking polychromatic terrazzo-floored porticoes, a porte cochere, and the addition of a substantial carriage house (originally designed to accommodate two horses and a cow, as well as three motor cars). The home rests 200 feet back from the street and a high, coursed limestone retaining wall marks the property's southern boundary.

Trimmed in mahogany, walnut, and quarter-sawn oak, the interior of the Keith residence, originally comprising 22 rooms, is defined by a center-hall plan with a large foyer between the formal living room to the east and the Palm Room to the west. Characterized by carved limestone slabs and hand-painted palms on plaster walls, the Palm Room opens by paired French doors onto the terrace and pergola with a view of the landscape. The northern half of the first floor, including the dining room and library, extends the formal design treatise, incorporating predictable yet highly crafted elements of Elizabethan, Georgian, and Jacobethan vocabulary.

Hare & Hare, a Kansas City firm, designed the elaborate landscaping for the 3-acre grounds. Many of the stable features of Hare & Hare's 1913 design—the overall grading, stone walls, and entry marker, the formal garden to the north featuring a water-lily pond, and the sweeping, forested southwest lawn—have recently been modified. Tatarian honeysuckle and rose-of-Sharon shrubs originally screened service areas on the west and rear of the house, thus creating two distinct areas: the back lawn and servants' access walkway. In the enclosed formal garden, typical of its time, the visitor could sit in the shade at either end and enjoy the plants in a sun-filled surrounding.

Although Keith's financial resources allowed for the luxury of planning such an opulent estate, deed restrictions set forth by the J. C. Nichols Company lent guidelines to the direction of the final design. At the time, it was one of the largest homes constructed in Kansas City.

During his early years with his father's company, Charles Keith studied mining and engineering in Missouri and Kansas, where he worked in mines. Subsequently, he became involved in the company's lumber trade and in 1903 was elected vice president of Central Coal & Coke. Following the death of his father's successor, W. C. Perry, Keith headed the company, operating in eight states under nine subsidiaries. After the company fell into receivership in 1931, Keith left the coal and lumber trades permanently.

Purportedly, Charles Keith was not comfortable in his palatial residence. In 1920, he sold the home to J. C. Nichols, who lived there until his death in 1950. Significant locally for its architecture and landscape design, the home and grounds were listed in the National Register of Historic Places in March 2000.

LONGVIEW FARM

ROBERT ALEXANDER LONG HOUSE

Lee's Summit (1913–1916)

ROBERT ALEXANDER LONG was a magnanimous lumber baron who changed the Kansas City skyline by commissioning the city's first skyscraper for his company headquarters. His country estate, Longview Farm, was notable as one of the farm groups that gained popularity in America at the turn of the 20th century. Like DuPont's Winterthur Farm built the same year and Louis Comfort Tiffany's farm group at Oyster Bay, Long Island, Longview Farm stood as a "paradigm of agrarian excellence." Designed by Henry F. Hoit (who also planned Long's residence, Corinthian Hall) with George E. Kessler as landscape architect, Longview allowed its owner to escape the city and indulge in a rich complex of country home and farming enterprise. Leading 19th century architecture critic Barr Ferree endorsed this lifestyle grown out of ideals of the American country house, while Alfred Hopkins, the dean of farmgroup architects, formulated prototypes for architectural layout and design.

Entrance facade

View through formal garden

Long's vast rural retreat and working farm originally comprised some 40 structures sited high on 1,700 acres of rolling farmland, allowing for maximum vistas, light, and air circulation. The imposing main residence, reached by a drive 900 feet long, was the centerpiece for this showcase of self-sufficiency. Measuring 138 feet in length, the 2½-story mansion is loosely based on Spanish Colonial and Arts and Crafts traditions. Its exterior comprises concrete fluted Tuscan columns, generously sized multipaned and often ribboned wood sash windows, buttery stucco walls, a red tiled roof, and flanking gabled bays. The house sets the stage for the entire ensemble of visually pleasing and highly efficient buildings, from the monumental horse barn to the modestly scaled workers' houses. Sawed and planed in Long's Louisiana lumber mill, a mortised cyprus fence painted lustrous white stretched the nine-mile perimeter.

Aside from the house itself, Longview was essentially divided into four categories: floral, dairy, horse, and hog—and each category had its own specialized building type, groupings, and associated structures. Two greenhouses, originally supplying flowers and starts for the farm and for Long's city estate, eventually turned commercial as the public demand for gardenias and roses grew. The dairy barn and milk house, connected by a covered walkway, housed Long's purebred Jersey cows, some of them actually from the Isle of Jersey. Hoit provided the dairy stock with filtered water kept in a 100,000-gallon "Tin Man"-style

Entrance hall

Dining room

View of the grounds from the porch

water tank. Designed for comfort, quality, and supreme sanitation, the stalls featured cork block flooring that newspaper accounts described as "yielding to the feet and soft as a Brussels carpet."

Although the dairy barn and related buildings housed the main commercial activity at Longview, it was the equestrian complex for which the farm was best known. Long's daughter, Loula Long Combs, was a celebrated horsewoman who won top national and international prizes throughout a lifelong career. An H-shaped show horse barn held stalls for 30 saddlebred and hackney horses, living quarters for horse trainers, and a 175-foot-long indoor arena with cork floors and steel trusses. Hoit employed the most advanced standards in design for the horses' health, while incorporating the salient eclectic architectural vocabulary of the main residence.

Kessler, working with Hoit, was masterful at unifying the complex with formal and informal elements. Gravel roads following the contour of the terrain connected the myriad buildings, while two rows of elm trees and electric lights lined a formal 60-foot-wide roadway leading past the stucco and red tile entrance gate. Lush formal gardens, fountains, and lily ponds, decorative wells, a 20-acre lake, and a precast concrete pergola with classical ornamentation completed the landscape.

Pergola

The lily pond

The Longs' daughters, Loula Long Combs and Sally Long Ellis, inherited the property in 1934. In 1964 the sisters bequeathed 146 acres to Longview Community College and in the 1980s, the U.S. Army Corps of Engineers flooded 950 acres for Longview Lake, a recreational and camping site. Used today for private and public events, the original mansion, Loula's barns, and a few remaining structures sit among a new generation of suburban settlements and strip malls.

Show barn

Rendering of race track and grandstand

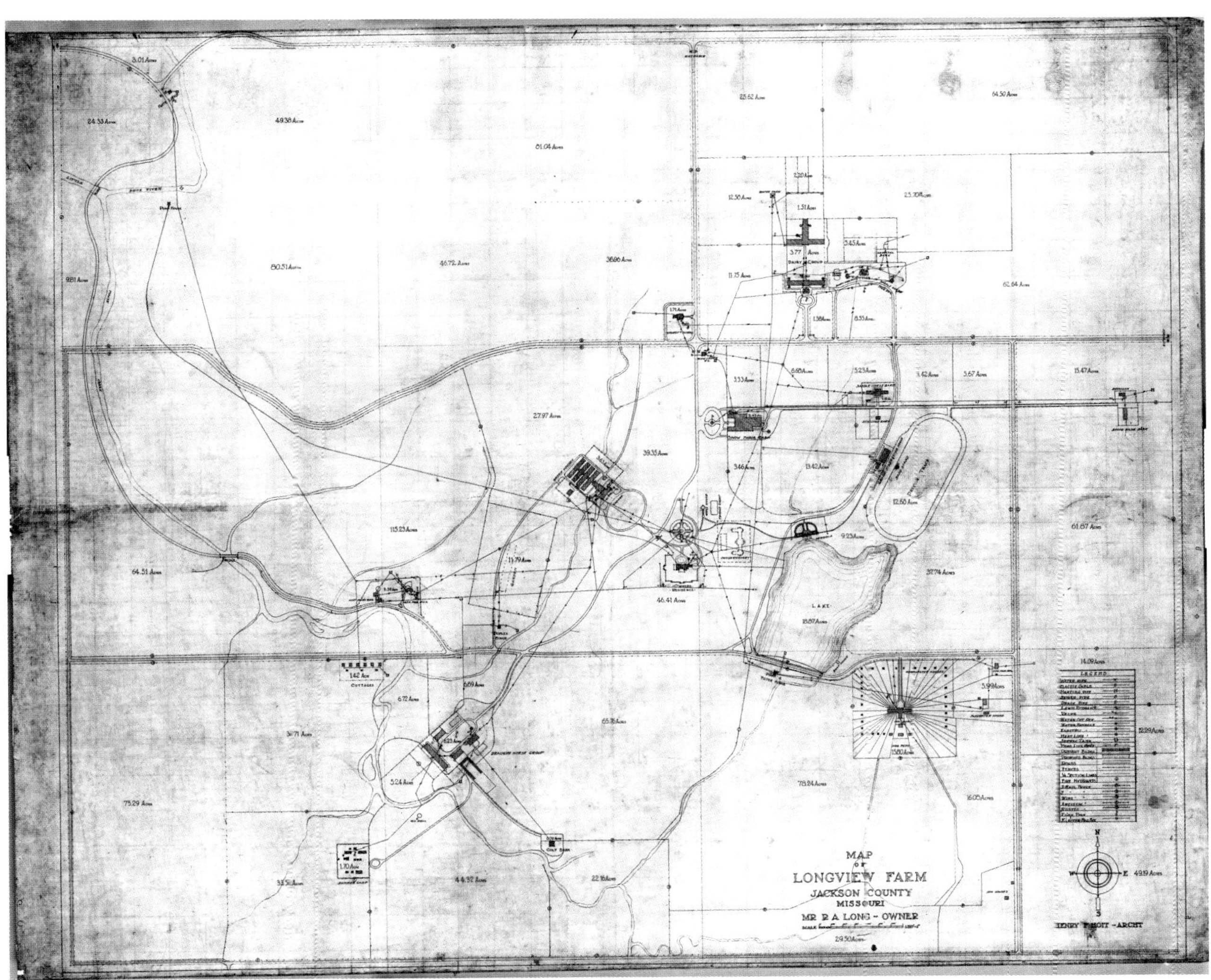

Original site plan

ALSWEL

WILLIAM J. LEMP JR. HOUSE

St. Louis County (1914)

JOHANN ADAM LEMP, originally from Eschwege, Germany, started the Lemp Brewery of St. Louis in 1842 for the commercial production of beer. The firm grew to be the largest brewery in the city—Anheuser & Company (now Anheuser-Busch) being the second—and revolutionized the local brewing industry with the introduction of lager beer. The light effervescent beverage was stored in "lagering" caves under the city streets and kept cool with ice cut and transported from the Mississippi River in the winter. The Lemp brand, Falstaff, with the tag line, "the choicest product of the brewer's art," first appealed to the city's large German population, but by the 1890s was being shipped coast to coast. Operating as a profitable business for 60 years, the company passed from Adam Lemp's son (whose son-in-law was Gustav Pabst of the Milwaukee brewing family) to his grandson, William J. Lemp Jr. By 1922, Prohibition and a family history plagued by tragedy and suicide resulted in the company's dissolution.

Main facade

Side and rear view of main house

William J. "Will" Lemp Jr. chose to spend the $10 million he inherited at his father's death in 1904 on a flamboyant lifestyle. His servants dressed in livery and his first wife was known as the "Lavender Lady" for dressing herself from head to toe in all shades of the color. The 33-room Italianate family mansion in the city was apparently too staid for the third-generation brewer, who lived amid an eclectic assortment of bibelots, furs, and Asian art. Although several successful German businessmen in the city built residences in a grand style dubbed "Brewer's Baronial," William J. Lemp Jr. chose characteristically individual architecture. Lemp built "Alswel," a name created using the first letters of his children's names, on a bluff overlooking the Meramec River valley and situated at the end of a mile-long poplar-lined drive on 192 bucolic acres south of the city. The residence's stylistic allusion to a Bavarian chalet is in keeping with the family's heritage but also makes reference to Andrew Jackson Downing, to Newport cottages designed by Richard Morris Hunt, and to the work of architect Leopold Eidlitz in particular.

Born in Prague, Eidlitz trained at the Vienna Polytechnic and later immigrated to the United States, where he practiced and wrote on the subject of architecture. Lemp may have seen Eidlitz's design for a "rural home" published in *The American Cottage Builder* in 1854, which is strikingly similar to the cottage Eidlitz built for himself at 86th and Riverside in New York City. Alswel shares characteristics of both in its low, spreading roofline, deep eaves, decorative sawn balustrades, parapets, and brackets. It may have been Eidlitz's interest in the "science of the beautiful" and in reconciling art and technology that influenced Lemp staff architect, Guy T. Norton, to whom the residence is attributed. Clearly Norton's interest was in the practical aspects of design, echoing Eidlitz's belief that technology and engineering were as valuable as aesthetics.

Alswel's exterior is clad in cypress; its delicate and decorative effect, employing scalloped shingles and cut-work balustrades, contradicts the building's steel frame and reinforced concrete foundation. The interior of the house has exposed trusses, beamed ceilings, and half-timbering detailed with an exotic mix of mahogany and Japanese cypress. The blue terrazzo porch, parquet flooring, granite, mica-flecked limestone, and gray-brown brick with gray mortar combine to produce a polychrome effect. "Bull's-eye" glass, a stained and leaded glass skylight and book cases, Craftsman motifs, and portieres ornament the public spaces. Massive fireplaces warm the dining room and main hall. Two of the eight bedrooms have dressing rooms and baths.

Servants resided in two separate houses built on the property, both miniature versions of the main house. The West House had eight rooms, the East House, five. Outbuildings on the property included the keeper's residence, a dairy, a two-story garage, machine shop, kennels, and a pavilion that overlooked a 200-foot drop to the Meramec River.

Lemp committed suicide, the fifth person in his family to do so, after the brewery's failure in 1922. Alswel is still extant (albeit severed from its original context). It is now part of a gated community of luxury homes.

Side view of the West House

Mack B. Nelson Residence

Kansas City (1914)

PROMINENTLY SITED on the southwest corner of 55th Street and Ward Parkway, the Mack B. Nelson residence was the first to be constructed on Kansas City's grandest thoroughfare, the "Gold Coast" of George E. Kessler's park and boulevard plan resting in the middle of J. C. Nichols' highly coveted subdivision. The house's conspicuous site in the area's most prominent residential section may be no coincidence—Nelson was a fearless self-made man.

In 1886, at the age of 14, Nelson began prospecting for gold in the Sierra Madres. Eventually he struck it rich, although by other means. In the mines of Mexico, Nelson came to realize that the business was riddled with duplicity, indolence, and danger. He returned to work as a clerk in a lumberyard in Arkansas; he advanced to become president of the largest lumber company in the world at the time, Long-Bell.

Henry Hoit, in planning Nelson's 30,000-square-foot mansion, took his cue from the Beaux Arts residence of R. A. Long, Long-Bell board chairman, which he had designed in 1909. Unlike Long's mansion,

Main facade from Ward Parkway

Main facade

Reer facade

Stair hall

Nelson's is an amalgamation of revival styles as characterized by its general detailing, yet it adheres closest to the vocabulary of the neoclassical tradition with multiple two-story fluted Corinthian columns placed at the full-height porch, a roofline balustrade, and broken pediments. Hoit was greatly influenced by the exhibitions at the World Columbian Exposition in 1893 before he began his studies at MIT and the symmetrical facade of Nelson's 2½-story brick residence shadows the traditions espoused at the fair.

A full-height enclosed courtyard with a Tennessee marble floor, colossal wood columns, and a retractable skylight is the focal point of Nelson's palatial residence, also home to his mother-in-law, two sisters, and their families. Off the courtyard at the first floor are the living room, library, dining and kitchen areas, salon, reception hall, and billiard room. A balcony surrounding the courtyard at the second story provides access to the four bedroom suites. Servants' quarters were at the attic level.

Nelson also engaged the services of the local landscape architectural firm of Hare & Hare to design the gardens of his three-acre site. Although the house has a Ward Parkway address, access to the house and grounds is by a curving driveway placed at 55th Street that leads to a rose bed at its center. Hare & Hare planned a formal tea garden and pergola at the south end of the grounds, accessed from the rear of the house off the continuous terrace. The southwest corner of the yard featured a formal bed for

Living room

Dining room

Garden view through pergola

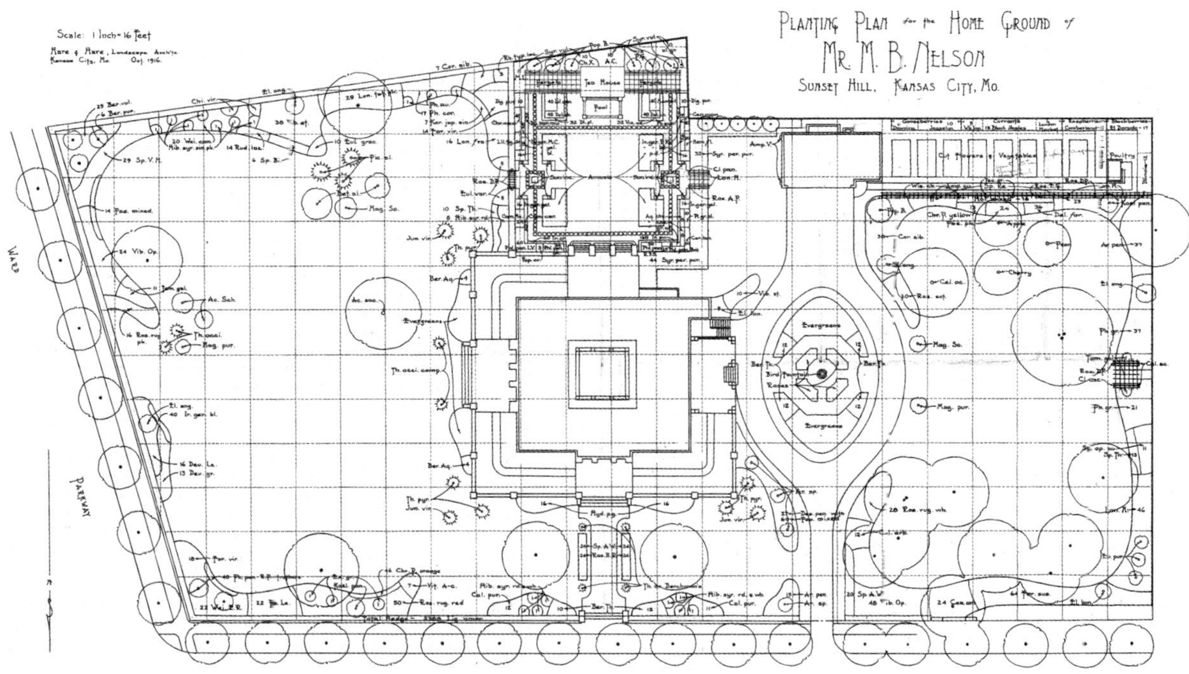

Site plan

vegetables and cut flowers. The remainder of the site, filled with more natural groupings of beds and trees, was planned in contrast.

After the deaths of Mack Nelson and his wife, May, in 1950 and 1951 respectively, May's two sisters inherited the house. In 1956 Mary Hudson Vandergrift purchased the Nelson residence through auction; subsequently it sat vacant for several years and suffered vandalism and neglect. In turn, Vandergrift bestowed her investment to the University of Missouri-Kansas City. Today, the Mack B. Nelson residence is privately owned. Both house and grounds have been sensitively renovated.

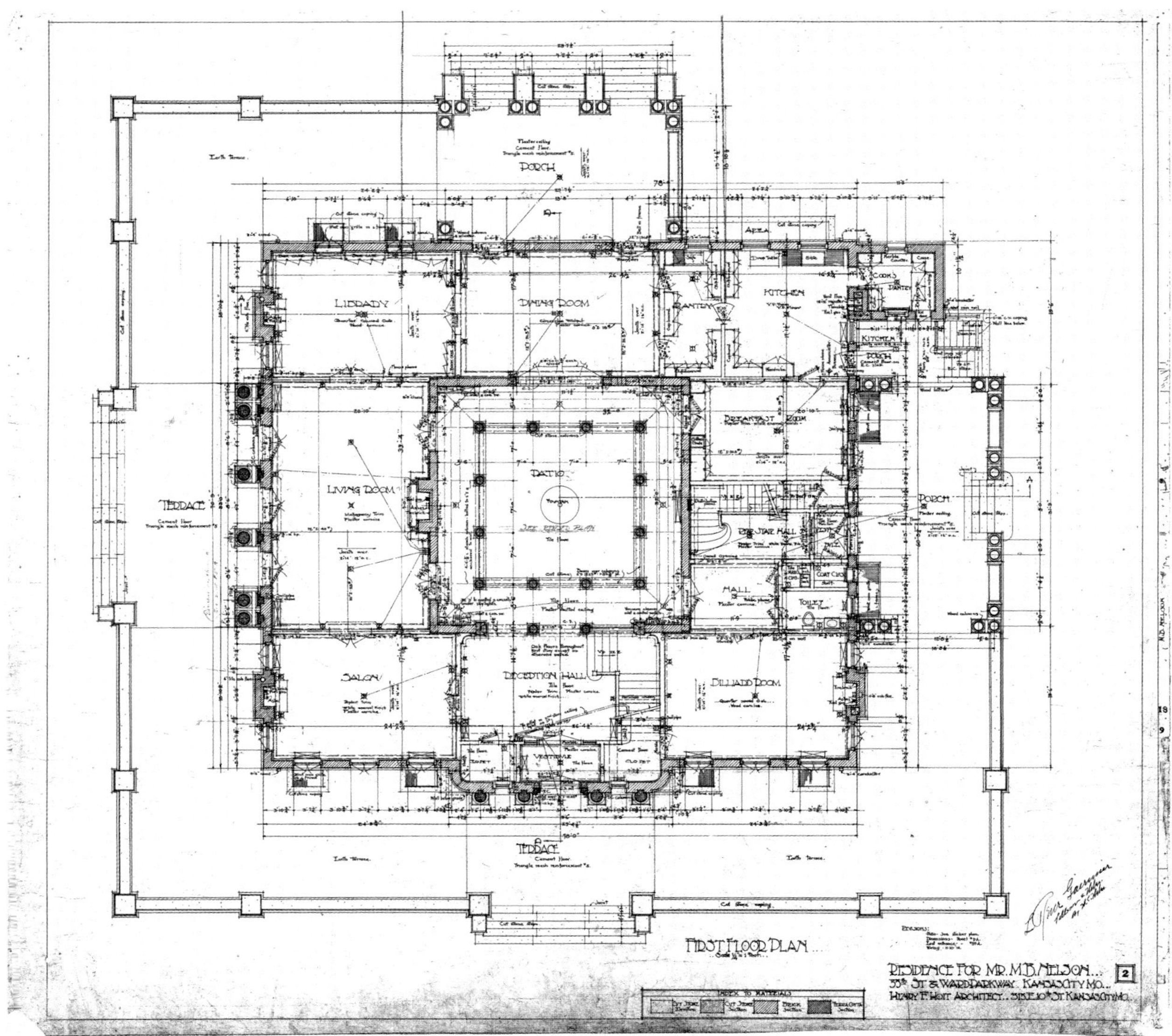

Original first floor plan

Daniel Catlin Sr. Residence

St. Louis (1915)

PLATTED BY JULIUS PITZMAN in 1888 as the Forest Park Addition, the suburban enclave attracted the city's most prestigious families, who chose to isolate themselves from the dirt, clang, and bustle of the city. Celebrated as the finest private streets in the city, Westmoreland and Portland Places are located here. By 1920, nearly 90 residences had been built along these roads just north of Forest Park (site of the 1904 World's Fair) and west of Washington University. Despite their being grand and

Courtyard facing Westmoreland Place

sophisticated, the houses' placement close to the street and to each other creates a sense of community, albeit a privileged one. Of these fine residences, one of the most unique is that built by Daniel Catlin Sr. and his wife, Justina Kayser Catlin.

By amassing a personal wealth of $20 million, Daniel Catlin Sr. earned the nickname "the Astor of St. Louis," in part from tobacco; his business became the American Tobacco Company. He was also the founder of St. Louis Union Trust and a director of State National Bank. He and his wife's interest in the arts is reflected in their contributions to the Mercantile Library and the St. Louis Symphony Orchestra, and in Justina's donation of a collection of 19th-century French oil paintings to the City Art Museum upon her husband's death in 1916. She resided in the house another 30 years.

Catlin's residence was one of 14 in the neighborhood designed by James P. Jamieson and firms with which he was associated. After 12 years in the St. Louis office of Cope & Stewardson of Philadelphia, he began his own practice in 1912. Jamieson became one of the most prolific designers of Tudor and Collegiate Gothic, and was known in particular for "neatly correct adaptations" of Georgian architecture. His taste was impeccable and his solutions original; he had an innate ability to mesh historical prototypes with contemporary requirements, creating solutions for fireproofing and the placement of garages, for example. It is in the design and plan of the Catlin Sr. house that Jamieson's ability to join style and function effectively is most apparent.

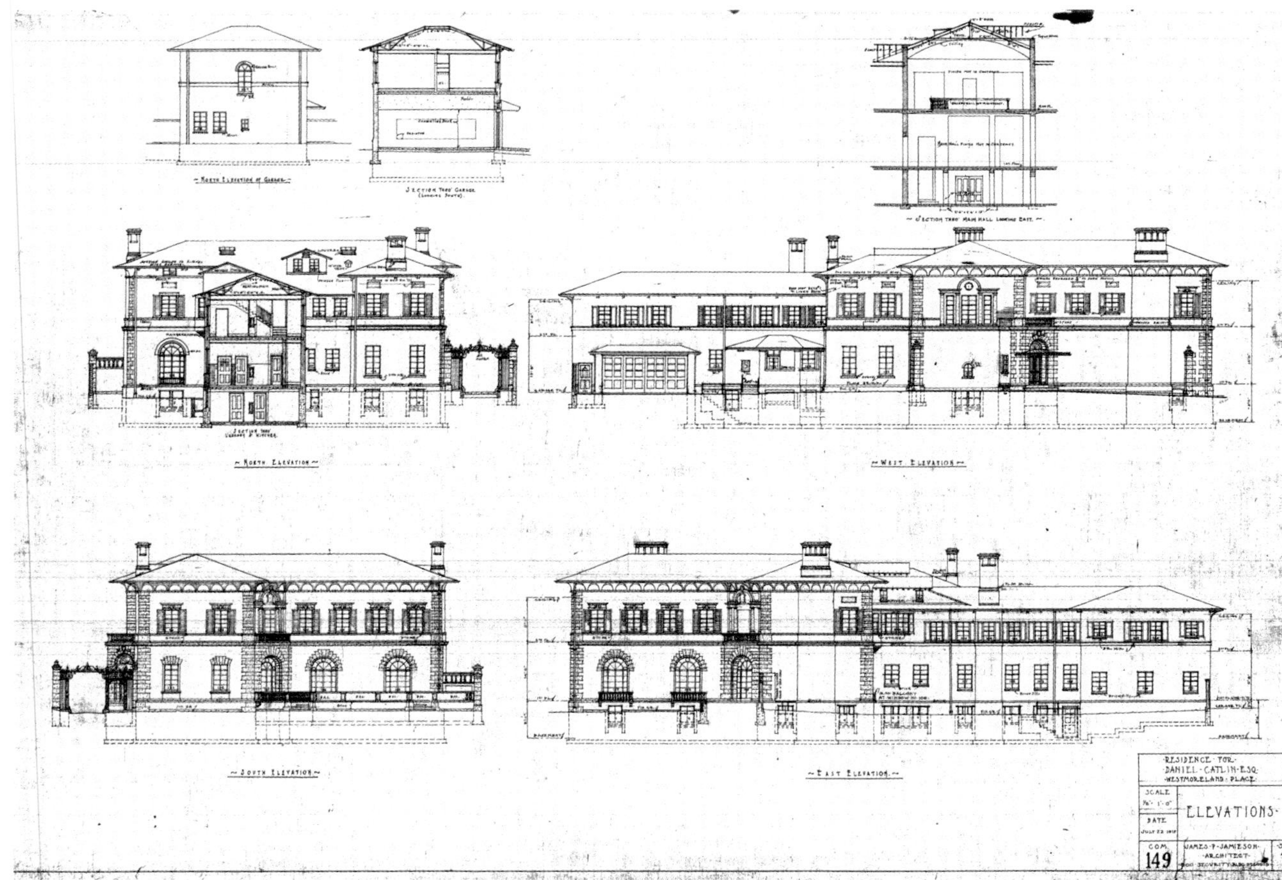

Elevation drawings

Rotunda

For this residence, Jamieson (who also designed the Daniel Catlin Jr. house at 41 Westmoreland Place) chose the Renaissance Revival style, using red brick with limestone keystones, quoins, and entablatures, complete with a Palladian-arched loggia on the garden facade. Italian craftsmen built this great domed hall, constructed of various colored marble, and its curvaceous staircase; the stained glass at the landing incorporates Catlin's monogram. Within the L-shaped plan Jamieson arranged the main public rooms toward the southeast (locating the main entrance on the west side) to allow views across the parklike space that separates the north and south sides of Westmoreland Place. Another of Jamieson's strengths is his ability to integrate views and vistas both outdoors and in, by means of rooms arranged enfilade, providing glimpses of green that enrich the experience of the place.

Jamieson oriented the house on the lot so as to present its back to Union Boulevard, the public street to the west, and to reject the strict gridlike order traditionally found in St. Louis' private places. Such decisions reflect his careful deliberation on orientation and use and his sensitivity to context: the

Living room

Parlor

relationship of houses one to another and to the street are happily resolved at the Catlin residence. They also represent Jamieson's growing awareness of landscape, as seen in the picturesque planning in nearby Brentmoor Park, on which he collaborated so successfully with designer and urban planner Henry Wright.

WESTVUE

CHARLES C. PETERS HOUSE

Kansas City (1915–16)

CHARLES AND JOSEPHINE PETERS may have named their 19-room Georgian-style residence "Westvue" because it borders the Kansas state line to the west. But more than likely, the name referred to the view of the expansive landscape designed by Hare & Hare.

From a 20-foot-wide, L-shaped terrace on the south and west sides of the house, the Peterses could enjoy the sight of densely planted groves of trees—hickories, walnuts, ashes, redbuds, and oaks—lining the driveway and the walled perimeter, and the pond at the foot of their property toward the south.

So th facade and terrace

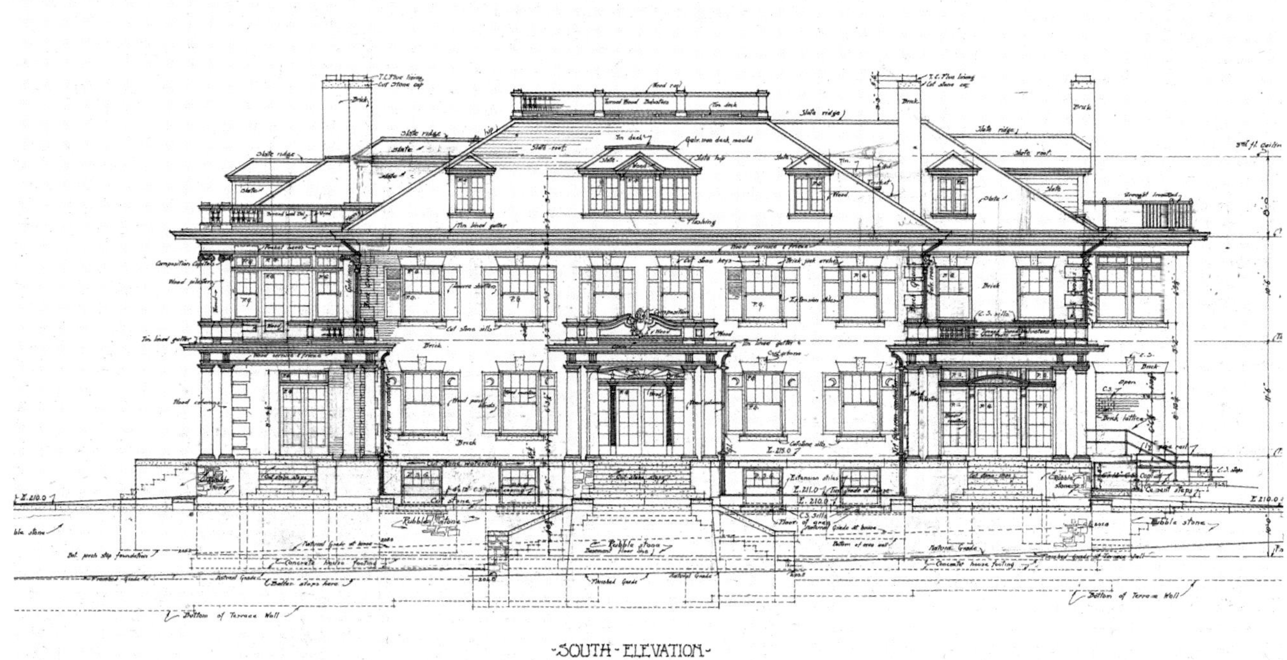

Original south elevation

"The Georgian house," observed John Burchard and Albert Bush-Brown in *The Architecture of America*, "set on a broad lawn became the characteristic image of residential America and the lawn was as important as the building."

Hare & Hare's informal, naturalistic scheme remained a clear distinction to the exacting paragon for the traditional house designed for the Peterses by leading architect Henry F. Hoit. Prior to the purchase of the lot, the 4-acre site was described as "pasture."

Charles Peters, a self-made businessman who settled in J. C. Nichols' heavily restricted Sunset Hill Subdivision, spent his career in the mercantile world. Born in Danville, Illinois, Charles started work as a floorwalker at Emery, Bird, Thayer Company (originally the Bullene, Moore & Emery Company), Kansas City's most cherished department store. In his half-century of employment at EBT, Peters rose to secretary of the company, working with Joseph T. Bird, the president. Interwoven with his steady work life were numerous pivotal civic positions that influenced the city's development. When the New Deal created the National Real Estate Association, President Roosevelt named Peters to serve in the recovery campaign of 1933. Both Peters and his wife, Josephine, dedicated themselves to community causes and charitable activities, but shunned public recognition.

Hoit, like most architects of his generation, read myriad architectural publications endorsing the Georgian Revival movement that became symbolic of the upper-class suburban American home; Westvue was one of these. The main block's symmetrical arrangement with its extended entry porch, double-hung sash fenestration, and flat deck with turned wood balusters at the crown of the hipped roof draws on the

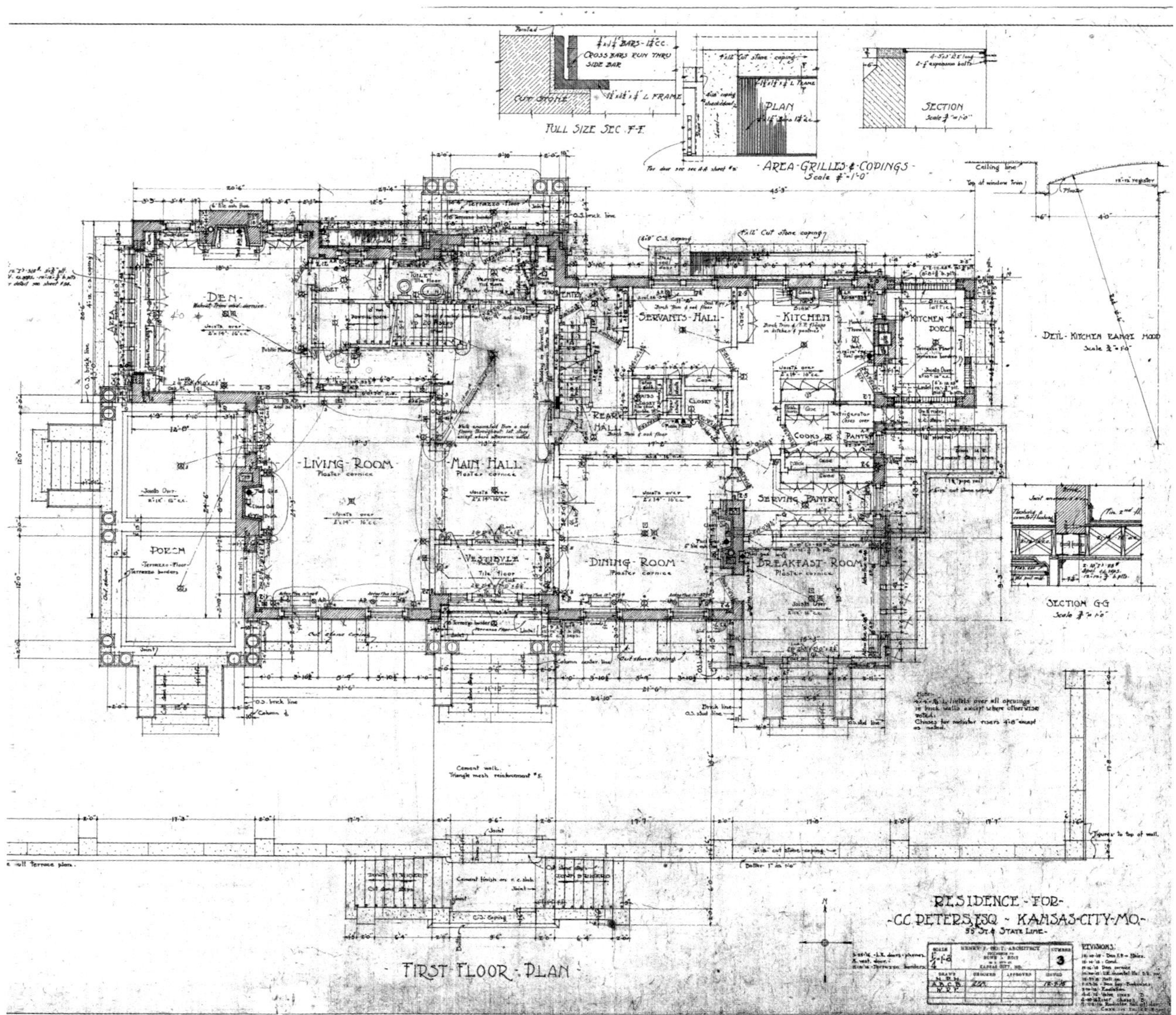

Original first floor plan

neocolonial tradition; nevertheless Hoit seems to have sidestepped the strict Revival canons by tucking one-story porches at the end bays.

The interior of Westvue, according to Hoit's original plans, called for white enameled plaster trim and oak floors throughout, with few exceptions. At the first floor, the 19- by 24-foot living room featured quarter-sawn oak, and a den was trimmed in black American walnut. Five bedrooms filled the second floor; servants' quarters were at the attic level. A card room, billiard hall, and fruit closets, all with walls of rustic stone, were located in the basement. Like the lives of the Peterses, the rooms of Westvue allowed for maximum privacy.

In the early 1930s, the Peterses moved from Westvue, as Josephine's health was failing. The residence remains in private hands.

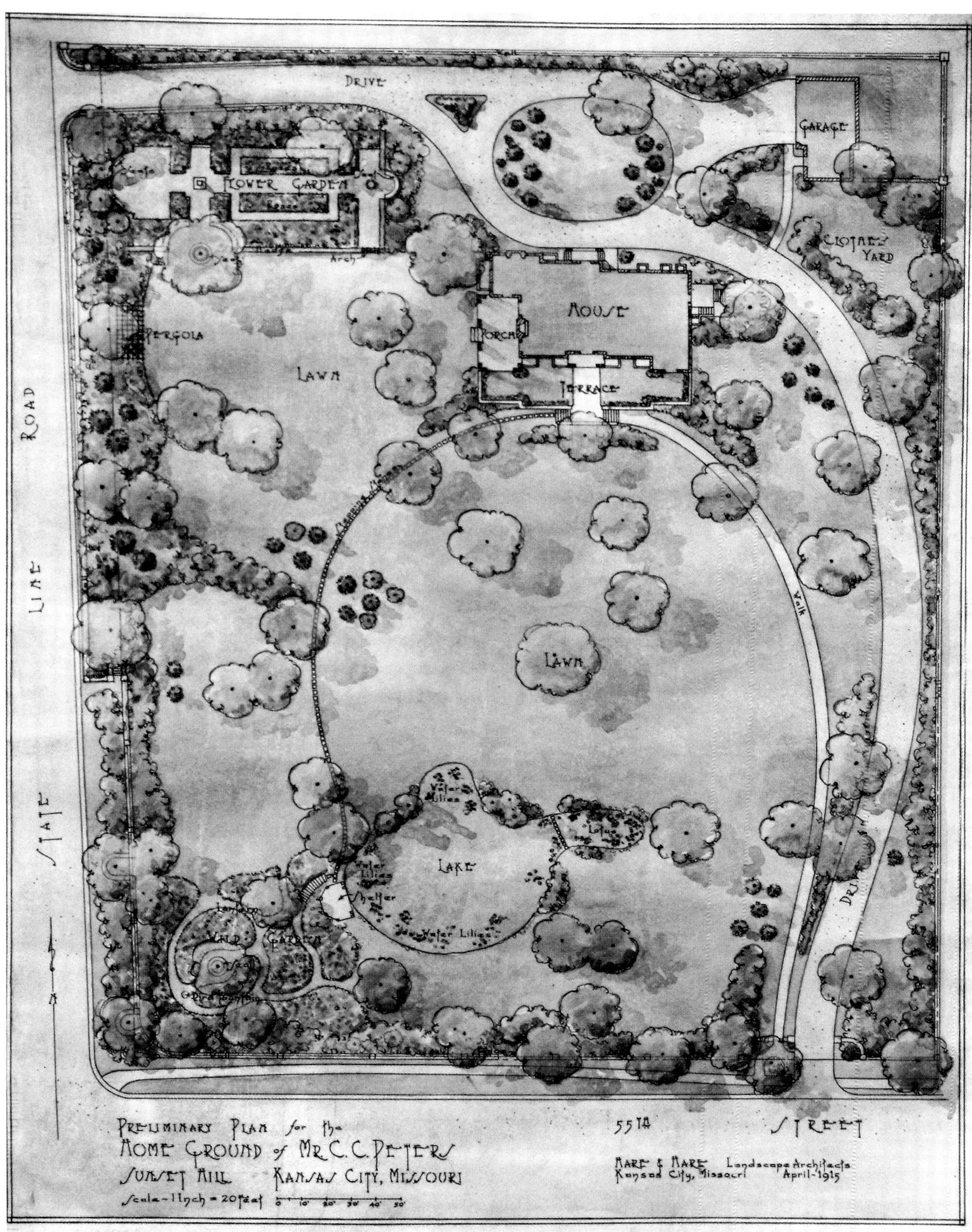

Ground plan by Hare & Hare, 1915

George E. Nicholson Residence

Kansas City (1917–1918)

The architect brothers Thomas Wight and William Wight were born in Halifax, Nova Scotia. Thomas studied architecture while traveling in Italy and Greece, while younger brother, William, was educated in Canadian schools and in ateliers. As draftsmen, both brothers worked in Boston and New York City with McKim, Mead & White; Marcus Whiffen, an architectural history scholar, notes that it was the "firm of McKim, Mead & White [that] set the pace of the Neoclassical Revival." As Wight & Wight, architects for the 2½-story Neoclassical Revival residence of George E. Nicholson, they were responsible for many of the Kansas City area's most celebrated, monumental classically-inspired institutional and commercial buildings.

Thomas began practicing architecture in Kansas City in 1904 with local architect and friend, Edward T. Wilder. The firm's first major commission, the marble-faced Neoclassical Revival First National Bank, brought Wilder & Wight instant recognition. From then on, Wilder & Wight and the successor firm of Wight & Wight fully embraced the Neoclassical Revival style with creative intuitiveness and completeness.

Main facade

Main hall

Living room

Sunroom

Of English descent, George E. Nicholson began in his teens to assist in his father's business constructing zinc and lead smelters in Kansas and Missouri. From that beginning, Nicholson built his own zinc plants, eventually branching out into the cement, brick, and natural gas businesses, and culminating in an empire reaching throughout the Midwest and South. Before moving to Kansas City from Baldwin City, Kansas, he was said to be the richest man in the state, with a fortune publicly estimated at $4 million.

Located in the Sunset Hill addition of the Country Club district, the Nicholson house is one of only six known residential designs by Wight & Wight. The stucco residence encompasses 3,611 square feet in an irregular shape, its main facade featuring a commanding full-height tetrastyle entry porch. The slender fluted Corinthian columns at the central block, supporting a bare frieze (except for roundels positioned directly above the columns), corresponding pilasters, and a modillioned cornice draw heavily from Greek Revival prototypes, not atypical of houses designed in this style during the first decades of the 20th century.

Fenestration, also reflecting the characteristic appearance of this popular domestic style, combines symmetrically placed groupings of double-hung sash units and multipaned casement windows separated by fluted pilasters, crowned at the center with molded plaster arches and keystones. The main entrance displays the trademark broken pediment. Although the whole crescendos from the roofline balustrade to the centered, gabled dormer, it is the colossal portico that triumphs.

Wight & Wight adhered to the neoclassical style in detailing throughout the house's interior. The central main hallway, measuring 14½ feet by 47 feet and displaying an ogee cornice above a Doric frieze, sets the architectural tone for the remainder of the interior. Featuring fluted pilasters flanking windows and doors, the 22- by 35-foot living room also maintains the tenor of the exterior. Most elaborate in its decor is the dining room, where recessed paneling at the ceiling's perimeter displays oil paintings on canvas. In addition, quarter-sawn-oak flooring, mahogany wainscoting, and birch and walnut trim pervade the first floor.

As with many houses in Kansas City's Country Club district, the landscape design was the work of Hare & Hare, who in 1918 planned for formal rose gardens, brick terraces, formal beds, and a vegetable garden behind the gabled garage and chauffeur's quarters.

With few exceptions, the George E. Nicholson house has maintained its historic integrity since its completion. It was listed in the National Register of Historic Places in 2005 and remains privately owned.

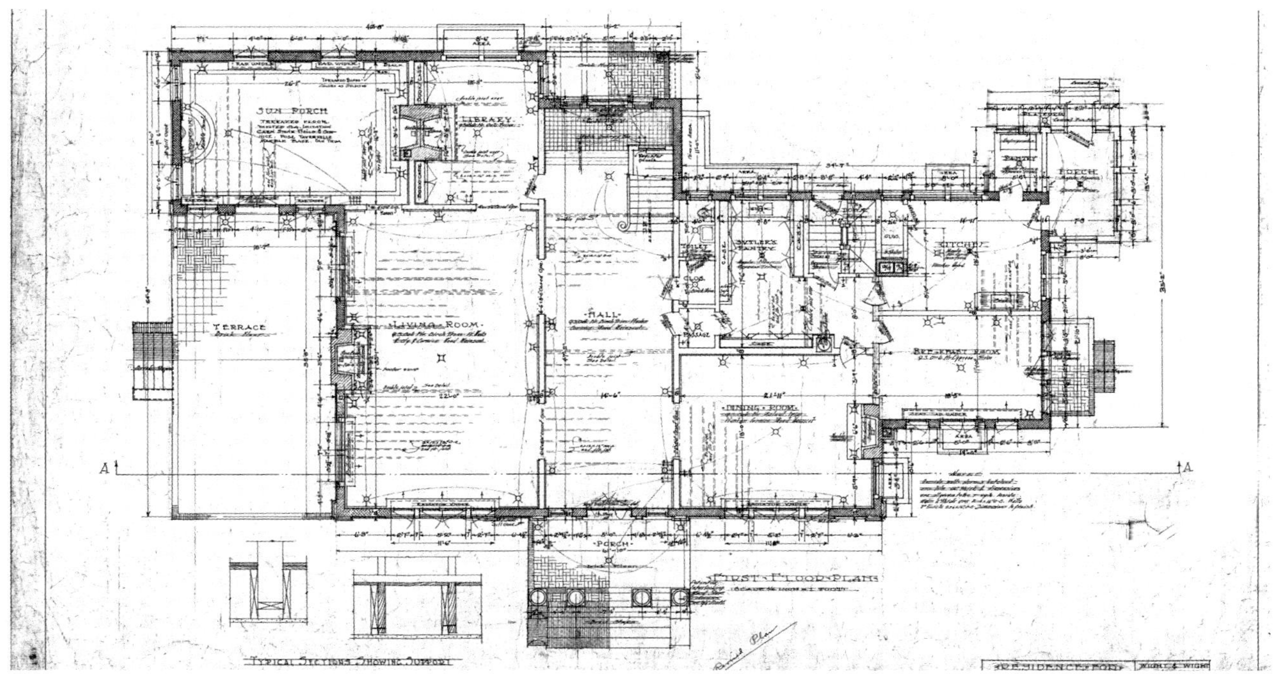

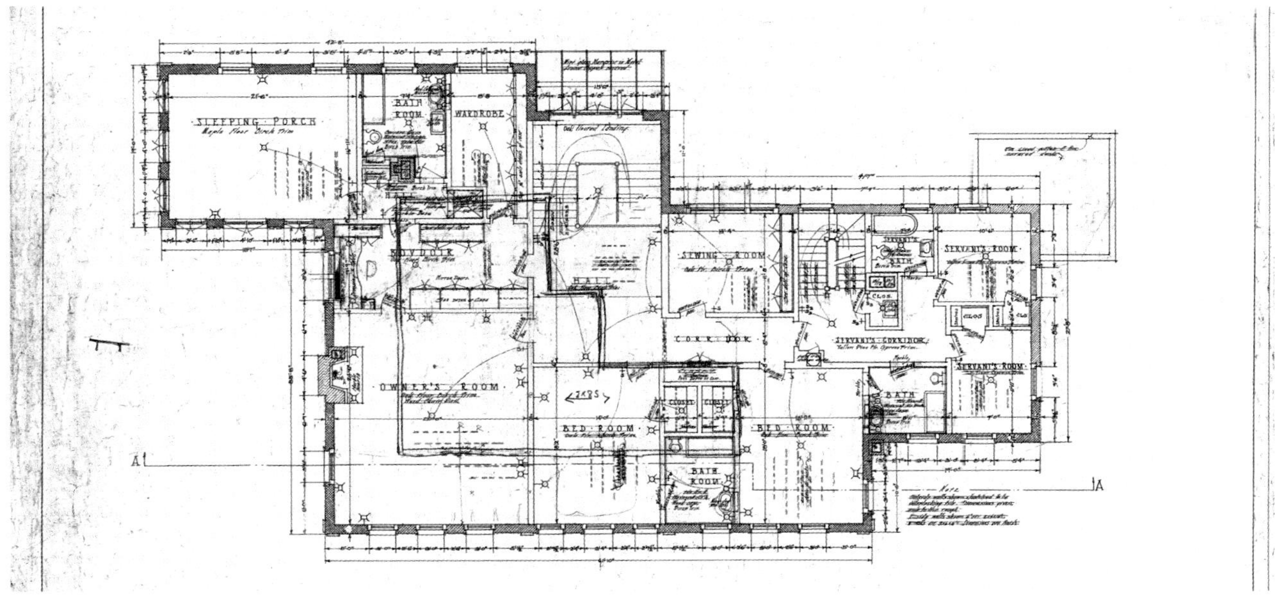

First and second floor plans

Charles A. Braley Residence

Kansas City (1918–1919)

One of the last residences Henry F. Hoit designed before joining in partnership with Edwin M. Price and Alfred E. Barnes Jr. in 1919 was that of Charles A. Braley. Braley's three-story Jacobethan Revival–style house was originally sited on a tract of land 300 by 200 feet, reached from Dunford Circle off Ward Parkway or by a secluded pedestrian path off of State Line Road, known as Dunford Way.

Hoit's client, Charles Braley, was born in River Falls, Wisconsin, and educated at Dartmouth College and Boston University School of Law. In Kansas City, Braley formed a partnership with J. M. Trimble, a law firm that served as counsel to Arthur E. Stilwell, the founder of the Kansas City Suburban Belt Railway—a railroad with lines that went throughout the Midwest and as far south as the Gulf of Mexico. In 1917, Braley was named vice president of the Sinclair Consolidated Oil Corporation plant in neighboring Argentine, Kansas; it had a capacity of 7,000 barrels of crude oil a day. It was reported at the time that the

Watercolor rendering of the Braley Residence

Main facade

Garden facade and terrace

Main hall

Kansas plant was the second "greatest" refinery in the country, just behind Standard Oil Company's Bayonne, New Jersey, facility.

The Braley house displays Hoit's understanding and skillful exposé of the Jacobethan Revival style, the characteristics of which are richly displayed on all four facades. Long, narrow casement windows dominate from the ground up, most often set in multiples and some with leaded glass. Cut stone mullions, quoins, and label surrounds continue the design program. Paired gables and dormers have parapets. Battlements and a single, false half-timbered gable rising behind the east entrance bay hint at the Tudor style. A winding drive at the east leads to the main entrance, recessed in a semi-hexagonal, buttressed bay. The rear or west facade, anchored by a wide, rambling rubble-stone, balustraded terrace, is reached off the loggia at the center bay.

Contemporary accounts of the Braley home affirm that the living and dining rooms are exact replicas of those found in an "old English manor house," although the source remains unknown. Certainly, the richness of the woodwork, the carved mantel and stairway detailing, and the thick profiled plaster strapwork in the main rooms on the first floor suggest early 19th century English prototypes.

Public spaces off the main hall and loggia, including the living and dining rooms, and a breakfast room with serving panty, occupy the main block of the first floor. The northern end of the first floor takes in the servants' dining hall, cooks' pantry, and a cardroom. The southern end has a large sun porch accessed from the living room through French doors.

Salon

Sitting room

Typical of dwellings in the Sunset Hill subdivision, the landscape of the Braley house is a Hare & Hare design, although much more subdued than most in its overall layout. The arrangement suggests that mature trees were incorporated into a plan augmented by a vegetable garden at the southeast corner of the lot, with stone paths to the pedestrian walkway leading to State Line Road. The natural, curvilinear pattern of the trees is reflected in the contour of the main entrance drive and the pool off the sun porch, counterbalancing the profile of the cul-de-sac where the residence is set.

In excellent condition, the Braley residence has maintained a high degree of its historic integrity. It remains privately owned, sited on its original isolated acreage.

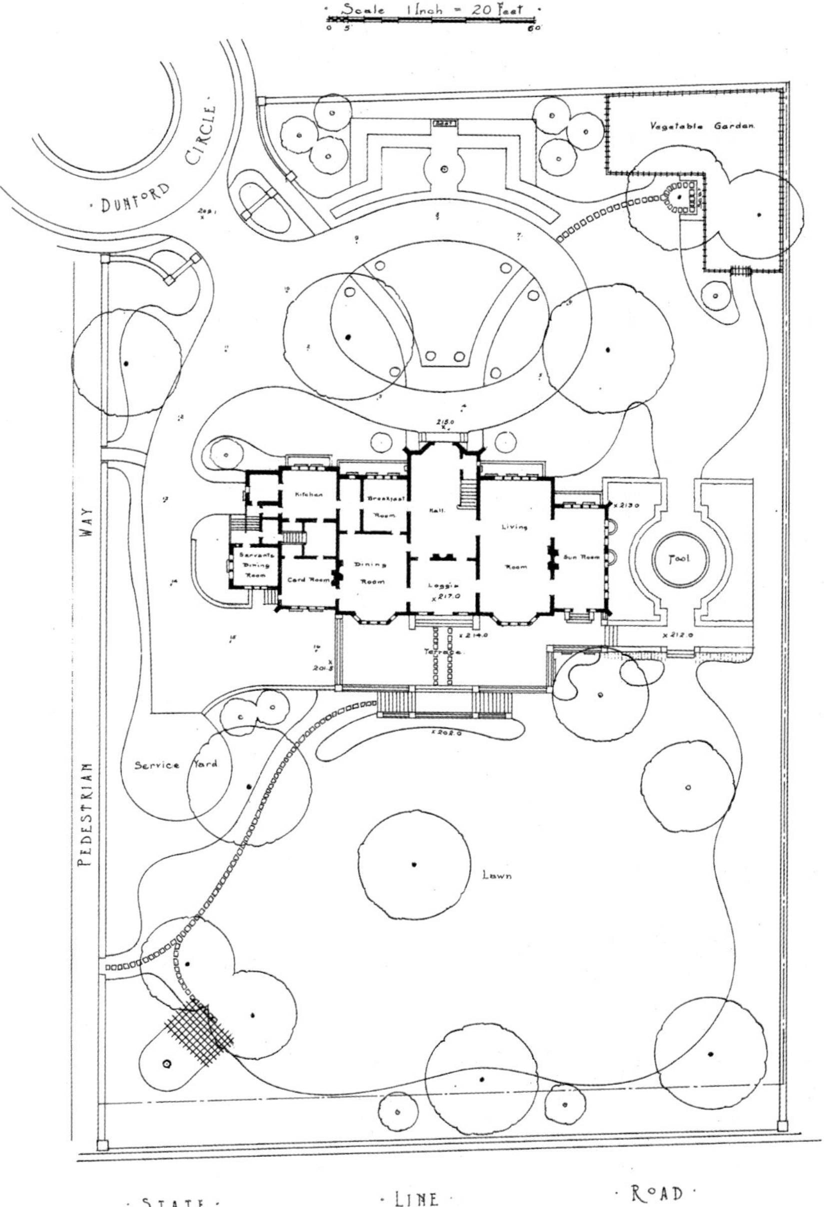

Site plan

Wyethwood Estate

Huston Wyeth House

St. Joseph (1918–1922)

Northeast of St. Joseph's central business district stands Wyethwood, built for Huston Wyeth, the only son of William Maxwell Wyeth, a descendant of pioneer New England stock and founder in 1859 of a St. Joseph wholesale hardware business. Following in the footsteps of his enterprising father, Huston Wyeth was typical of St. Joseph's jobbers, bankers, cattlemen, and industrialists who helped raise this western Missouri town into one of the "wealthiest cities per capita in the nation" during the close of the 19th century. When Huston Wyeth became president of Wyeth Hardware & Manufacturing

Garden facade

Aerial view of Wyethwood amidst farmland

Company after his father's death in 1901, he furthered the success of the harness and saddle-making business in his native city.

The three-story Wyethwood, steeped in the Italian Renaissance Revival tradition, represents the burgeoning prosperity of 19th- and early 20th-century St. Joseph, originally a trading community with strong ties to the opening of the western United States. The smooth-faced 22,000-square-foot house perches high beyond the bluffs of the Missouri River. Designed by Eckel & Aldrich, one of St. Joseph's most prominent architecture firms (descended from the several partnerships of Edmond J. Eckel), Wyethwood breaks from the earlier tradition of the many Italianate and Romanesque residences built during Eckel's partnership with Mann.

In contrast to many of the predecessor firm's late 19th-century designs, Wyethwood preserves the visual tradition of the City Beautiful in its classical, symmetrically massed facade, yet inspires in its unconventional application. The projecting front porch sets the overall design idiom of the residence with its multiple French doors topped by fanlights and deeply recessed sidelights. These elements repeat systematically on the first story, while the second story is punctuated solely by narrow casement

General view of property

fenestration. The repetition of design components makes the whole somewhat monolithic in tone, despite the hipped dormers, multiple chimneys, and massive red tile roof.

Unpredictable in plan and private in its overall arrangement of space, the front entrance of Wyethwood is not at the south facade's enclosed porch off the main drive, but at the west. Here another enclosed porch, wider than the one at the south, features black-and-white tiled flooring with a "puzzle" pattern at its center, stone benches, and sculpted metal cranes. The porch functions as a grand hall through which one reaches the oversize living room and a small vestibule (once displaying a rare collection of swords and coats of armor) that leads to the servants' wing, kitchen, and butler's pantry at the north and to an informal dining porch in the east wing.

An elevator off the hallway to the east of the vestibule provides access from the basement to the third floor. The main unit of the second floor houses the master bedroom, with separate baths for Huston and his wife Leila Ballinger Wyeth, along with three guest rooms, and sleeping porches at the wings; the servants' quarters are in the rear wing. Additional servants' rooms, a billiard room, a storage area, and a garage with a turntable for ease of egress are on the basement level.

Main entrance detail

Built as a country home adjacent to wooded pastureland, the 35-room Wyethwood was originally sited on 40 acres of land. Extensive vegetable gardens and orchards and a man-made pond with a stage at its southwest edge filled part of the expanse. A separate three-story brick carriage house had a dairy barn on the ground level, a stable and carriage storage on the main floor, and an apartment and hay bins on the top floor. The estate also had a modest gatekeeper's house. Now an office building in private hands, Wyethwood nevertheless maintains much of its historic integrity as a palpable link to St. Joseph's Golden Age.

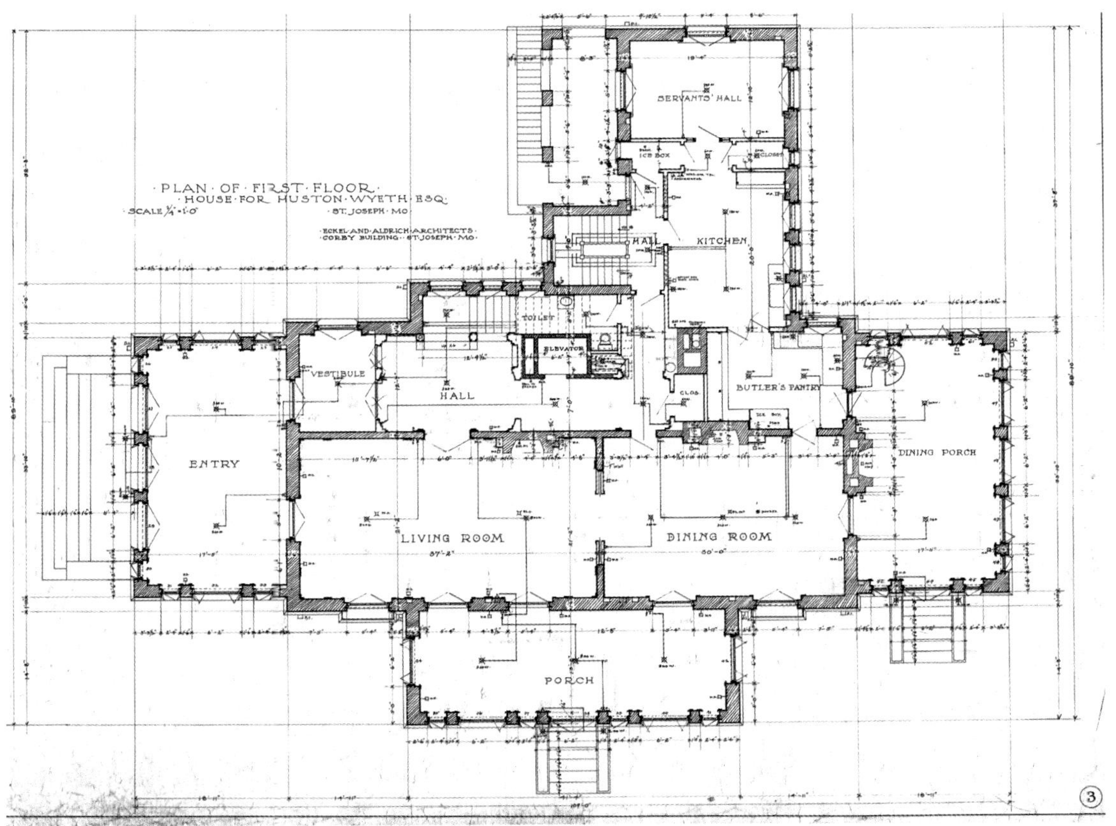

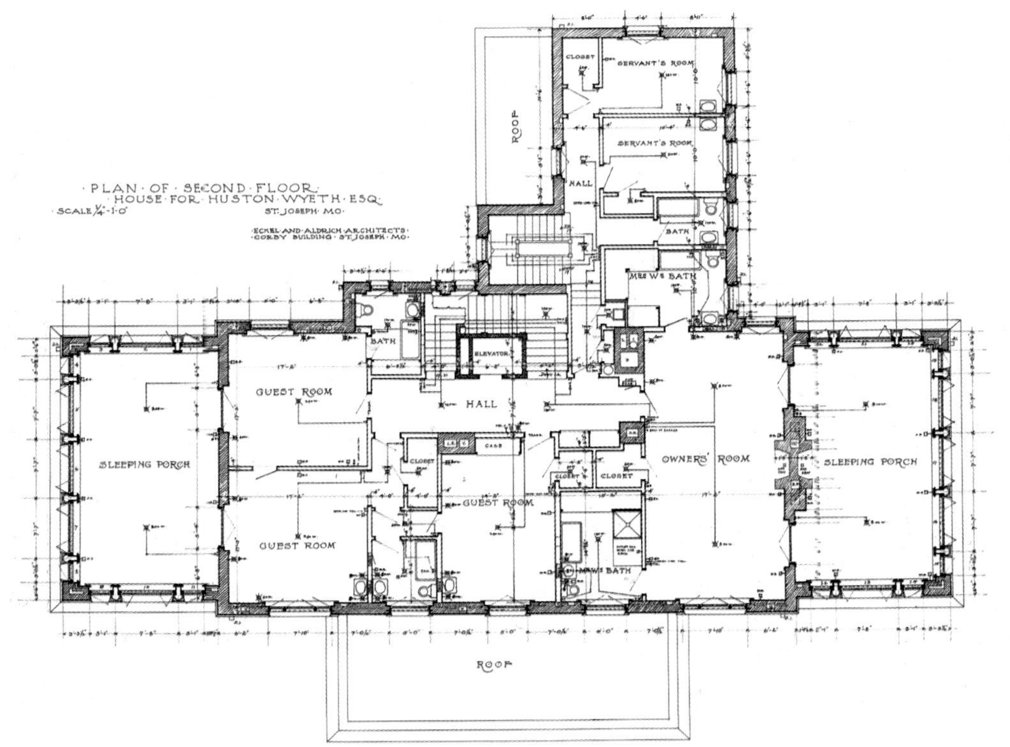

Original first and second floor plans

HAWTHORNE HALL

URIAH SPRAY EPPERSON HOUSE

Kansas City (1919–1923)

EPPERSON HOUSE, originally known as Hawthorne Hall, was designed by Kansas City architect Horace LaPierre for Uriah Spray and his wife, Elizabeth Weaver Epperson. A prominent Kansas City industrialist and banker who made his fortune, in part, in the insurance business, Epperson long dreamed of building a house in the style of an English country manor. His wish came true in 1919 when construction began on the 48-room mansion.

Sited on four acres on a hill in the Southwood Park development, the historic former residence is an amalgamation of architectural idioms, including Tudor and Gothic Revival, Elizabethan, and early Jacobethan. Assisted by architect Frederick R. Stuhl, LaPierre produced more than 1,500 detailed

Main facade and entry gate

Limestone stair detail

Detail of living room and organ loft

drawings, some of which incorporated notes and sketches Epperson had made during his many trips to Europe, for this commission. The 140-foot-long residence, which Elizabeth jokingly referred to as "Epperson's Folly," was completed in 1923 at a cost of $450,000.

One reaches the limestone and brick crenelated mansion by a winding drive of cobblestones past the front of the house, through a tunnel to a porte cochere at the east facade. A stone balustraded staircase leads from the front lawn to the pointed, arched entrance and connects to a sweeping veranda that curves east to the French doors of the sunroom. At the time of its completion, the views from the elevated terrace captured mostly undeveloped, wooded acreage in all directions.

Epperson's wealth accumulated from his "inter-insurance exchange" for grain elevators and lumber manufacturers. After he relinquished the inter-insurance exchange, Epperson focused on the Lumbermen's Underwriting Alliance, an organization he founded in 1904 that later became the Epperson Land and Investment Company. Epperson's civic involvement included joining a small group of Kansas City businessmen who raised money for the rebuilding of a convention center where William Jennings Bryan was nominated president of the United States.

The Eppersons' appreciation of and involvement in social, cultural, and philanthropic activities was part of the impetus for building such an eccentric and elaborate showplace. Some of the more notable (and unusual) features of LaPierre's design include a 48-foot-long living room with an elevated stage and

Carved oak staircase

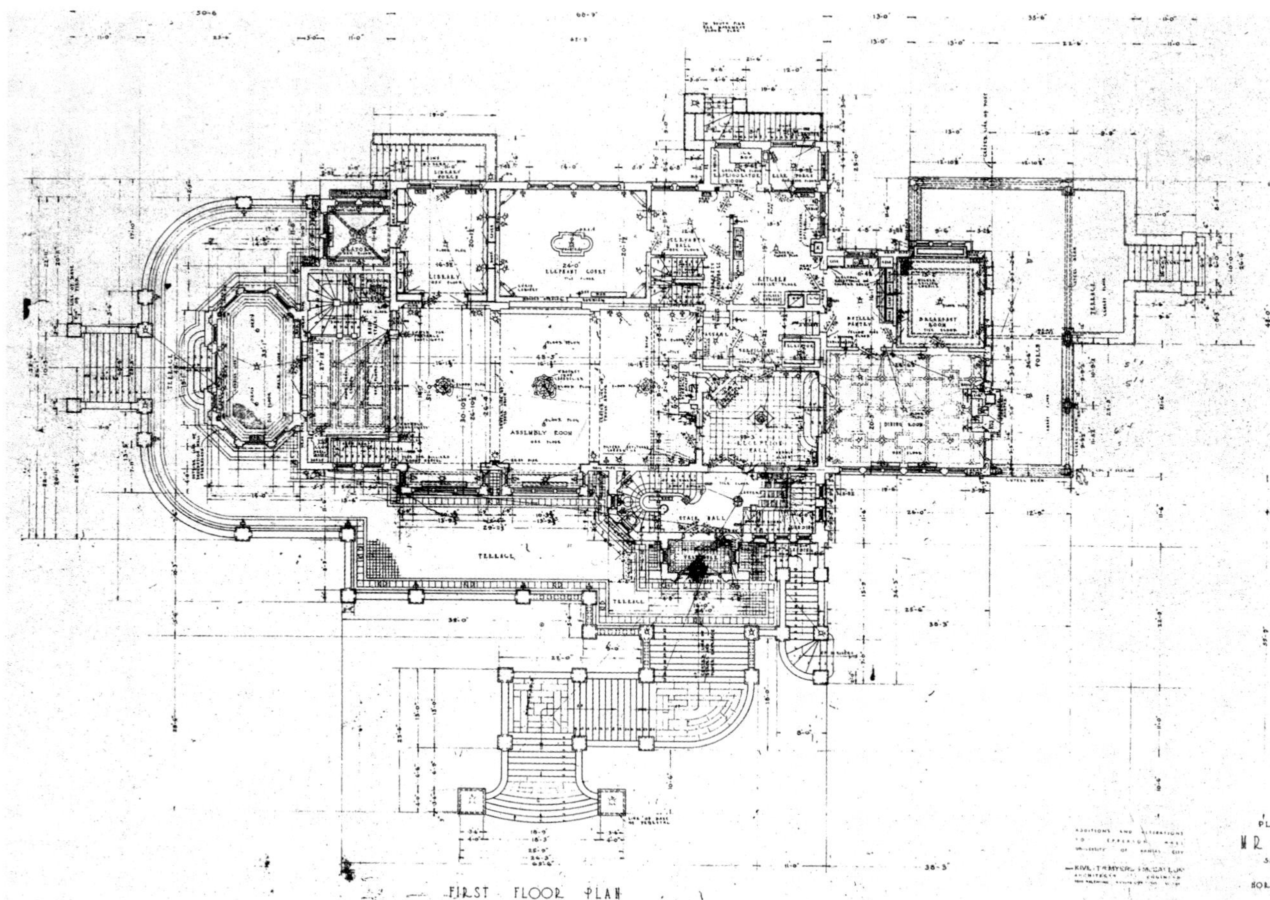

Original first floor plan

proscenium arch, where trapdoors in the ceiling could be lowered, allowing for scenery changes for amateur plays; an Elizabethan-appointed organ gallery above the living room; and the "Elephant Court," planned just off the south side of the living room as a museum to house Elizabeth's extensive collection of rare elephant carvings and statues. LaPierre also planned for a tile and marble Pompeian swimming pool in the basement and an oratory with hand-tooled leather walls and an ivory ceiling. A deeply carved oak baluster and newel post, still extant, embellishes the main staircase.

Although apparently robust, U. S. Epperson lived in his dream house for only four years, passing away in 1927 at the age of 66. Under the provisions of his will, title to the property passed to his nephew and business partner, James J. Lynn. Upon Elizabeth's death in 1939, the property was converted into a club for military transport pilots. Lynn had intended to make the mansion into an office for the Epperson Underwriting Company, but adjacent property owners opposed the plan.

In 1943, Lynn deeded Hawthorne Hall to the University of Kansas City for use as a men's dormitory and a venue for visiting professors, poets, and authors. Thirteen years later, Hawthorne Hall became classrooms and faculty offices. Since 1988, it has housed the architecture and environmental design studies program at the University of Missouri–Kansas City.

Fred Wolferman Residence

Kansas City (1923)

As a German émigré, Louis Wolferman struggled with the English language, which hampered his business dealings in the New World. And so, despite his son's wish to become a doctor, Louis drafted the aspiring 17-year-old Fred into a new enterprise: in 1888, with $750 in financing secured by mortgaging the family residence, the father and son bought a bankrupt stock of groceries. Their new business was an immediate success. By 1895 their motto "Good Things to Eat" was ubiquitous, as they sold delicatessen, baked goods, and liquor, and specialized in unrivaled homemade foods. The item that became their trademark was a giant homemade muffin, for which Fred developed the prototype shape using tuna cans.

Main facade

Gabled entrance detail

With the success of his business, Fred installed his family in a grand Tudor-style manor house designed in late 1922 by the Kansas City architectural firm, Wight & Wight, creators of some of the city's most impressive early 20th-century institutional and residential buildings.

The distinguished, sprawling house approximates a J shape, as the western portion rounds a curve from the grand foyer at the main facade. The half-timbered, patterned-brick and stucco residence is no mere semblance of this once highly popular style—it captures the Tudor tradition by a remarkable feat of craftsmanship. Carved wood lintels and vergeboards, pierced wood grilles, and cut stone trim define the exterior, while coved ceilings with foliated plaster strapwork, carved wood paneling, and wide plank, random-width, quarter-sawn-oak flooring, and zenitherm walls characterize the interior.

The exterior complexity and asymmetry are restated in the interior in an organic and inseparable fusion. The architects of the Wolferman home spun the typical center-hall plan into a combination of a seemingly indeterminate flow of one room into another at the first floor, while the second floor, with its strict divisions, suggests the design philosophy of Charles Francis Osborne and Eugene C. Gardner. The atypical placement and configuration of the six bedrooms, two sleeping porches, and separate sewing and linen rooms seem to indicate a close working relationship between architect and client.

Bathhouse and pool

The house plan takes exceptional advantage of its unusual site, with the individual rooms oriented to benefit from the Hare & Hare-designed landscape. The deeply recessed second-story gabled porches afford intimate spaces with views to the outdoors.

The words displayed in a casement window of what was originally the servants' dining room exemplify the household's generous hospitality: "Is't a time to talk when ye should be munching." Food and friends were paramount.

Besides the terraced lawns to the south, and the service gardens and pergola to the rear of the house planned by the Hare & Hare father-and-son team, the steep, 3-acre site featured a separate stone bathhouse and pool (one of the first private pools in the city) designed by Kansas City architect Jesse F. Lauck. Set under a dense planting of trees and featured in the popular magazine *Country Life*, the pool house had a second-story diving board, accessed from inside the picturesque structure. Because of the pool's popularity, the Wolfermans hired a full-time lifeguard. Eventually tiring of the responsibility, however, they filled in the pool sometime during the 1940s. The bathhouse was later demolished.

Stair hall

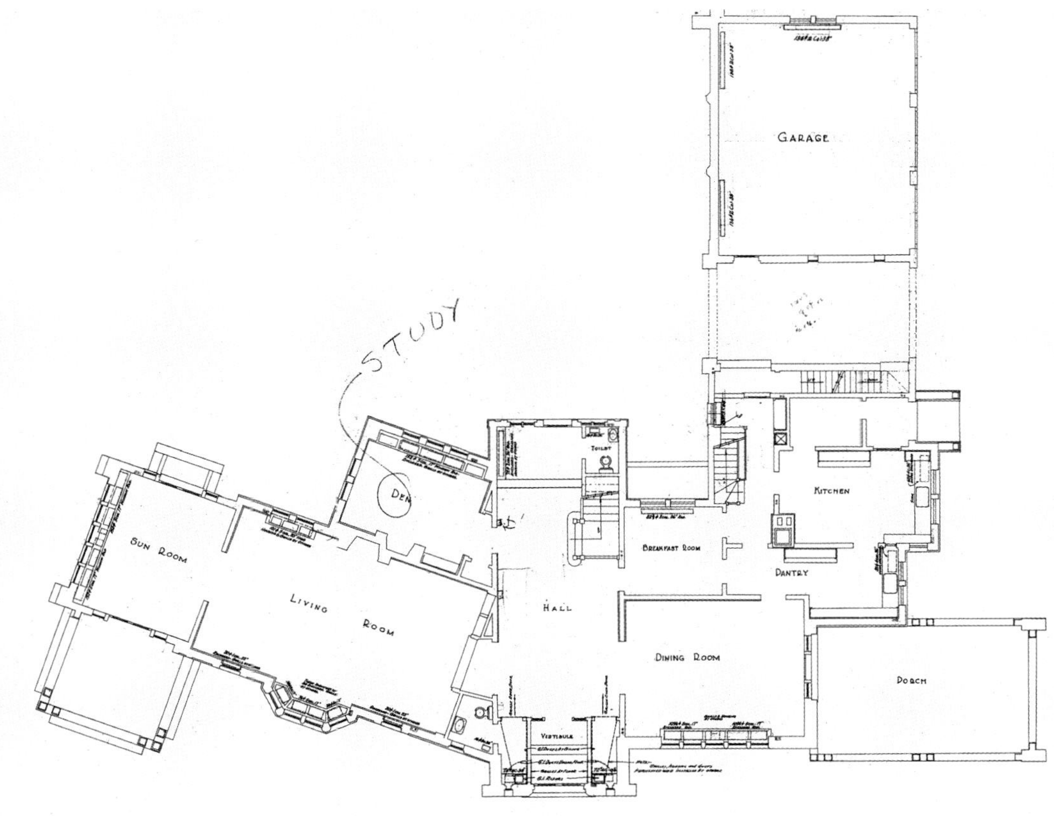

First floor Plan

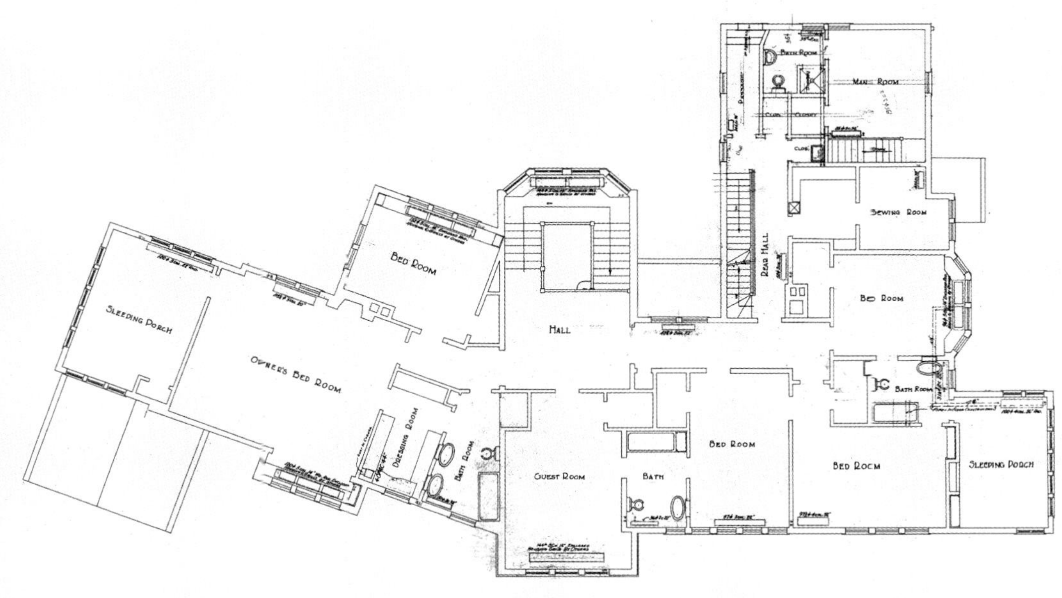

Second floor plan

Harry French Knight Residence

St. Louis County (1923)

Harrie T. Lindeberg designed his finest country houses in the 1920s and the Harry French Knight house belongs to this select body of work. Labeled Tudor Revival, it is an exercise in polychrome Pennsylvania traprock and Vermont slate that reflects the architect's ability to interpret history in innovative ways, free of direct reference to period style. The house crowns the hilltop site (chosen and marked by the architect from the passenger seat of Knight's airplane) and fits within the topography of the countryside with no reference to cardinal points. Palatial in its number of rooms, constructed of monolithic oak beams and finished with graceful wood paneling, all at a cost of $1 million, the interior expresses the intimate quality desired in a country house.

Lindeberg designed country houses for the country's elite and if Harry Knight, local stockbroker, did not fit into the most eminent of such circles, his new wife, Lora Small Moore, surely did. She contributed

Entrance facade

View across grounds

financially to the building of their house with the $93 million estate left to her by her deceased husband, James Hobart Moore, founder of United States Steel. Her taste is evident in the urbane mix of French and English furnishings (one bedroom was warmed by an Adam fireplace), gold-plated bath fixtures, and parquet and marble floors. Her husband's priorities were perhaps better represented by the telephone room tucked away in the chestnut-paneled entrance hall and the wine cellar hidden on the lower level and protected during Prohibition behind a vault door.

The entrance hall, with views through the gallery out onto the terrace, anchors the main block of the building; just inside the front entrance are ladies' and gentlemen's dressing rooms. The dining and living rooms, nearly equal in size, flank the entrance hall. Beyond the living room, the library (with a porch) overlooks the formal garden. On the second floor are four bedrooms (two for the owners and two for guests, each with separate bath) and a sleeping porch that overlook the rear of the property. A long gallery links them to the northeast wing, which houses the "linen room" and five servants' bedrooms.

The chauffeurs, butler, and servants in the Knight household enjoyed nearly as much room as the owners. On the main floor, in a wing to the northeast beyond the kitchen, pantry, and sewing room, was the chauffeur's apartment—four rooms, including his own living room—and a butler's room. The plan also indicates a "servants' hall," or living area, and large porch for their use on the main floor. The service

Entrance detail

court and garage are on the lower level, tucked into the hillside beneath the chauffeur's apartment. Landscape architect Warren Manning met with the Knights and Lindeberg in November 1923 to discuss plans for the grounds.

Lora Knight lived at the house for only three years (she divorced Knight in 1927); Harry Knight stayed on another two years. The year prior to selling the property, one of his guests was Charles

Window details

Lindbergh, who spent the night there before leaving for his historic transatlantic flight to Paris (Knight was a financial backer of the trip).

Too large for the needs of most owners, the property has been subdivided and the gatehouse and main house were sold separately.

Library

Entrance hall detail

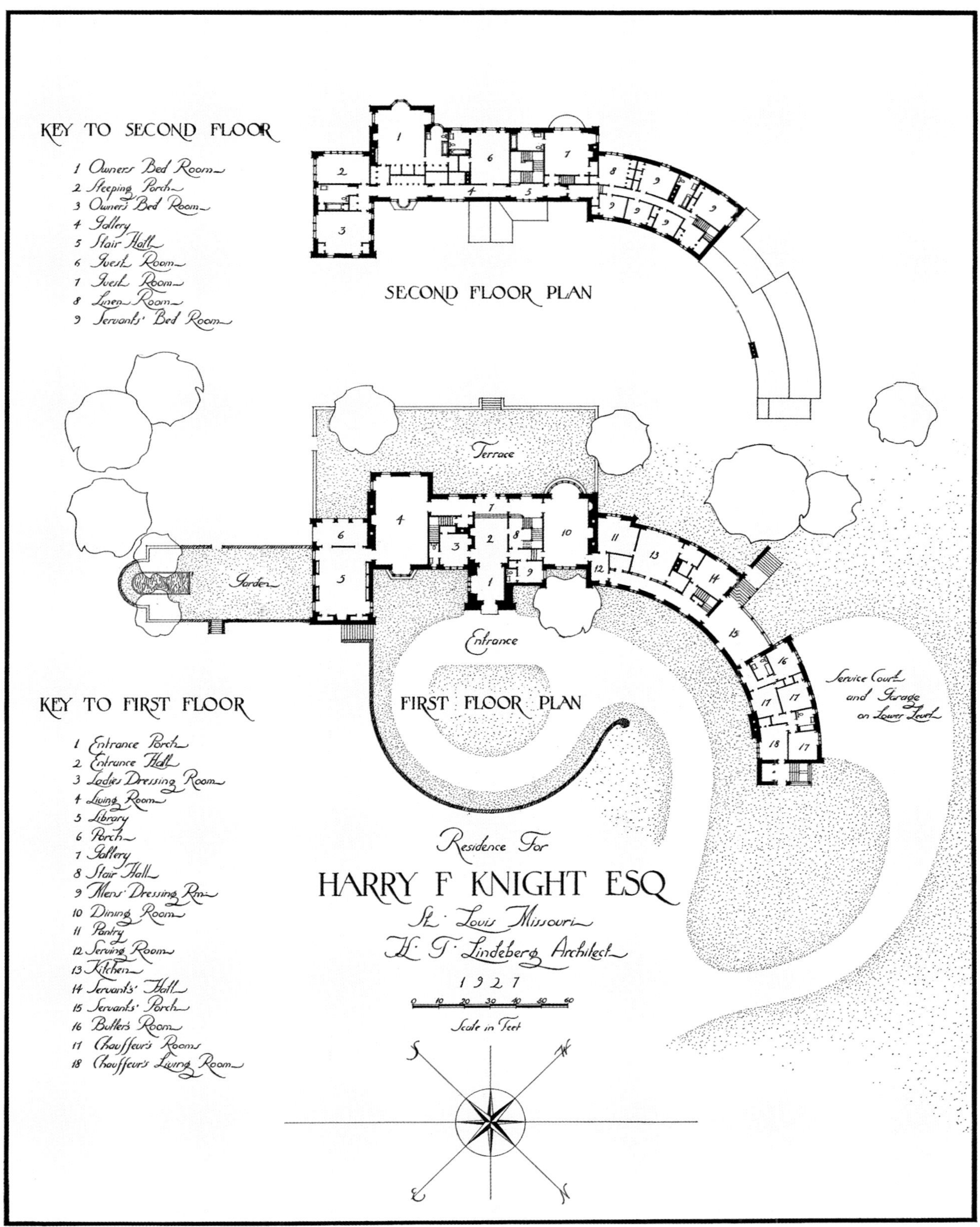

Architect's plan

Oscar Buder Residence

Clayton, St. Louis County (1925)

THE OSCAR BUDER RESIDENCE is one of only 23 houses in picturesque Carrswold, a private subdivision in the affluent city of Clayton. Nearly all were built in the 1920s and 15 of them were designed by the local architecture firm, Maritz & Young, known for a creative interpretation of period houses, often Tudor Revival in style. Most of the houses have grounds of at least an acre and they share a 10-acre park planned by midwestern landscape architect Jens Jensen in 1922. It is the sense of place created by Jensen's naturalistic aesthetic and choice of plantings that make Carrswold one of the most sophisticated neighborhoods in Clayton dating from the early 20th century.

Side and rear view

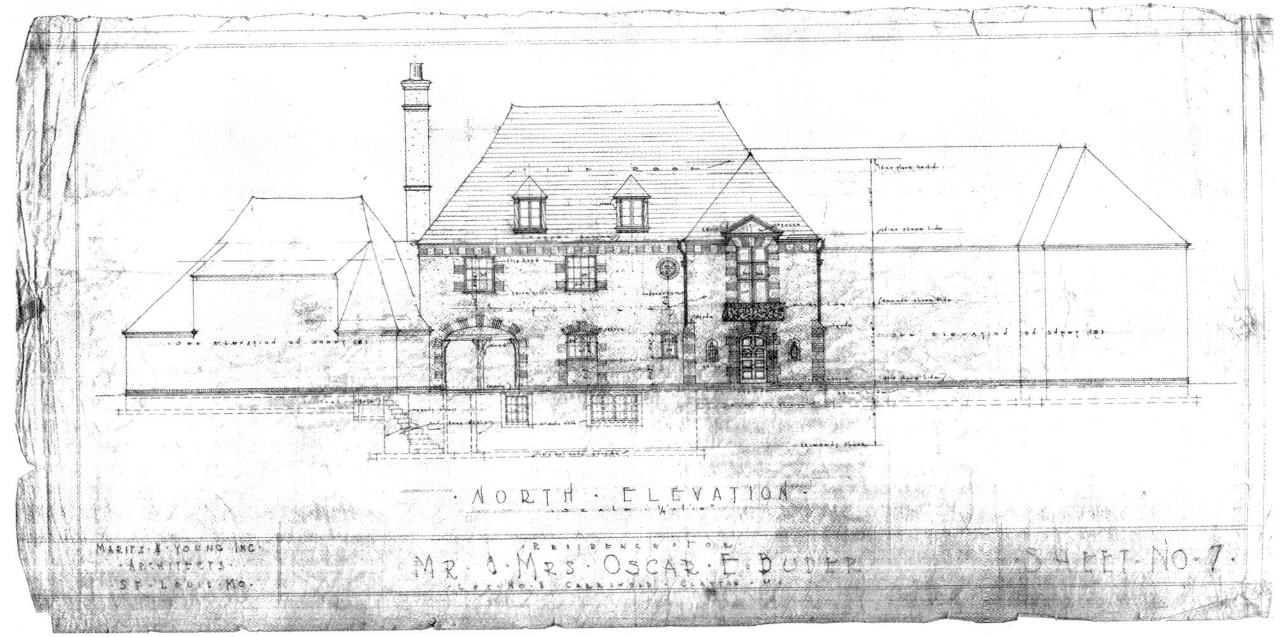

Architect's drawings

As late as 1900, much of Clayton was still rural. What would become Carrswold had been described as one of the handsomest places in the county. Carved from the heavily wooded and undulating landscape of Robert E. Carr's country estate, the group who purchased the 35-acre tract easily recognized the site's potential. In the same year the purchase was finalized, the group retained Jens Jensen to create a landscape and planting plan for the entire project.

Central hall

Jensen's distinctive design principles are evident at Carrswold. The main drive follows the "lines of nature" curving through the undulating terrain, creating a sense of mystery. The houses sit high on their lots, overlooking park and drive, in an open lawn that allows them to emerge in full sunlight, as Jensen planned. Fifteen-foot strips along both sides of the drive are heavily planted to create shade and shadow, and provide privacy. There is a player's bowl (a green space for outdoor theater or play), and rustic stonework. Masses of native plants—crabapple, sumac, dogwood, redbud, sugar maple, and Jensen's favorite, hawthorn—"bind together forest and meadow." No fences were permitted to destroy the peacefulness of the scene. Honeysuckles drape the bridge, ferns line the ravine, and the forest floor was to be planted with violets and trilliums.

The Buder residence faces north, with its back to the road, and away from the sloping south lawn. The third house built in Carrswold, it anchors a corner of the subdivision that is actually two lots. One of the most eclectic and representative examples of Maritz & Young's work, it is hard to classify stylistically, but it is reminiscent of English Arts and Crafts, specifically William Morris's Red House, in its irregular massing and rustic red brick, flagstone "stoop," red tile roof, and timber-framed sleeping porch. The five-bay center block is flanked by wings—one 1½ stories with hipped dormers; the other, two stories, set at

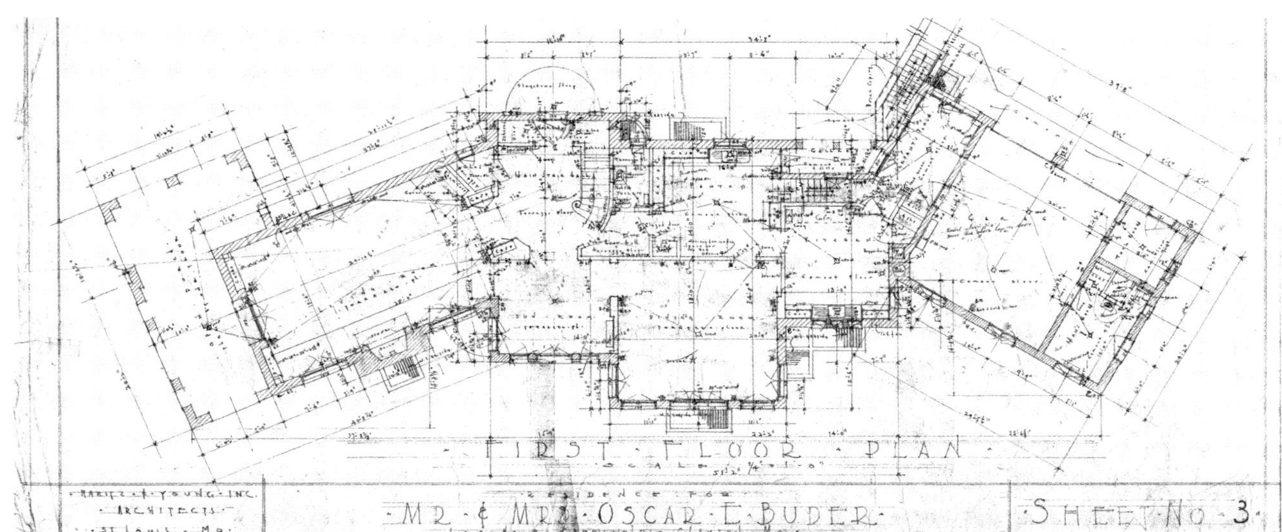

First floor plan

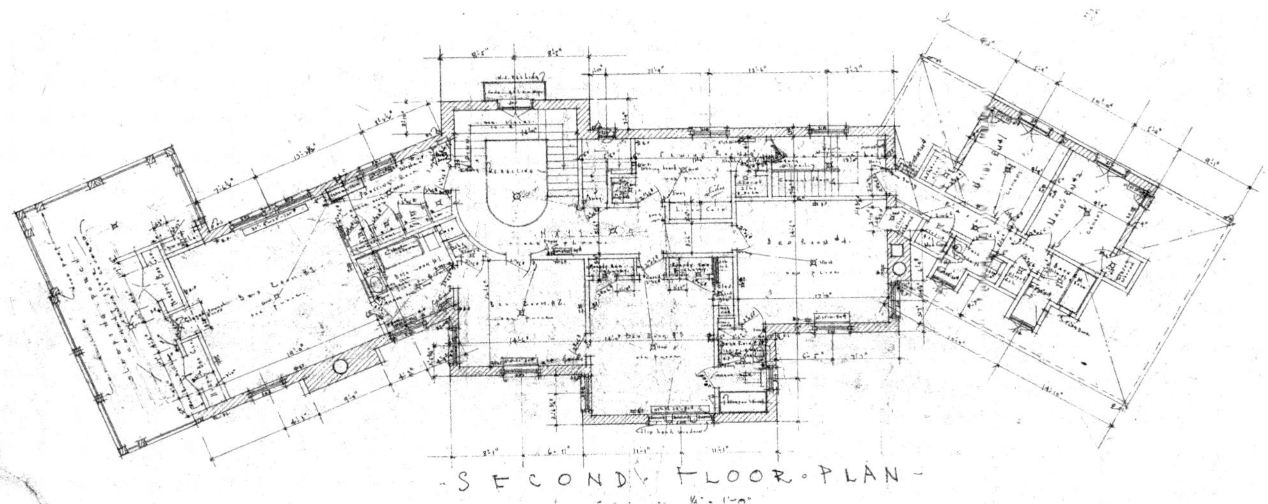

Second floor plan

oblique angles. The circular main hall is double height and links the living room, dining room (the actual center of the house), and sunroom. On the second floor are four bedrooms (two of which have Murphy beds), three baths, two maid's rooms, and a sewing room. The floors upstairs are oak, with terrazzo in the living and dining rooms. The plan indicates a "fruit closet" in the basement and a "man's room" next to the garage and tool storage area. The architects designed a charming playhouse for young family members, complete with bunks, that echoes the style of the house.

It has been more than 80 years since Maritz & Young designed the Buder house and Jensen planned Carrswold, and both have aged gracefully. Jensen's handling of the landscape continues to endow the neighborhood with pastoral appeal: the trees have matured, providing a majestic canopy that shades the grounds, and the drive along the park is still draped in shadow. Carrswold is listed in the National Register of Historic Places; its houses remain privately owned and used as primary residences.

FOUR GATES FARM

MARVIN GATES HOUSE

Kansas City (1925–1927)

SCENIC LITTLE BLUE ROAD is a rambling, tree-lined pathway that hugs the midsection of Jackson County. From the outskirts of Kansas City, this curving, two-lane road leads to Four Gates Farm, built for Marvin and Medill Gates and their two children. When constructed, Four Gates Farm was well outside the city limits, and that feeling of "somewhere else" still pervades the more than 120 acres overlooking a valley near the Little Blue River.

Objectively, the Little Blue is merely a tributary of the Missouri. Its real significance is historical: it is the site of Native American traces, the 1804 Lewis & Clark Voyage of Discovery (at its delta), and the Battle of the Little Blue, one of the area's most significant Civil War skirmishes—"the last tactical maneuver by the Confederacy to gain control of Missouri and portions of Trans Mississippi Territory."

After the Civil War, farms dotted the fertile lands of the Little Blue, including the acreage that became home to the Gates family. Mary Rockwell Hook and Mac Remington, architects for the brick and

Garden facade

Main entrance detail

Side patio

Living room

Dining room

Stone-lined terrace and circular pool

limestone house, incorporated into it the existing fieldstone house and barn, conical-roof water tower, and servants' quarters, placing them all a quarter-mile above the creek that flowed through the property's thickly wooded eastern terrain. Today, Four Gates Farm retains a "commanding view of the countryside."

Marvin Gates, a Yale graduate with a degree from the old Kansas City School of Law, was a noted Kansas City real estate developer and the son of Jemuel Gates, a key developer of the city's core after the Civil War. Once a cowboy in New Mexico, Marvin served as lieutenant colonel under General Pershing in World War I. Kansas City native Medill Smith Gates was "rated Kansas City's best amateur actress" in 1935; along with Mary Rockwell Hook, she was a founding member of the Comedy Club, later the Kansas City Theater. With Medill's commitment to the performing arts, it is no wonder that she and her husband commissioned Hook and Remington to design their country house. Not only was Hook an acting colleague, she had a penchant for building stages into her residential designs. The pairing of Medill and Hook was ideal.

Four Gates Farm is a collaboration between Hook and Remington, but Hook seemed to dominate, as her signature is everywhere, in the arched doorways, multipane casement windows, balconies, multiple fireplaces, Italian plaster walls, and large wooden interior beams. To accommodate Medill's performances, a platform in the living room served as a stage, and Hook provided built-in cabinets for costume storage. Like Hook's other designs, Four Gates sits on a sloped site, yet the major part of the house is on one level. Hook and Remington's sensitive use of local materials, ingenious combination of textures, simplicity of style, and overall mastery of proportion for this rural retreat (in addition to Hook's family house) echoes the architectural work of David Knickerbacker Boyd in his design from the same period for Philadelphian Charles Walton.

The only formal area of the 15,000-square-foot house is the east, or main, section, where the living room features intricate molding, white plaster walls punctuated with Classical Revival notes, and an onyx terrazzo floor. In contrast, the rear of the first floor uses uncoursed limestone (the walls of the house are 18 inches thick), firebrick, exposed beams, and patina-stained concrete flooring, as seen in the dining room. The second story has six bedrooms, with sleeping porches at both ends of the lengthy hall. Early on, Hook and Remington had planned for a stone-lined terrace and a circular pool off the rear of the house.

Most of the original farm buildings on the property prior to the construction of Four Gates no longer exist, yet even today, with housing developments encroaching in the Little Blue River Valley, Four Gates retains its identity as a unique rural retreat in the ever-shrinking countryside of Kansas City.

Mary Rockwell Hook Residence

Kansas City (1927)

"If I have made any contribution to architecture in Kansas City," Mary Rockwell Hook avowed, "it has been my pleasure to try things out. I joy in experiment. I have kept myself free to do this. Houses are fun to plan and fun to build and should be fun to live in. Most people take houses too seriously."

Even as she genuinely held that sentiment, Hook is to be recognized as a pioneer female architect of Kansas City. Born in Junction City, Kansas, to a wealthy family, Mary Rockwell Hook was also one of the nation's early female architects, enrolled in the School of Architecture at the Art Institute of Chicago in 1903, after graduating from Wellesley College.

Mary and her four sisters enjoyed the unconstrained support of their parents, Bertrand and Julia Rockwell, who sent their children on extended European and Asian tours. Mary sailed with her father and

Gabled main entrance, present-day view

sister Florence to the Philippines in 1902 to visit General Adna Chaffee, an uncle who was assigned the military governor of these tropical islands by President Roosevelt.

Her uncle's residence, situated right on the sea with a wide, continuous balcony and commanding outdoor spaces, made a lasting impression on Mary, as she reminisced in her autobiography, *This and That*. "It was during this trip home from the Philippines that I decided someone needed to improve the design of buildings used by our government abroad. I made up my mind to go home and study architecture."

Mary Hook never worked on government structures, but she designed more than 50 residences (many for family and friends), a resort hotel, and the initial buildings for the Pine Mountain Settlement School in Harlan County, Kentucky. Her career in Kansas City began in 1908 with the design for a bungalow, the elements of which became a constant in her later residential schemes—balconies, casement windows, and adaptation of an asymmetrical plan to a sloping site. As they did with this project, her parents purchased vacant lots in new subdivisions to help launch Mary's career.

Situated on a heavily wooded hillside cul-de-sac is the residence that Mary planned for her own family. It is one of her most successful, and perhaps, most challenging residential projects. During the early 1920s, the Rockwell and Hook families purchased three contiguous lots in prestigious Sunset Hill. The Rockwell Hook residence, the last of the houses that she designed at this location, is "a rambling aggregation of intersecting wings and extruding gables, dormers, decks, and porches."

At first glance, the Rockwell Hook residence is reminiscent of the Tudor Revival with its period elements, including multiple gables and chimneys, abundant casement fenestration, brick veneer, and stone trim. Yet Mary's trademark idioms are everywhere—multiple levels, integration of indoor and outdoor

House and garden, present-day view

Main entrance and stairs, present-day view

Mary's studio

Courtyard and pool

spaces, a large courtyard, and stages for amateur theater. The rear of the house, which affords the best views of the surrounding rugged terrain, descends more than 60 feet from the south.

Mary also refrained from tradition with the arrangement of the interior rooms: the first floor features a kitchen and living and dining rooms placed around a courtyard and swimming pool—originally the quarry for the house's limestone masonry. Mary employed recycled materials everywhere—fireplaces from Italy and Kansas City, railroad bridge beams, paneling, and lanterns salvaged from demolished houses. The brick face was purchased for $6 per thousand; the marble for the swimming pool came from a defunct hotel in Topeka, Kansas. "This house is made of discarded materials, relics of the past."

The Rockwell Hooks occupied the house until 1972. It is listed in the National Register of Historic Places as a contributing resource to the residential structures in Kansas City by Mary Rockwell Hook and remains privately owned.

FERRIERES

VIRGIL A. LEWIS HOUSE

Ladue, St. Louis County (1927)

MORE SPARE than its 19th century namesake—the Château de Ferrières outside Paris, built by Baron James de Rothschild—architect Beverly T. Nelson's interpretation of a French manor was a sophisticated and reserved addition to Ladue in 1927. Ladue was not yet a city at the time (it remains primarily residential) and the heavily wooded hills of this 5-acre property shared the same rural character as the French countryside. Against this rustic backdrop sat Ferrieres, the residence of Virgil A. Lewis. Its curving drive approaching from the north, the public rooms of the residence were situated along an east-west axis, opening out to the south. Clematis scrambled over the balustrade of the stone terrace, and boxwood bordered a sweep of lawn.

Garden facade

Side elevation with garden

Entrance facade

The architecture, severely plain to some tastes, provided the perfect context for Lewis's collection of fine French furniture that had been in his family for a century. A black-and-white marble floor was the single decorative element in the entrance hall, yet other rooms provided a narrative of French design that spanned the reigns of several kings. To the east was a Louis XV period salon, its palette of pale yellow and cream complemented by red and ivory Toile de Jouy fabric; to the west was a walnut-lined dining room. Rococo boiseries—wooden panels carved with shells and tendrils—and paintings of frolicking angels were worked into the overall design of the drawing room. The salon held a 1789 clavacin, a variety of harpsichord.

The grounds of Ferrieres included a swimming pool with a charming bathhouse, its steeply pitched hip roof mirroring that of the main house. A garage and servants' quarters with a conical tower flanked the drive. The house is still privately owned.

Garage and servants' quarters

VOUZIERS

JOSEPH DESLOGE HOUSE

St. Louis County (1927)

VOUZIERS IS SITED on land settled by Jesuit priests near the confluence of the Mississippi and Missouri Rivers at Portage des Sioux. The area, which came to be known as Florissant, had attracted wealthy St. Louisans early in the 19th century with its fresh air and flourishing green landscape. Built by Joseph Desloge in 1927, the residence evokes the French architecture and culture he defended as a soldier in World War I and is named after the village where he met his future wife. The primary residence for the family was a formal house in the Central West End of St. Louis, near Forest

Main facade

Stair hall

Gallery

Park, but it was at Vouziers, in the grand underground ballroom and on the terraced expanse of lawn, that gala parties and philanthropic events were held. And here in the country, the Desloge children swam in the river, raised rabbits and wolfhounds and found their presents—ponies left by St. Nick—in the gallery on Christmas morning.

The four-story Bedford limestone chateau is over 15,000 square feet, has ten bedrooms, eight baths, and an elegant interior of marble, walnut, and teak. The long gallery, with its Louis XVI furniture and an Aubusson carpet, connected dining room to drawing room and was ornamented with carved wooden panels representing agriculture, music and the arts. The Gothic Library, embellished with finials, arches and tracery, is exceptional. Although details such as locks and hinges were inspired by those at a chateau near Chalons, France, it is English Gothic in effect, similar to Horace Walpole's fanciful library at Strawberry Hill, Twickenham, England. From the windows of this gothic retreat one can see the Missouri River, the view along the allée in the garden, and weather permitting, to the St. Louis Arch in the distance.

Drawing room

Perhaps the most unusual aspect of the chateau is the *sous sol,* or underground complex, which Desloge added in 1938, to provide more room for social functions such as his daughter's debutante ball. To create the *sous sol,* which was purportedly placed underground to prevent hindering the view, portions of the house were elevated allowing the basement to be transformed into an elaborate space worthy of entertaining. An underground passageway connected the 3,500 square foot underground ballroom to the house. Guests could access this glittering mirrored space lit by chandeliers from an underground receiving hall or the elegant front hall in the house proper. Later Desloge added the "carriage house," or garage, equally French with its mansard roof, turret-like pavilions, and triple-arched entry. The grounds included riding trails, tennis courts, a swimming pool, and a teahouse.

Many other country houses in the state, Selma Hall and Greystone among them, were built on the high bluffs overlooking the Mississippi River but none had such elaborate formal grounds as those at Vouziers. A 1000-foot allée of Siberian elms created an axis from house to grounds, the lawn dropping, via a series of terraces, to the ballroom. Such formality—a marked contrast to the surrounding

Balustrade overlooking the Mississippi River

landscape—so surprised English landscape architect Russell Page (who spotted it from the air as he flew into the city) that he insisted he see it.

Until 1997, it was believed that Moise H. Goldstein was the architect responsible for Vouziers but original plans found that year credit Francis J. MacDonnell, of New Orleans, who worked with the local firm of Study and Farrar. Later additions were the work of Harry I. Hellmuth. Vouziers was sold by the Desloge family in 1977. It is presently owned by the Boeing Company, who has added a state-of-the-art Learning Center, and uses the site for corporate training.

Garage, or "carriage house"

Garage detail

Chatol

F. Gano Chance House

Centralia, Boone County (1939)

CHATOL, the residence of F. Gano Chance, lies surrounded by farmland on the outskirts of Centralia, a small town in rural Boone County. Contrasting starkly with the neighboring fields of hay and cattle, its Art Moderne horizontality and streamlined curves may seem an unusual choice for a conservative midwestern businessman—but they make perfect sense.

F. Gano's father, Albert Bishop Chance, started a family business in the area in 1907, specializing in industrial and telephone technology. He became known internationally for his invention of the "Never-Creep Anchor," an innovation in earth anchors used to support waterfront piers and telephone poles. The company survived the Depression and diversified between 1940 and 1980 to increase its productivity and assets. Patented inventions such as Epoxiglass plastic insulation contributed to its continued success.

Architect's drawing

Aerial view

As an engineer with his father's company, F. Gano incorporated into his house the innovative techniques and materials that he was familiar with from his business: steel "snowshoe" footings to stabilize the building (its site was once marsh and lacks bedrock) and the same spring system was attached to stabilize walls in the Empire State Building. Chance relied on little-known Kansas City architect Sam W. Bihr Jr. for plans and drawings, but he was very hands-on in design and construction (in fact, he altered the architect's design for the east facade).

Chance and his wife traveled the world and Chatol (a conflation of the Chance surname and his wife's maiden name, Toalson) represents their collection of both art and ideas. They brought back silk wallpaper hand-painted with bamboo and peonies from the Orient and a mahogany dining-room set from Honduras that had been exhibited at the 1933 Chicago World's Fair. Their travels also endowed them with an

View of the house through the woods

appreciation for modernism in architecture. That Chatol seems to be a vernacular interpretation of Le Corbusier's Villa Savoye (1929) prompts speculation that the Chances may have been familiar with that "machine for living."

The house's modern conveniences included dual furnaces for better heat control, alarm and intercom systems, and paired sets of attic fans for summer cooling. The building's modularity, curved and planar surfaces, window bands, and entrance supported by *pilotis*, or tall thin piers, suggest a relationship to both early International-Style and American Art Moderne architecture, and clearly to Chance's interest in efficiency and innovative design.

Curved spaces and motifs repeat throughout Chatol's interior, in the shape of the sunroom, and dining and living rooms. The breakfast room's oval ceiling features recessed lighting, and silver and bleached mahogany banding complements the pale green color scheme. Other decorative elements include a freeform teak bar on the first floor, "Never-Creep Anchor" depictions as a motif around the pool, and a

Entrance detail

glass and stainless-steel baluster designed by Chance for the central stairway. No longer extant on the grounds are the original steam-heated dog kennel, orchard, tea house, and fish pond.

Listed in the National Register, Chatol was used as a meeting- and guesthouse by the A. B. Chance Company, now a subsidiary of Hubbell Incorporated, manufacturer of products for the electric utility, telecommunications, and construction industries. The house was recently purchased by a Chance family relative, who plans to make it a small luxury inn.

Stair hall

Dining room

Walter E. Bixby Sr. Residence

Kansas City (1935–1937)

It comes as a surprise that Edward W. Tanner—the architect of over 2,000 predictably popular and well-crafted period revival-style residences in the Kansas City area during the 1920s and 1930s—planned for the first International Style house in this Midwestern metropolis. But Walter E. Bixby Sr. insisted on breaking with the traditional styles of architecture that pervaded the J. C. Nichols Company developments in the area when he contracted Edward Tanner to build his house in the exclusive Country Club District.

In 1923 Walter Bixby Sr. married Angeline Reynolds, the daughter of J. B. Reynolds, president and later chairman of the nationally recognized Kansas City Life Insurance Company, organized in 1895. Shortly thereafter, Bixby's father-in-law coaxed him to join the company. He ultimately rose to chairman of the board in 1964, a position he held until 1972, the year he died.

Main facade from the northwest

Main entrance detail

Terrace at rear

Side patio

Rumpus room

Circular bar with diorama

Bixby's residence was a collaboration between Edward Tanner and the Los Angeles-based industrial designer Kem Weber, who brought "a tradition-free, machine-age creativeness to American interior design." Together, Tanner and Weber effectively transformed the simple streamlined house with built-in and movable furniture into a unified expression of the new era of architecture.

Practitioners of the International Style, such as Le Corbusier and Walter Gropius, erased the razzle-dazzle of the Art Deco style in favor of clean, unadorned surfaces. Tanner's bold exploration of form and shape in the Bixby residence follows in this tradition, eschewing the ornamentation of revival styles and the colonial elements of the newly popoular ranch house.

Well sited on a sloping terrain atop natural limestone, the asymmetrical house comprises a 2-story (plus basement) core flanked by two-story wings; curved, one-story expansions and cantilevered balconies supported by sleek, tubular steel columns break the primary rectilinear composition. Fenestration includes ribboned bands of single-light casement windows, plate glass units, glass block, and a few double-hung sash windows, all set in aluminum frames. Poured concrete paretta terraces (with a surface of protruding pebbles) further relieve the otherwise tight cubic character of the Bixby house. Tripartite incised bands, threading seemingly uninterrupted at the roofline, are essential to the whole.

Working together, Tanner and Weber designed the 13-room interior of the reinforced concrete and stucco house, which comprises more than 15,000 square feet. Having been influenced by work with Bruno Paul early in his career, Weber evolved from a master cabinetmaker to a designer of Machine Age

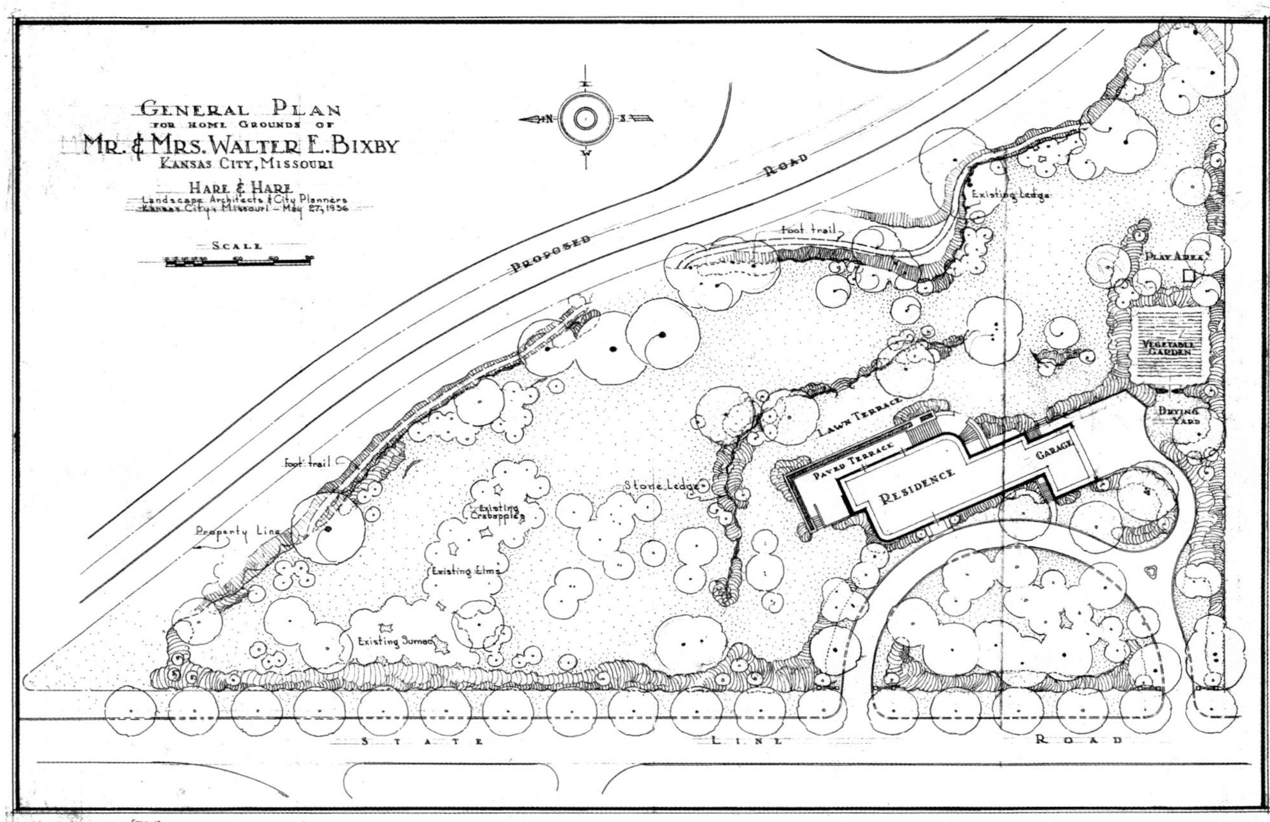

Site plan

mass-produced objects. To allow for a "full view of the interior space" of his plans for streamlined, curvilinear furniture, Weber presented his client with drawings in which the interior walls were transparent.

A focal point of the house is the circular, two-story main staircase; it has Baccarat glass posts set between aluminum alloy railings. Long corridors link the living, dining, and breakfast rooms, six bedrooms, and Walter Bixby's study; a rumpus room at the basement level has a circular bar, the shape of which is echoed in a diorama of Bixby's ranch in Wyoming. Weber used a highly saturated palette throughout the house and machined Streamline Moderne materials and details—brushed aluminum was everywhere. Listed in the National Register, the house was the backdrop for the 1990 film *Mr. and Mrs. Bridge.*

Weber commented in a 1929 lecture that "it must be our ambition to express beauty in our daily commodities, through the most simple, most logical, most graceful and proportioned forms and designs . . . and the most natural development based upon the understanding of the problem, will be retained as the best possible solution." Weber attained his goal in the Bixby house, but sadly, with few exceptions, his innovative interiors and furnishings have not survived.

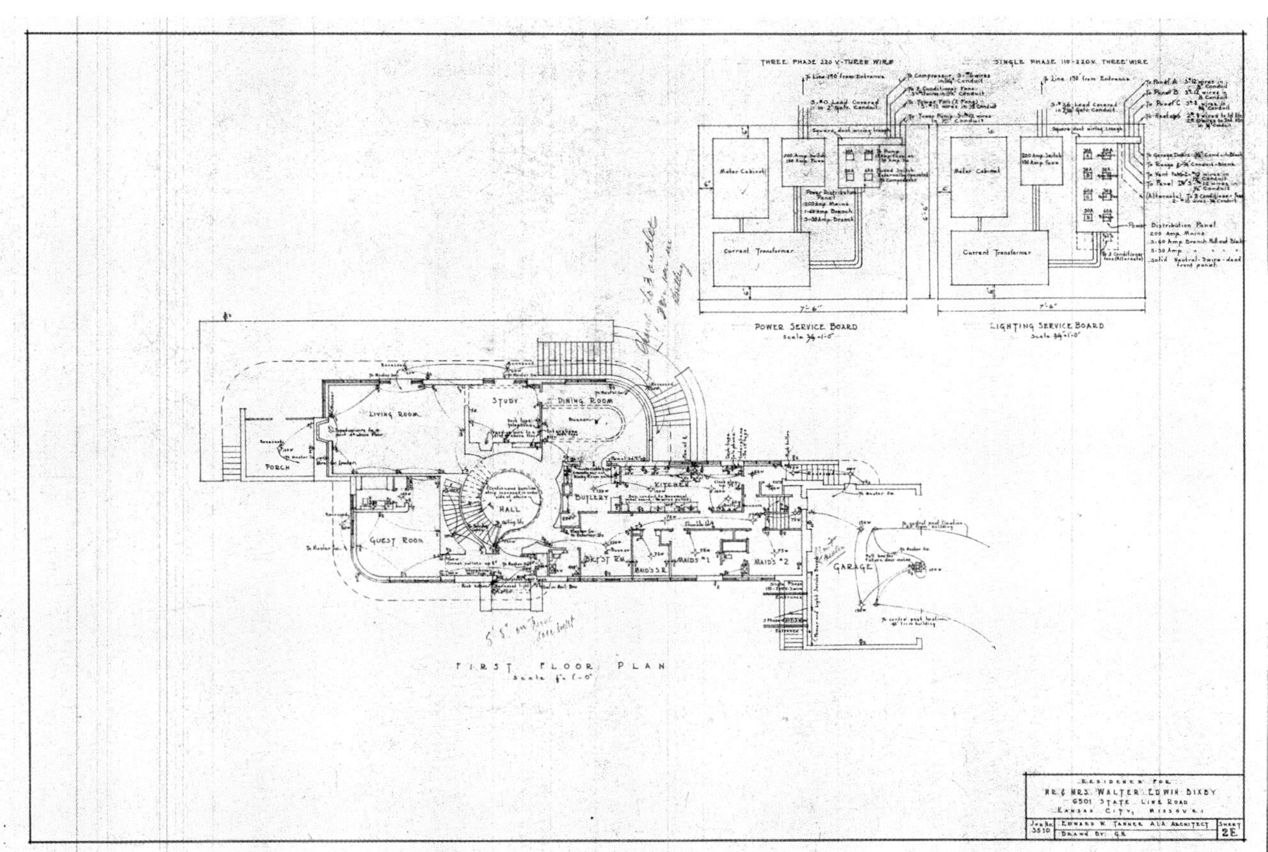

First floor plan

Arnold Maremont Residence

Clayton, St. Louis County (1939)

The move out of St. Louis to suburban surroundings resulted in neighborhoods of similar stature and prestige in the county, such as Brentmoor and Carrswold and the Wydown-Forsyth District. The last portion of this district to be platted (in 1922) was Ellenwood which shares the attributes of its sister neighborhoods, albeit on a smaller and more modest scale. Wydown-Forsyth is known for its period and

Street elevation

Entrance hall

Living room

revival style architecture—tasteful Georgian, Colonial, Spanish and French Eclectic examples—but tree-lined DeMun Boulevard in Ellenwood is distinguished by two delightful proto-modern houses. Located adjacent to one another and related stylistically, the Arnold Maremont house and that built for Thomas Sherman (music critic for the *Post-Dispatch* newspaper and friend of architect Frederick Dunn), acknowledge the historic sources around them while being forward-looking and idiosyncratic.

Designed by the architectural firm of Nagel and Dunn and built for real estate executive Arnold Maremont, the cubic three-by-three bay brick house (painted white) has spare ornamentation in the form of brick lintels in a meander pattern and banding on the high basement. The entrance and secondary porches, located to the side rather than the front and back of the house, mirror one another and assert the symmetry of the plan. The firm's trademark bull's eye windows are incorporated on the street facade (on the Sherman house next door they flank the side chimney). Brick and ironwork—both traditional materials used often in St. Louis in the 19th century—are used, but here the ironwork is sleek and stylized, and the windows punch through the brick facade with mechanical precision.

Dressing room detail

The architects were known for their ability to synthesize tradition and modernity and the Maremont facade—a reduced and spare relative of Georgian predecessors on one hand and vaguely reminiscent of a temple front on the other—is an example. A contemporary of Frederick Dunn noted his absolute understanding of Georgian architecture. Alhough grounded in history, Nagel and Dunn collaborated with designers and architects such as Ralph Cole Hall and Victor Proetz, who were known for their streamlined and functional work.

Kitchen with signature bull's eye window

The interior is a tasteful use of a small space—the efficient kitchen and dressing room are examples as tricks were used to visually expand space such as floor-to-ceiling mirrors in the living room and bold, graphic wallpaper in the entrance hall. The balance inherent in the plan and facade is evident in the entrance hall: the doors that flank the central niche hide a guest bathroom to one side and coat closet to the other but are read by the eye as a sophisticated whole. Dunn's interest in integrating art and architecture is evident also in the living room in the trompe l'oeil Ionic columns painted onto the walls.

Julius Pitzman designed many of the city's unique private places, such as Westmoreland and Portland Place in the 19th century, and it was the Pitzman Company that planned Ellenwood's curving streets and sited lots to make best use of the undulating topography. The neighborhood has retained these qualities, and the Maremont house, which ushered modernism into the neighborhood, and its "twin" next door, remain private residences.

Morton May Residence

Ladue, St. Louis County (1942)

In the Ladue residence of May Company department store scion Morton "Buster" May, Chicago architect Samuel Marx deftly crossed Streamline Moderne with International style. Marx's urbane creativity—whether applied to a Pullman railroad car or a flagship retail store on the Wilshire Boulevard "Miracle Mile" in Los Angeles—was a solid match for his patron's appreciation for cutting-edge design and fine art, be it pre-Columbian or German Expressionist. Humanizing the modern aesthetic with the use of natural, often exotic, materials—such as shell-strewn Cordova stone, grass cloth, hand-woven fabrics and leather—Marx softened all reference to the "box" that was quickly becoming the model for contemporary housing.

Front elevation

Side elevation

Marx merged interior and exterior space in the May plan. The basic T shape was extended by borrowing visually from the sweep of lawn to the south, the walled garden on the west, and the porch connecting the two. The 2,300 square feet of ground-floor living space was articulated by sliding leather screens, the architect's precise placement of furniture and carpet runners, and a 10-foot sunken planter that linked both space and provided a visual stop at the end of the main axis. Low-slung linearity—conferred by a 56-foot curtain wall—and the horizontal emphasis of window bands were juxtaposed with circular motifs repeated in a courtyard screen and site sculpture. Just inside the main entrance, set at right angles to the main facade between the library and the living/dining core, was perhaps the most spectacular element in the composition, and another of the circular motifs: a dramatic curving staircase at once baroque and modern—a giant transcendent spiral so organic in feel that it belied its steel and plaster composition—led to the upstairs bedrooms, sundecks, and darkroom (Buster May was an amateur photographer).

Like many of the great works of architecture from this period, the plan suggests a relationship to Cubist and contemporary painting in the balance of solids and voids, and the bold line inherent in modernism set against the organic forms of nature Marx incorporated. Likewise, the period's renewed interest

Main staircase

Living room

Dining room

Kitchen

in art and craft as a component of good architecture is evident here. Fabrics were the product of American textile designer Dorothy Liebes, who was strongly influenced by Bauhaus tenets of design. Marx himself designed virtually all the furniture, and Chicago-based Franz Lipp was the landscape architect for the project, which comprised nine acres, including a pool and pool house. Resident architects were Study & Farrar of St. Louis.

Marx's "machine in the prairie" was an iconoclastic exception in pastoral but pastiche-prone Ladue. Few people aspire to the level of taste May cultivated or to the financial commitment he was able to make in the name of good architecture. The house was sacrificed to redevelopment pressures and demolished in 2006. The new owners have subdivided the property into smaller parcels.

Upstairs bedroom

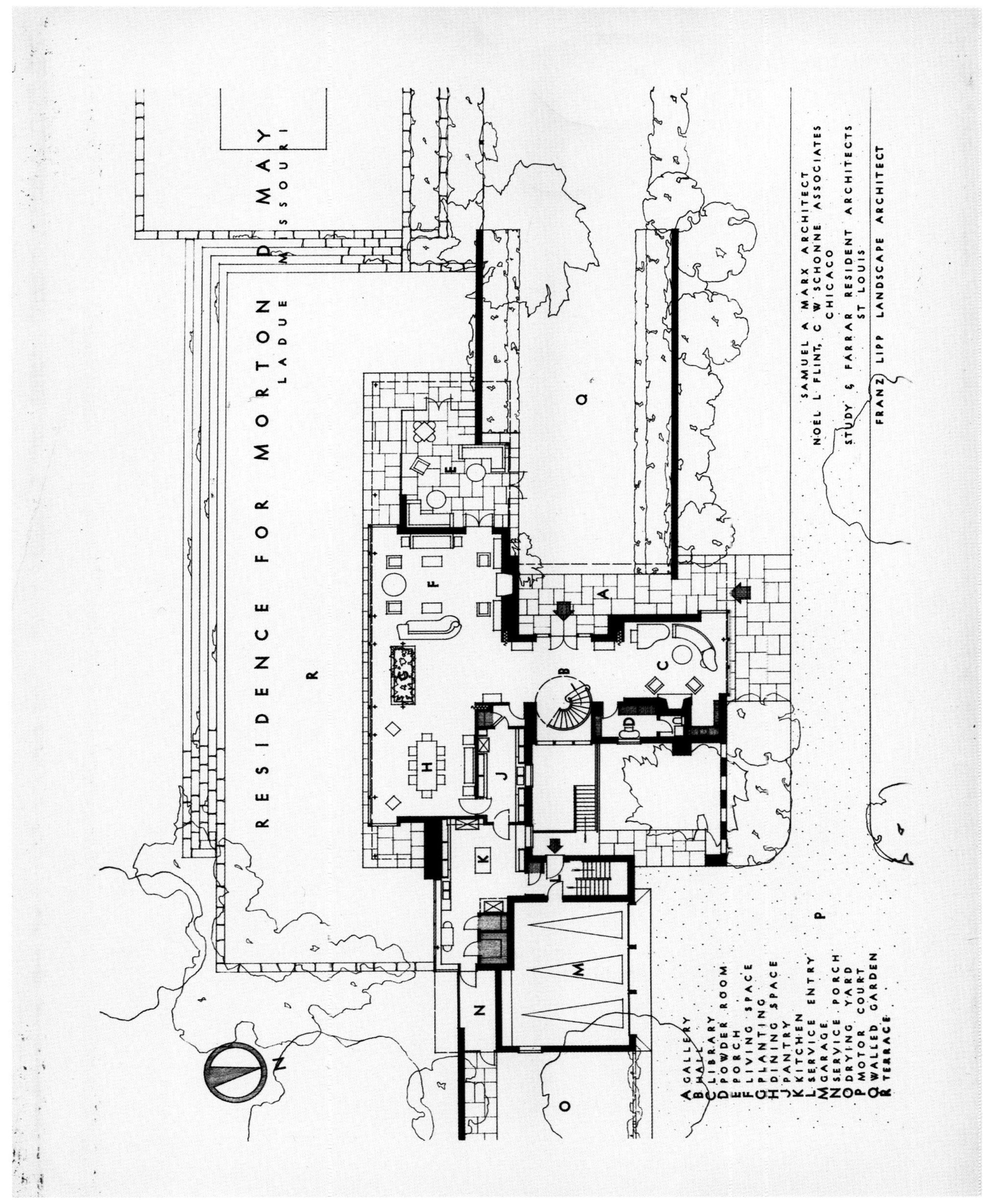

Architect's plan

APPENDICES

1911. St. Louis County residence of brewery mogul Augustus Busch Sr.
Widman and Walsh, Architects
Private residence

Portfolio of Houses
1876–1938

Ca. 1876. Kansas City residence of livestock commissioner Cornelius C. Quinlan
Edmond J. Eckel (attrib), architect
Demolished

1882. Kansas City residence of pioneer physician
Dr. I. M. Ridge
Architect unknown
Demolished

Ca. 1885. Kansas City residence of rancher and president/founder Union National Bank David T. Beals
Architect unknown
Demolished

1886. St. Louis County residence of investor and banker
John R. Lionberger
H. H. Richardson, architect
Demolished

1887. Kansas City residence of First National Bank president James L. Lombard
Burnham & Root, architect
Demolished

1889. St. Joseph residence of banker Joseph W. McAllister
Harvey Ellis, architect
Private residence

Ca. 1889. Kansas City residence of attorney Henry Smith
Architect unknown
Demolished

1890. Kansas City residence of real estate investor George F. Winter
William S. Matthews, architect
Demolished

Ca. 1890. Independence residence of real estate investor Logan O. Swope
Architect unknown
Demolished

Ca. 1890. Joplin residence of bakery businessman George W. Keller
T. R. Bellas, architect
Demolished

1891. Carthage residence of Carthage Stone Company president Curtis Wright
C. W. Terry, architect
Private residence

1891. Carthage residence of lead and zinc mining investor Thomas Davey
Architect unknown
Private residence (remodeled)

Ca. 1895. Joplin residence of mining investor Julius Hewitt
A. C. Michaelis, architect
Demolished

1897. Pike County residence of real estate investor Edward Dameron
Shepley, Rutan & Coolidge (with John L. Mauran), architects
Private residence

1897. St. Louis residence of Missouri governor and 1904 World's Fair president David Francis
Eames & Young, architects
Demolished

Ca. 1900. Kansas City residence of furniture businessman William L. Abernathy
James Oliver Hogg, architect
Demolished

Ca. 1900. Kansas City residence of real estate investor Elmer Williams
John W. McKecknie, architect
Demolished

Ca. 1900. Carthage residence of mining and real estate investor James Luke
Architect unknown
Private residence

1901. Albany residence of E. L. Peery and Company, dry goods, president Samuel Peery
E. J. Eckel, architect
Private residence

1904. Maryville residence of Nodaway Valley Bank president James B. Robinson
Alexander A. Searcy, architect
Private residence

1904. Kansas City residence of Phenix Stone & Lime Company president and manager of Phenix Cut Stone Company Calvert Hunt
John W. McKecknie, architect
Private residence

1905. Cape Girardeau residence of railroad executive and real estate investor Louis B. Houck
Jerome B. Legg, architect
Demolished

1906. University City (St. Louis County) residence of Lewis Publishing Company treasurer and University Heights Realty owner Francis V. Putnam
Herbert C. Chivers, architect
Private residence

1906. University City (St. Louis County) residence of shoe importer David Ralston
Herbert C. Chivers, architect
Private residence

1907. Kansas City residence of United States Mexican Trust Company assistant secretary William Lee Karnes
Wilder and Wight, architects
Private residence

1910. Kansas City residence of Hall Baker Grain Company president Herbert F. Hall
Wilder & Wight, architects
Demolished

1911. University City (St. Louis County) residence of Roberts, Johnson & Rand (shoes) founder and president, International Shoe Company, Frank C. Rand
Theodore Link, architect
Private residence

1911. University City (St. Louis County) residence of Johnson-Stephens and Shinkle Shoe Co. vice president Bradford Shinkle
Theodore Link, architect
Private residence

1912. Clayton (St. Louis County) residence of coffee and tea importer and president Evens-Howard Fire Brick Co. Cecil Dudley Gregg
Howard Van Doren Shaw, architect
Private residence

1912. Ladue (St. Louis County) residence of milling entrepreneur Samuel Plant
Norman Vegely, architect
Private residence

1913. Kansas City residence of T. W. Ballew Lumber Company representative Ben C. Hyde
Shepard Farrar & Wiser, architects
Private residence

1915. Kansas City residence of physician and surgeon Dr. Samuel Ayres
Selby Kurfiss, architect
Private residence

1924–1927. Kansas City residence of real estate investor George Wright
Horace LaPierre, architect
Private residence

1927. OAK HILL, Macon County residence of Independent Telephone Co. head Theodore Gary
Edward Buehler Delk, architect
Private residence

1935. Huntleigh (St.Louis County) residence of bond and stock broker and owner of Carton's Importers
Leo De Smet Carton
Maritz, Young & Dusard, architects
Private residence

1935. Glendale (St. Louis County) residence of 1947 Nobel Peace Prize winners and physiologists
Carl and Gerti Cori
Harris Armstrong, architect
Private residence

1935. FERCREST, North St. Louis County residence of Mesker Bros. Iron Company vice president Francis Mesker
Study & Farrar, architects
Private residence

Ca. 1935. Clayton (St. Louis County) residence of hotel executive Morris Corn
Maritz, Young & Dusard, architects
Private residence

Ca. 1936. Huntleigh (St. Louis County) residence of Anheuser-Busch president and chairman of the board
Percy J. Orthwein
Maritz, Young & Dusard, architects
Private residence

1938. Poplar Bluff residence of Moore Ford Motor Sales owner and real estate developer J. Herbert Moore
J. Herbert Moore, builder
Private residence

Biographies

Architects, Landscape Architects, and Planners

George Ingham Barnett

The first professional architect to practice in St. Louis and the best known of the mid-19th century, George Ingham Barnett (1815–1898) earned the title dean of architects. Born in Nottingham, England, and trained in London under Thomas Hine, he arrived in Missouri in 1839. His classical design idiom reflects travel in Italy and a return to England, where he noted the work of Christopher Wren and the design of English parks. For a limited time he was in partnership with Charles H. Peck, and he collaborated with Henry Shaw in designing Shaw's town house (in 1849) and country house, Tower Grove, on the grounds of the Missouri Botanical Garden. He also designed Shaw Place, a private block of 10 houses intended to generate income for the Botanical Garden.

Along with his many churches and institutional and commercial buildings, Barnett designed park pavilions that still contribute to the original character of the Botanical Garden and the nearby Tower Grove Park. Other extant Barnett buildings include the Corinthian-style Grand Avenue Water Tower, St. Vincent de Paul Church in St. Louis, and the Governor's Mansion in Jefferson City. Barnett's role as mentor to aspiring architects is one of his most important contributions to the field. He is buried in St. Louis in Bellefontaine Cemetery, the city's foremost example of the rural cemetery movement of the 19th century.

Barnett, Haynes & Barnett

George Dennis Barnett (1863–1923), Tom P. Barnett (1870–1929), and John I. Haynes (1861–1943) were, respectively, the sons and son-in-law of the premier St. Louis architect, George I. Barnett. Stylistically, they inherited the patriarch's classical approach to design, and in that sense, they carried his legacy into the 20th century. The firm's residential work sits along St. Louis's private streets in Kingsbury, Lewis, and Portland Places, and its range suggests the partners' ability to meet client needs.

Besides houses, institutional buildings, theaters, and hotels, they designed the Palace of Liberal Arts at the Louisiana Purchase Exposition (the 1904 World's Fair) and the Romanesque-style Cathedral of St. Louis (completed in 1914). Projects outside Missouri include 1 Wall Street in New York City, the Illinois Athletic Club in Chicago, and the Adolphus Hotel in Dallas. Honored as fellows of the American Institute of Architects, George Dennis Barnett and John I. Haynes may have been as successful as the senior Barnett; in fact, their reputations eclipse his when considering the varied locations of their projects.

Samuel Wilks Bihr Jr.

Little is known of Samuel Wilks Bihr Jr. (dates unknown) save his work in Kansas City and the Midwest dating primarily from the late 1920s through the 1950s. Bihr, whose office was at 912 Baltimore Avenue in Kansas City, was fluent in the design of institutional buildings, including commercial, religious, educational, and governmental types. Between 1920 and 1930, the firm of Madorie & Bihr designed the Normandy Building and Crowley Apartments on Main Street, Fire Station No. 31 on Troost Avenue, and the St. James Rectory and Recreation Center, all in Kansas City. In later years Bihr worked independently (and briefly with architectural engineer Ralph E. Kiene Jr.) on buildings for the Puritan Compressed Gas Corporation, Haas &

Wilkerson Insurance Company, and the Immaculate Conception Catholic School, also in Kansas City. Bihr's work outside the state includes the design of the Art Moderne Fox Theaters in Hayes and Atchison, Kansas, circa 1950. It is likely that Bihr collaborated closely with F. Gano Chance on Chatol, Chance's house in Boone County, as Chance was also a designer and engineer.

CANN & CORRUBIA

M. Franklin Cann (1891–1967) and Angelo B. M. Corrubia (1884?–1943) were partners in a St. Louis architecture firm from 1915 to 1921, after which they took on some notable projects with a variety of other architects. Their work includes the Collegiate Revival Duncker Memorial Hall at Washington University (built in 1923, in association with Jamieson & Spearl) and Charles H. Duncker's personal residence in Brentmoor Park. Cann studied architecture at Washington University and landscape architecture at the University of Illinois. He represents several generations of practicing architects in his family; he trained under his father, W. A. Cann, and later worked with his son.

Corrubia also studied at Washington University and at MIT after coming to the United States from Italy at the age of 18. Corrubia's partnership with Gale Henderson circa 1926 resulted in the St. Louis landmark, Garavelli's Restaurant, a variation of a Renaissance palazzo richly ornamented with terra cotta, and houses on the grounds of the St. Louis Country Club and in Westmoreland Place. A man of catholic interests, Corrubia was associated with the Clinton-Peabody Terrace, an early public housing project, and he painted landscapes.

HERBERT CALEB CHIVERS

Architect Herbert Caleb Chivers (1869–1946) worked in St. Louis between 1891 and 1906 and thereafter in California. His best work was for businessman Edward Gardner Lewis in University City, Missouri. Born in Windsor, England, and having lived in Fort Leavenworth, Kansas, Chivers began his career in St. Louis as a draftsman on the Union Station project under architect Theodore Link. He later worked with Missouri architect Jerome Legg, who designed several courthouses in the state, and the Houck house in Cape Girardeau (included here in the portfolio). The extent of Chivers' professional training is unknown but to his credit are commercial buildings, at least five churches, and hundreds (purportedly thousands) of houses. Several of his outstanding plans failed to be built for financial reasons.

Chivers and his client Edward Gardner Lewis shared an interest in self-promotion that bordered on excess. Lewis developed University City and several of its first major businesses, and for five years, beginning in 1901, Chivers designed dramatic buildings to house these projects. Among them were a remarkable Egyptian Revival temple (built circa 1905 and demolished in 1931) and the world-class Magazine Building, an octagonal French Renaissance work, which today serves as the city hall for University City. Chivers designed houses, Lewis's own residence in University Heights Number One is attributed to him, and he published a catalog of house plans titled, *Artistic Homes*, which appeared in such journals as *Country Life* between 1896 and 1910. Purportedly 2,000 of his Stick-style, Queen Anne, Craftsman, Colonial, and Tudor Revival plans were built in 26 states and Canada. (Two other houses attributed to him, the Francis Putnam and David Ralston houses, are in the portfolio here.)

Chivers worked briefly in San Francisco, and in 1908 he moved to Oakland; from there he submitted an entry for the Canberra, Australia, capital competition. Just prior, he had proposed City Beautiful improvements for St. Louis, such as a monumental gateway to the Eads Bridge on the Mississippi River and a 26-mile network of parkways that would link the city's parks to the river. He had hoped to expand his body of work to include landscape architecture and urban planning—he appealed repeatedly to city planner John Nolen for employment in the early 1920s—but he did not succeed. He died in Tecumseh, Kansas, on May 13, 1946.

COPE & STEWARDSON

Although known primarily for introducing Collegiate Gothic architecture to U.S. college campuses, including 10 buildings for the new campus of Washington University in St. Louis (1899), Walter Cope (1860–1902) and John Stewardson (1858–1896) designed several fine houses in the Wydown-Forsyth District. Their academic training—Cope at the Pennsylvania Academy of Fine Arts and Stewardson at Harvard University and the Ecole des Beaux-

Arts—is reflected in their skillful interpretation of historical prototypes and their use of fine materials and craftsmanship. The firm's primary office was in Philadelphia; the St. Louis office was run by James P. Jamieson, who carried on their reputation after the office closed in 1912, following the early deaths of both partners. Considered among the best of their generation of East Coast architects, Cope & Stewardson is one of the relatively few firms "imported" by wealthy Missouri clients to design their houses.

ASA BEEBE CROSS

Born in Camden, New Jersey, Asa Beebe Cross (1826–1894) was Kansas City's first professional architect, and he transformed the town in its nascent years. Although he started as a carpenter, Cross's architecture career began in New York, working for A. B. Stone, and in St. Louis, for John Johnson, with whom he formed a partnership in 1851 that endured until 1858. He established the A. B. Cross & Company, a lumber business, in Kansas City in 1858, while he worked concurrently as an architect.

His first work of considerable prestige was the Mechanics Bank (1860), followed by Vaughan's Diamond (1869), one of Kansas City's first notable office buildings. His other commissions include the Pacific Hotel (1860), Union Depot (1878), the Gillis Opera House (1883), the second Jackson County Courthouse (1892), and several railroad depots, including those for Denver, Colorado; Peoria, Illinois; and Atchison, Kansas. Cross served one term as Kansas City's city treasurer and as supervising architect for the county. Among the honors he earned in his prolific career was election as the founding president of the Western Association of Architects, which later merged with the American Institute of Architects. Cross may have designed more than 1,000 buildings throughout Kansas City and the Midwest, but only a handful of his work remains.

LOUIS S. CURTISS

One of the most enigmatic and progressive architects working in Kansas City and the nation during the late 19th and early 20th centuries was Louis Singleton Curtiss (1865–1924), a native of Belleville, Ontario, Canada. Trained in architecture at the University of Toronto and allegedly at the Ecole des Beaux-Arts, Curtiss moved to Kansas City in 1887. He worked at one time as a draftsman for Adriance Van Brunt and served as assistant superintendent of buildings for Kansas City.

In collaboration with his supervisor, Simeon E. Chamberlain, Curtiss conceived an innovative type of caisson pier that "preceded by at least three years the tentative attempts at caisson foundation under Adler & Sullivan's 1893 Chicago Stock Exchange building." At the same time, he and his partner, architect Frederick C. Gunn (in the firm Gunn & Curtiss, 1890–1899), enjoyed success with courthouse designs for Huntington, West Virginia, and Fort Worth, Texas. Together, they designed the Missouri State Building at the World's Columbian Exposition in 1893.

With this impressive beginning, Curtiss was commissioned to design the Renaissance Revival–style Baltimore Hotel (built in 1899 in Kansas City; demolished in 1939) and its several expansions through 1907. Other works in Kansas City by Curtiss include the Italianate Standard Theater (1900), the ornately embellished Beaux Arts–style Willis Wood Theater (built in 1902 and since demolished), and the Boley Building (1908–1909)—arguably the first curtain-walled construction The Santa Fe Railroad and the Fred Harvey enterprise also commissioned Curtiss to design "depots, office buildings, hotels and 'eating houses' from Moline, Illinois, through southern Missouri, Oklahoma, and Texas to Santa Fe and the Grand Canyon." Design elements found on the array of structures in Kingsville and Lubbock, Texas and Joplin, Missouri, predate the defining characteristics of the Corrigan residence in Kansas City. The Art Nouveau–influenced Mineral Hall (1903–1904) and the Tromenhauser and Hoel residences also represent the exemplary vision of Louis Curtiss.

EAMES & YOUNG

William S. Eames (1857–1915) toured Europe studying architecture after graduating from the St. Louis School of Fine Arts in 1878. Thomas Crane Young (1858–1934) attended Washington University and studied at the Ecole des Beaux-Arts and Heidelberg University. On his return Young worked briefly in the Boston office of Van Brunt & Howe (just prior to Van Brunt's move to Kansas City).

Like other top St. Louis architects, the firm designed houses in the city's private places, but they are best known for their public buildings, such as the Art Building for the 1898 Trans-Continental Exposition in Omaha, Nebraska, the Palace of Education for the 1904 World's Fair, and the Title Guaranty Building. The firm competed against Cass Gilbert; McKim, Mead & White; Carrere & Hastings; Shepley, Rutan & Coolidge; and winners Cope & Stewardson of Philadelphia for the Washington University campus plan in 1899. Architectural journals of the period praised their Cupples Warehouse project, built for Robert S. Brookings, as a sophisticated solution to the functional demands of freight handling and storage. Other important commissions include federal prisons in Atlanta, Georgia, and Leavenworth, Kansas.

Eames, whose brother was the father of designer Charles Eames, was the founding president of the St. Louis chapter of the AIA in 1890 (Young served as president in 1909–1910), and in 1904 was elected president of the national organization. After Eames died, Young continued to operate the firm under the same name until 1927, also running a practice in Chicago with Alfred H. Granger. Both Eames and Young lived in Shingle-style houses in Webster Groves, a St. Louis suburb, where Young served as mayor. In 1927 the local chapter of the AIA praised the work of Eames & Young as "a civic asset," one that fulfilled its duty to the public. Architect Cass Gilbert described their work as "distinguished, scholarly, and notable."

ECKEL & ALDRICH

George Robert Eckel (1882–1959) was the son of Edmond Jacques Eckel (1845–1934), a prominent St. Joseph architect. A graduate of MIT, George joined his father and William Stein Aldrich in 1910 in Eckel & Aldrich, "recognized as one of the oldest [architecture] firms operating in the country." Chicago-born William S. Aldrich (1865–1947), like the younger Eckel, attended MIT, although it is uncertain that he graduated. Prior to moving to St. Joseph in 1910, Aldrich's varied career included work for the New York firm of Lord, Hewlett & Hull and the prestigious McKim, Mead & White on two separate occasions, in the late 1890s and from 1903 to 1910. During the two tenures he participated in such projects as the Boston Public Library, the Pennsylvania Railroad Station, an addition to the Metropolitan Museum of Art, and the Brooklyn Institute of Arts and Sciences, among others. Several of Aldrich's measured drawings of historic Colonial buildings from his early years were published in contemporary journals. Aldrich was director of the American Academy of Fine Arts in Rome from 1897–1898. Eckel & Aldrich completed two notable commissions: a factory for the National Biscuit Company (Los Angeles, 1926) and the St. Joseph City Hall (1927), steeped in the Beaux Arts tradition. The firm was active until the 1959 death of George Eckel.

FULLER & WHEELER

Albert W. Fuller (1854–1934) and William Arthur Wheeler (dates unknown) started the firm of Fuller & Wheeler in Albany, New York, in 1883. They worked together until 1897 (after 1900, Fuller had other partners), most often in the Richardsonian Romanesque mode. Although the firm specialized in educational and YMCA buildings—their design for the Albany YMCA was repeated in Hartford, Connecticut; Montreal; Oakland, California; and Paris—they also designed apartment houses, banks, churches, a hospital, and a police station. In 1882 Fuller published *Artistic Homes in City and Country.* Their design for the Henry Clay Pierce house has at times been incorrectly credited to Canadian architect Thomas Fuller, who designed the capitol building in Albany, New York, and the Parliament buildings in Ottawa.

ROGER GILMAN

Relatively unfamiliar in Missouri, Roger Gilman (1874–1964) was a native of Cambridge, Massachusetts, and a cum laude graduate of Harvard University in 1895. After a brief teaching career, he traveled to Paris to study at the Ecole des Beaux-Arts for four years. In the *Fiftieth Anniversary Report of Harvard College*, Gilman wrote

> The first 25 years after my graduation were given up to architecture. It was fascinating but for me an exacting profession. Whether as a student in Paris, as a draftsman and designer in New York, or as a practicing architect in Kansas City, it absorbed the greater part of my time and thought.

After World War I (when he volunteered for overseas service), he worked in "Burnham's largest office" in Chicago, with Pierce Anderson, another Harvard graduate. Employed in the New York office of Post & Sons, Gilman was given the commission for the Walter Dickey residence in Kansas City. In 1920, Gilman alluded to the Dickey project as his "only one real success" in Kansas City. Gilman served as dean of the Rhode Island School of Design from 1919 to 1929; from then until his retirement in 1941, he served as publicity director of Harvard's Fogg Art Museum. Gilman also authored *Great Styles of Interior Architecture* and painted for pleasure. Aside from the Dickey residence, no other works by Gilman are known in Kansas City.

HARE & HARE

Sidney J. Hare (1860–1938) formed a landscape architecture firm with his son S. Herbert Hare (1888–1960) when landscape architecture in America was still a fledgling profession. A native of Louisville, Kentucky, Sidney Hare had no formal landscape training, but as a high school student, he studied horticulture, civil engineering, geology, surveying, and photography. Hare worked from 1881 to 1896 in the city engineer's office in Kansas City; there he was introduced to George Edward Kessler, who inspired the elder Hare's interest in landscape design. In 1896 Forest Hill Cemetery in Kansas City hired Sidney Hare as superintendent, and during his tenure, he earned a national reputation for his landscape theories. At a national convention of the Association of American Cemetery Superintendents in 1901, Hare discussed the cemetery as botanical garden, bird sanctuary, and arboretum—probably the first formal discussion on record in the design evolution of the modern cemetery—which led to his election as a fellow of the American Society of Landscape Architects (ASLA). In 1902 Hare established a landscape architecture firm in Kansas City; it became Hare & Hare eight years later, when his son S. Herbert joined him in practice.

Born in Kansas City, S. Herbert Hare studied landscape planning at Harvard's School of Architecture with Frederick Law Olmsted Jr. Although he never completed his degree, the younger Hare was one of the first landscape architects in the United States to prepare formally for the profession, and like his father, he was elected a fellow of ASLA.

During their 28-year association, Sidney preferred park and cemetery projects, while Herbert mastered community planning and design. In 1913 Hare & Hare planned approximately 2,500 acres for J. C. Nichols' famed Country Club District, as well as the grounds for many of the residences within the development. By 1925 Hare & Hare had completed projects—cemeteries, college campuses, subdivisions, parks, military housing, and master plans—in 28 states. Some of their more outstanding commissions include Wagner Place in Jefferson City, Missouri; Point Defiance Park in Tacoma, Washington; the University of Kansas campus; and the design for the new town of Longview, Washington, the largest preplanned city of its time outside Washington, D.C. Their later projects include the Country Club Plaza (designed along with Edward B. Delk), the setting for the Nelson-Atkins Museum (now the Nelson-Atkins Museum of Art), plans for several Missouri state parks (Arrow Rock, Bennett Springs, Mark Twain, Table Rock, and Wallace), college campuses throughout the region, and a variety of projects for the private sector in 33 states, Canada, and Costa Rica.

HELFENSTELLER, HIRSCH & WATSON

Established in 1906, this firm comprised senior partner Ernest Helfensteller Jr. (1873–1925), William Hirsch (1871?–1964), and Jesse Watson (dates unknown), all members of the St. Louis chapter of the American Institute of Architects (AIA). Helfensteller and Watson trained locally, as did Hirsch, who went on to work in the Chicago office of Henry Ives Cobb on buildings for the 1893 World's Fair. All were involved in designing a building for the Liederkranz Society, the cultural hub for the city's German population; they also designed the colorful Moolah Temple (1913) on Lindell Boulevard and the classical Nathan Frank Bandstand in Forest Park (1925), which replaced the original Moorish folly on the site. For Edward Gardner Lewis, the St. Louis businessman extraordinaire and publisher specializing in women's magazines, they designed Prairie-style meetinghouses. Each member of the firm served at one time as the head of a local professional architecture organization: Helfensteller was president of the St. Louis Architectural Club in 1903, as was Watson in 1904, and Hirsch was president of the St. Louis chapter of the AIA in 1923. The firm constructed houses in Parkview, where Hirsch built his personal residence in 1908, and in nearby Compton Heights. The firm continued to be active in St. Louis into the 1940s.

FREDERICK HILL

He designed many of Kansas City's early buildings, but the career of Frederick Elmer Hill (1860–1929) is nevertheless poorly documented. Born in Minnesota, Hill enrolled in the State University of Minnesota for one year (1887) and later studied at MIT as a special student in architecture (1880–1881). Following his studies in Boston, he was employed at the New York office of McKim, Mead & White (1882–1885), after which he moved to Kansas City. For a brief period Hill gave up practicing architecture to work as an auditor for the United States Housing Corporation in Washington, D.C. Hill was the supervising architect for the McKim, Mead & White–designed New York Life Building in Kansas City. Other of his commissions include the first and second convention halls for Kansas City (1890s and 1900), Grace Church (1893), and a variety of residences and commercial buildings. He practiced as an architect in Kansas City until 1901; however, most of his known work there has been demolished.

HENRY HOIT/HOIT, PRICE & BARNES

Hoit, Price & Barnes, a leading architecture firm in Kansas City history, can trace its beginning to 1901, when Chicago-born, MIT-trained Henry Ford Hoit (1872–1951) moved to Kansas City to join the firm of Van Brunt & Howe. Prior to his arrival, Hoit worked for the Boston firm Cabot, Everett & Meade, after a short stint in a lithographic business. Following the death of Van Brunt in 1903, Hoit and William H. Cutler became partners in the firm. Howe, Hoit & Cutler designed the R. A. Long Building (1906), one of the earliest skyscrapers in Kansas City, and the Beaux Arts–style Independence Boulevard Christian Church (1905). Two years after the firm became Howe, Hoit & Cutler, Cutler passed away, and Howe died in 1909. The passing of his two partners left Hoit the principal architect; he worked on his own for four years. In 1913 Edwin M. Price (1885–1957), one of Hoit's draftsmen, became a partner. When Alfred E. Barnes Jr. (1892–1960), a grandson of the noted Kansas City architect Asa B. Cross, joined the partnership in 1919, the firm's name changed to Hoit, Price & Barnes.

One of the most prolific architecture firms in Kansas City, Hoit, Price & Barnes "received commissions for a wide range of projects from skyscrapers to single-family residences," including the Kansas City Athletic Club (1918, 1922), the Southwestern Bell Telephone Company building (1919, 1929), the Fidelity Bank & Trust Company building (1930), and the Kansas City Power & Light building (1930–1931). In association with Gentry, Voscamp & Neville, the firm planned the Municipal Auditorium in 1933. Hoit, Price & Barnes remained active until Henry Hoit retired in 1941; the firm dissolved shortly thereafter.

JAMES OLIVER HOGG

Wisconsin-born James Oliver Hogg (1858–1941) studied architecture at the University of Illinois, under the guidance of M. C. Rickes. He later worked as an apprentice to the well-known Chicago architect S. S. Beman before moving to Kansas City around 1886. There he established the firm of Coddington & Hogg, and in 1887 he partnered in the firm Nier, Hogg & Byram. The union was brief, and in 1888 Hogg decided to practice on his own, but only for a while. From 1889 to 1893, Hogg worked with architect W. W. Rose, forming the firm Hogg & Rose, with offices in Kansas City, Missouri, and Kansas City, Kansas. During this period the firm designed buildings for the Kansas City, Kansas, school district. In 1894, Hogg split with Rose and undertook solo practice, while serving as the inspector and superintendent of buildings for the city of Kansas City, Missouri. Hogg's early work includes the Romanesque-influenced Grand Avenue Storage Company (1902), the Globe Storage Building (1902), the Advance Thresher Company building (1907), and the Abernathy residence (1901–1902). Additional designs by Hogg include Mackay Hall on the Park College (now Park University) campus in Parkville, Missouri; the Ft. Smith, Arkansas, courthouse; and buildings in Hannibal, Missouri, where he lived with his family during his childhood. Hogg practiced architecture in Kansas City for 45 years.

MARY ROCKWELL HOOK

"As a woman and a practicing architect, Mary Rockwell Hook (1877–1978) was a pioneer, opening a path for other women to follow, and thus making a significant contribution to the history of American architecture." One of five daughters, Hook was born in Junction City, Kansas, to a wealthy family and spent a good part of her youth traveling throughout Europe, the Philippines, Japan, and China. Her formal education included Wellesley College, from which she graduated in 1900, the Art Institute of Chicago, and the Ecole des Beaux-Arts in Paris. After moving to Kansas City with her family in 1906, Hook sought work at the Kansas City architecture firm of Wilder & Wight; they refused her, even as an unpaid intern. Subsequently, the office of Howe, Hoit & Cutler hired Hook, and she purportedly worked there for one year.

In 1908, Hook's career as an independent architect took off; most of her early commissions were for family and friends in Santa Rosa, California; Wellesley, Massachusetts; and Kansas City. Her first major commission was to design several buildings for a school for underprivileged children, the Pine Mountain Settlement School in Harlan County, Kentucky. After working for the American Committee for Devastated France in Blerancourt, Hook practiced with Mac Remington from 1924 to 1929 in Kansas City. Their partnership and her solo practice produced plans for eclectic hillside residences in Sunset Hill and Mission Hills, Kansas, Jackson County, and Woodside, California. Hook's uncommon career extended to Siesta Key, Florida, in Sarasota, where she continued to work through the 1940s. She died there on her 101st birthday.

JAMES P. JAMIESON

Born in Scotland, James P. Jamieson (1867–1941) arrived in Philadelphia in 1884, and 10 years later traveled throughout Europe as the first recipient of an architecture scholarship awarded by the University of Pennsylvania. After working at the firm Cope & Stewardson until the closing of its St. Louis office in 1912, he continued designing for wealthy and prestigious clients, many of whom he met through his connections at Washington University. The most prolific architect in Westmoreland and Portland Places, he designed 14 houses there in all; many houses in the Wydown-Forsyth District and Brentmoor Park are also his designs. His houses reveal the ability to interpret Federal, Tudor Revival, Chateauesque, and Georgian Revival modes, the latter of which was his strength. He often gave the rear (usually southern) elevation primary importance, drawing upon the European tradition of a formal garden facade. In 1918 he partnered with George Spearl; their designs for academic buildings at Washington University, the University of Missouri-Columbia, and Stephens College in Columbia rival those of Cope & Stewardson.

ERNEST C. JANSSEN

A native of the Midwest, Ernest C. Janssen (1857?–1946) is representative of several architects who specialized in houses for fellow German-Americans on the South Side of St. Louis. To his credit are 14 houses in Compton Heights, most of which are in the Tudor Revival style, the most elaborate being the salmon brick and terra cotta Stockstrom house at 3400 Russell. He also designed houses in prestigious Forest Ridge and what is now the Wydown-Forsyth District near Washington University. Janssen's work is grounded in lessons learned while studying architecture in Karlsruhe, Germany, where he earned a gold medal for best thesis. A member of the AIA, Janssen worked for three years around 1880 with partner Otto J. Wilhelmi, another local architect who trained at Karlsruhe, on houses in Compton Heights and Parkview. Aside from his residential work, Janssen specialized in brewery architecture, working on projects in St. Louis and as far away as Mexico. He designed the monumental entrance gates on Grand Avenue in Compton Heights and a commemorative granite obelisk in Benton Park, as well as the Witte Hardware building at Laclede's Landing in downtown St. Louis.

GEORGE EDWARD KESSLER

German-born George Edward Kessler (1862–1923) was the brilliant landscape architect who planned the parks and boulevard system for Kansas City, Missouri, and other cities throughout the United States. In Germany, Kessler studied landscape gardening at the Belvedere in Weimar, the *Neue Garten* in Potsdam, and civil engineering at the University of Jena. Frederick Law Olmsted Sr. recommended Kessler for his first professional job, managing a pleasure park for the Kansas City, Fort Scott & Gulf Railroad Company in Merriam, Kansas.

In short order, Kessler's growing reputation brought him commissions to plan residential subdivisions in Kansas City, Baltimore, Ohio, and Utah. Through his work in Kansas City, Kessler became acquainted with William Rockhill

Nelson and August Meyer. These two civic leaders influenced Kessler's appointment by the Kansas City, Missouri, Parks Board, as secretary and engineer in 1892 and as landscape architect (1893–1902). He remained affiliated with the board as a consultant until his death. Influenced by the City Beautiful movement, Kessler's plan for Kansas City was a brilliant integration of the "monumental and scenic" throughout the system. From his successful commission in Kansas City, Kessler went on to design park and boulevard plans for Memphis, Indianapolis, Syracuse, Cincinnati, Fort Worth, Pensacola, Dallas, and beyond. In 1900, he established an office in St. Louis for the purpose of working on the Louisiana Purchase Exposition, Forest Park, and Washington University. Concurrently, Kessler did community planning for Roland Park, Baltimore; J. C. Nichols' Country Club District in Kansas City; and Longview, Washington, where he teamed with Nichols and Hare & Hare. Kessler's planning spread even beyond college campuses, cemeteries, and fairgrounds. In 1917, he was one of the founding members of the American Institute of Planners (now the APA). Kessler's comprehensive plan for Kansas City is arguably the finest work of his career.

HORACE LAPIERRE

Architect and artist Horace LaPierre (1873–1945) was originally from Ottawa, Canada, and evidence of his work in Kansas City is plentiful, but little else is known about his educational training or personal life. Working early in his career with architect George Mathews, LaPierre codesigned the Armour Memorial Home, an institutional complex that also featured the work of Van Brunt & Howe. LaPierre designed an expansive house for U. S. Epperson, a Tudor-style dwelling for Dr. Hetherington (1925), and for George Wright, a monolithic Medieval Spanish–derived house built of huge coursed limestone. Outside Kansas City, LaPierre designed residences in Liberty, Missouri, and Okmulgee, Oklahoma. His other known designs include churches, hotels, and recreational cabins throughout the Midwest and the South. He was not as prolific or well known as some of his contemporaries, but Henry Van Brunt characterized LaPierre as "a diminutive Frenchman whose evocative enthusiasms were cheese dishes and oil painting, in both of which he was impressively efficient." His paintings and etchings reside in private collections.

JESSE LAUCK

A graduate of the University of Pennsylvania, Jesse F. Lauck (1888–1969) enjoyed a 40-year partnership with architect Elmer Boillot. The firm was well known in Kansas City for hotel and apartment design, including the Hotel Phillips and the Walnut Apartments. The firm designed many single-family residences in the Country Club District, and they collaborated with the noted Kansas City architect Nelle E. Peters on the Poet Group Apartments. Boillot & Lauck planned Ft. Riley, Kansas (and its remodeling for World War II), and their best work is quite possibly the Unity School of Christianity (1926–1929). This landmark group of Italian Renaissance Revival buildings in Unity Village (15 miles southeast of Kansas City) is the world headquarters for Unity Church. Lauck practiced solo after the death of Boillot in 1947.

H. T. LINDEBERG

Harrie Thomas Lindeberg (1879–1959), born of Swedish parents in Bergen Point, New Jersey, apprenticed in the office of McKim, Mead & White, the quintessential architects of the American renaissance, from 1901 to 1906. His knowledge of country house design traces back to his position as Stanford White's assistant on the James L. Breese house in Southampton, Long Island, circa 1890. After White's murder in 1906, Lindeberg went into practice with Lewis Colt Albro, a partnership that continued until 1914, designing country houses that became their trademark. Lindeberg was most prolific from 1915 to 1930—during the 1920s he had commissions (and offices) in the East, South, and Midwest—when he perfected his blend of historical style and modern sensibility. His work integrated vernacular building and fashionable idioms ranging from English Tudor to Georgian. Bold in massing and silhouette and rational in plan (reflecting his academic training), Lindeberg's work appealed to a new moneyed class in search of domestic spaces that clearly exhibited social standing. With a reputation built on ability rather than social connections, *Architectural Record* described him in 1924 as the "American Lutyens" for what would ultimately become his unique contribution to American country house architecture.

After 1930 Lindeberg experimented with new materials and technologies, designing plans for a cellular steel house and moderate-size residences stripped bare, with an emphasis on function, but modernism never won him over. He designed his only large-scale public works in the mid-1930s: consulates for Shanghai, Moscow, Helsinki, and Managua (commissioned by the U.S. Department of State but cancelled due to World War II). Logically, these complexes were based on a classical vocabulary of forms that communicated national identity (and stylistically represented a return to the architect's earliest work). Throughout his career, Lindeberg's conviction, to "build simply" regardless of style or size remained a core tenet of his most successful country house designs.

JOHN W. MCKECKNIE

Born in Clarksville, Ohio, John W. McKecknie (1862–1934) pursued his education in an itinerant manner: He attended Wilmington College, in Wilmington, Ohio; graduated from Princeton in 1886; and studied at the Columbia School of Mines in New York. He worked thereafter for various New York architecture firms and subsequently practiced on his own. Architecture was not his only ambition. McKecknie studied and taught art in New York City and Brooklyn and developed his love of photography into a separate career. After spending a year photographing in France and Italy, the Metropolitan Museum of Art commissioned him to enlarge and catalog his European photos. He intended to make art his profession but gave it up in favor of architecture; his interest in painting, however, remained strong throughout his life.

In 1896 McKecknie came to Kansas City, where he worked as an architect for the Hucke & Sexton Contracting & Building Company. By 1914, he had established a solo architecture practice. In the meantime, McKecknie pioneered the use of reinforced concrete construction, as exemplified in the six-story Gumbel Building, designed in 1905, followed by the Gloyd building in 1909. Other landmark works by McKecknie include the Grand Avenue Temple and office building (1909–1911).

In 1914, McKecknie partnered with Frank Edgar Trask, a native of Axtell, Kansas, who had studied architecture at Columbia University. Together McKecknie and Trask designed the Exchange Building (1929), the Federal Building, the Board of Trade Building, and the University Club. The partnership ended with McKecknie's death in 1934, after which Trask continued to practice under his own name. McKecknie's legacy to Kansas City includes the colonnaded apartment, a design he introduced in 1900 with the Pergola Apartments, now demolished.

FRANCIS J. MACDONNELL

Little is known of Francis J. MacDonnell (dates unknown), and he was credited only recently with Vouziers, the Desloge family country house in St. Louis County. MacDonnell worked in New Orleans, possibly with architect Moise H. Goldstein. His work is cited in the Jefferson City area of New Orleans (formerly part of Jefferson Parish, which was annexed into the city in 1870), specifically, in the design of Prairie-style architecture and the use of concrete.

MARITZ & YOUNG

During the 1920s and 1930s the St. Louis architecture firm of Maritz & Young built 25 houses in the affluent suburban neighborhoods of Carrswold and Brentmoor. These ranged stylistically from French Renaissance to Tudor Revival to Arts and Crafts, the last being possibly their most successful expression. Their work includes clubhouses for the new Westwood, Bridlespur, and Hillcrest country clubs in the county and houses nearby for more of the city's elite, including Adalbert von Gontard (the grandson of Adolphus Busch) and Mahlon B. Wallace Jr (the nephew of Robert Brookings).

As was the case with several local architects, Raymond E. Maritz (1894–1973) trained at Washington University (and briefly at the Ecole des Beaux-Arts), as did his partner, Ridgely Young (1893–1949). Their work excels in its richness of materials and attention to detail, and it demonstrates their ability to interpret traditional models with originality, particularly in terms of picturesque massing and composition. A 1929 monograph of Maritz & Young's work notes their interest in solving problems by adapting the practical and artistic aspects of a structure to the personality and requirements of the owner.

Prior to 1920, Maritz worked with Gale E. Henderson (who went on to work with Angelo Corrubia); after 1935 the Maritz & Young team worked with a third partner, Rime Dusard. With the death of Ridgely Young in the late 1940s,

Raymond Maritz founded Maritz & Sons with his twin sons (fresh from MIT), doing institutional designs for the Clayton City Hall and the Annunziata School in Ladue. The Raymond E. Maritz Professorship in the Washington University School of Architecture acknowledges his contributions to the city and continues his legacy.

SAMUEL ABRAHAM MARX

Architect and interior designer Samuel Abraham Marx (1885–1964) was born in Natchez, Mississippi, and graduated in architecture from MIT in 1907. He traveled in Europe and studied at the Ecole des Beaux-Arts before working in the Chicago office of Shepley, Rutan & Coolidge; he subsequently opened his own office. Marx balanced his spare modern aesthetic with the use of natural materials like cork, leather, exotic wood, and stone; he often used chunky textiles woven by Dorothy Liebes. Much of his architecture has an organic quality evident in curvaceous shell shapes and swooping arcs that embrace space.

His work includes the 1938 Pump Room in the Ambassador East Hotel in Chicago, the Famous-Barr department store in Clayton, Missouri, and the Streamline Moderne May Company department store on Wilshire Boulevard in Los Angeles (1939). Marx married Florene May, aunt of Morton "Buster" May of the May Company family. Over a lifetime they built one of the finest collections of modern art in the country—works by Braque, Picasso, Bonnard, Noguchi, and Matisse—which they donated to Museum of Modern Art and the Metropolitan Museum of Art.

MAURAN & RUSSELL (MAURAN, RUSSELL & GARDEN)

John Lawrence Mauran (1866–1933) and Ernest John Russell (1870–1956) teamed with two distinctive partners during their career: Edward Gordon Garden (1871–1924) and later William DeForrest Crowell (1879?–1967). Mauran, Russell, and Garden left the St. Louis office of Shepley, Rutan & Coolidge (successors to H. H. Richardson) when it closed around 1900 and worked together for nearly 10 years, designing some of the city's finest churches, libraries, and commercial buildings. Other commissions took them to beyond Missouri, Illinois, Texas, and New Hampshire. Their work is stylistically diverse, ranging from Tudor to Mediterranean, and many of their houses exhibit Prairie influence (attributed to Garden), trademark Palladian loggias, and the use of terra cotta and crisp brickwork in decorative patterns.

Mauran, who graduated from MIT and trained in the Boston and Chicago offices of Shepley, Rutan & Coolidge, lived in an Eames & Young house at 46 Vandeventer Place; he contributed an English flavor to the firm's work. Russell, born in London, appears to have had a supervisory rather than a creative role in the firm.

Edward "Ned" Garden, brother of Chicago modernist Hugh Garden, was born in Toronto and trained in Minneapolis as a draftsman for William Channing Whitney (he is known for his ability as a delineator). Like Mauran, a member of the St. Louis chapter of the AIA, Garden left the firm in 1909 and relocated to San Francisco, where he worked independently until two years before his death.

Crowell joined Mauran & Russell in 1911; their joint commissions include the Mediterranean-style St. Louis Country Club, the Southwestern Bell building (ornamented with Gothic ribs, finials, and setbacks), and 33 Portland Place, one of the finest houses on the private street, modeled on urbane 18th-century French prototypes.

NAGEL & DUNN

Charles Nagel Jr. (1899?–1992) and Frederick W. Dunn (1905–1984) worked as a team for only six years—from 1936 until World War II—before each went on to make important contributions to St. Louis. Dunn was born in St. Paul, Minnesota, and earned bachelor's and master's degrees at Yale, where he met Nagel, who was from the West End of St. Louis. Their partnership resulted in St. Mark's Episcopal Church (1939), its austere vertical facade (only 25 feet wide) punctuated with their signature bull's-eye window, and houses in Ladue such as the Putzel house (1938), an abstract and elegant Georgian interpretation.

After having been a curator at the Yale Art Gallery and serving in the Navy during World War II, Nagel returned to St. Louis and became director of the St. Louis Art Museum. In 1964 he and St. Louisans Victor Proetz and Robert Cunningham designed the National Portrait Gallery at the Smithsonian Institution in Washington, D.C. As a committee member, he helped oversee Jacqueline Kennedy's White House redecoration and helped choose Eero Saarinen's design for the St. Louis Arch (the Jefferson Memorial Expansion Project).

Described by his daughter as a man of the 18th century—his designs reflect a complete understanding of history—Dunn was nevertheless successful at reinventing traditional models for modern sensibilities. He appreciated that new solutions to the problems of building demanded adaptation of craft and material. This sensitivity to past and present may account for the firm's being chosen to handle the restoration of the antebellum Selma Hall after a massive fire in 1938.

Dunn practiced architecture with partners Nolen Stinson Jr. and Harry Richman for the remainder of his life. His nomination as a fellow to the AIA in 1962 cited three of his projects: the headquarters for the National Council of State Garden Clubs, the A. S. Aloe Warehouse, and the Steinberg Skating Rink at Forest Park. These buildings represent Dunn's spare, powerful architectural designs, and suggest the mark his work made on the city.

Beverly Tucker Nelson

The work of Beverly Tucker Nelson (1893?–1954), who was born in Salem, VA, ranged from the restrained French vocabulary of Ferrieres (the Virgil Lewis house) in Ladue to the Colonial Revival style of the Pierce Pennant Motor Hotel in Columbia, Missouri. The Pierce Pennant chain was one of the first to respond to the needs of automobile travelers on the new federal highway system; Nelson designed the Pierce Pennant Hotel and Gas Station in Tulsa, Oklahoma (1926), and the Columbia counterpart three years later. He designed more than a dozen houses in Ladue and several buildings in downtown Clayton prior to World War II. Nelson was working in London in the Foreign Buildings Office of the State Department when he died. His son, Beverly T. Nelson Jr. was an architect in Tulsa.

Guy T Norton

As the Lemp Brewery staff architect, Guy T. Norton (1873?–1940) designed the vast fermenting house and other elements of the Lemp complex at Cherokee Street and Broadway. Brewery design produced a distinctive type of architecture, and an important one in a city with so many breweries; Norton specialized in industrial designs that balanced form and function. Alswel, the "chalet" he designed for brewery heir William Lemp, exhibits his ability to combine polychrome decorative effects with the structural technology primary to larger industrial work. Norton lived on Russell Boulevard, located on the South Side of St. Louis. He practiced architecture for 35 years, retired at the age of 57, and died ten years later. He is buried in Mount Hope Cemetery in St. Louis.

Julius Pitzman

Considered the "father of the private place in America," surveyor, developer, and civil engineer Julius Pitzman (1837–1923) planned 40 private streets and subdivisions in the city and the county of St. Louis. Born in Halberstadt, Germany, he arrived in St. Louis in 1854 to work as an assistant in the family civil engineering company. He gained mapmaking experience during the Civil War, after which he returned to surveying in St. Louis. His first private place—and the prototype for many others—Benton Place (1866) featured the elements that would make his designs distinctive: gated streets to control traffic, central parkways or crescents creating picturesque landscapes, uniform setbacks, streets arranged in cul-de-sacs or grid patterns, enforced deed restrictions, and a governing board to oversee operations. With each subsequent project Pitzman refined the design and attempted to anticipate problems, but the encroachment of commercial development was a threat as the city grew, and one for which there was no solution.

A few of Pitzman's most important private streets and subdivisions are Vandeventer, Westmoreland, and Portland Places, Compton Hill, and his last, Parkview. As the 19th century progressed, a broader cross section of society grew to appreciate Pitzman's projects: they evolved from elite, exclusive places to neighborhoods that were home to greater numbers of middle-class St. Louisans. His influence is evident even in Houston, Texas; landscape architect George Kessler designed the neighborhood of Shadyside (circa 1919), near Rice University, on Pitzman's private place model. The Pitzman firm continues to work in St. Louis. Julius Pitzman is buried in Bellefontaine Cemetery in St. Louis.

George B. Post

George Brown Post (1837–1913) was born in New York City. In 1858, he received a degree in civil engineering from New York University, after which he studied architecture under Richard M. Hunt. By 1860 he had formed a partnership with Charles D. Gambrill. That same year Post became an associate of the American Institute of Architects; he was elected a fellow four years later. In 1907 Post was appointed an honorary corresponding member of the Royal Institute of British Architects.

Post designed the New York Produce Exchange, the New York Stock Exchange (1903), the Pulitzer Building, and the Cornelius Vanderbilt residence. Post's sons, William Stone Post and James Otis Post, joined the firm in 1904; in 1905 the firm's name changed to George B. Post & Sons. Although George Post built his career designing early skyscrapers, office buildings, and hotels, his sons greatly expanded the firm's scope. The senior Post died on November 28, 1913, and the practice continued to operate under his name with his son, William, as the principal designer.

The first of the Post brothers' projects to grab the architecture industry's notice was the plan for Eclipse Park in Beloit, Wisconsin, in 1918; the unifying theme was the American garden village. By the 1920s George B. Post & Sons had the knowledge and experience to design high-rise hotels and single-family dwellings and to do city planning. The business consequently grew and opened satellite offices throughout the larger cities in the East and Midwest. Some of the firm's more notable designs include a number of hotels for the Staler Hotel chain. George B. Post & Sons maintained an office in Kansas City from 1921 through 1926, with architect Alonzo H. Gentry as manager.

W. Angelo Powell

Having trained in New York City as a draftsman for Minard Lafever and studied civil engineering in Baltimore, W. Angelo Powell (1836?–1911) was one of few professional architects in the Midwest when he settled in St. Joseph in 1866. His formal training and appreciation for architectural pattern books as design guides distinguished him from other builders, as did his work on major federal projects under Robert Mills in Washington, D.C. Powell worked with Mills' firm during the U.S. Capitol expansion and construction of the Washington Monument and the U.S. Treasury. Another of Powell's commissions in Washington was the National Theater. He served during the Civil War as chief engineer for the 8th Army Corps, and before arriving in St. Joseph, was employed with the railroad. Powell's work is only now being identified and credited, but it appears that he contributed considerably to the architecture of St. Joseph and the Midwest in general. His designs include institutional buildings, several hundred residences, and parks and cemeteries, such as the picturesque Mount Mora Cemetery in St. Joseph. His work has been identified as far west as Colorado and the Dakotas.

Shepard, Farrar & Wiser

Charles E. Shepard (1868–1932) was the principal of Shepard, Farrar & Wiser, one of the most distinguished and productive Kansas City architecture firms working in the first decades of the 20th century. During his career, Shepard was the principal designer of buildings of every type found not only in Kansas City, but in Wichita, Kansas; Tulsa, Oklahoma; and Amarillo, Texas, as well. In the Kansas City metropolitan area, Shepard left a rich architectural legacy that encompasses the design of more than 600 residences in Hyde Park, Mission Hills, and the County Club District.

Shepard was educated at the University of Iowa, and prior to settling in Kansas City in 1887, was involved in designing the State Capitol at Des Moines. His first brief partnership was with architect Martin U. Vrydagh, who left for Pittsburgh in 1893, the year Ernest H. Farrar formed a partnership with Shepard that lasted through 1910. Works by Shepard & Farrar include the Loose Manufacturing Company building (1902), the 12-room Jacobethan residence for G. A. Gurley (1908), and the Prairie-style residence for J. J. Wolcott (1910).

Albert Wiser (1882–1937), a former apprentice and draftsman for the firm, entered into partnership with Shepard in 1911; despite Farrar's departure, the partnership retained the Shepard, Farrar & Wiser name from 1911 to

1918. This prolific, seven-year period saw some of the firm's most refined and remarkable residential works, with many early commissions in the Hyde Park neighborhood: the Colonial Revival house at 3530 Charlotte Street (1912) and the Benjamin Berkshire residence (1911) are two of the more illustrious examples. In 1927 the firm became Shepard & Pickett when Shepard and Frederick C. Pickett became affiliated.

EDWARD W. TANNER

Most recognized for his work with J. C. Nichols on the Country Club Plaza in Kansas City, architect and city planner Edward W. Tanner (1896–1974) initially designed the majority of the buildings in this renowned shopping district. He chose the Spanish- and Mission-style design idiom that distinguishes it "because of its humor."

Originally from Cottonwood Falls, Kansas, Tanner was in the first class that graduated from the University of Kansas School of Architecture and Engineering at Lawrence. His first professional job was with the noted Kansas City firm of Shepard, Farrar & Wiser.

Besides his eclectic designs for Country Club Plaza, Tanner completed more than 2,000 residential plans in the Country Club District; shopping centers such as The Landing and Prairie Village; Linda Hall Library; and the Kansas City Public Library and Board of Education Building. Tanner's career comprised both traditional and modern expressions, and it expanded with wartime to designing and building Whiteman Air Base in Knob Noster, Missouri, among other government complexes. His firm, Edward Tanner & Associates, designed a low-cost residence that *Better Homes and Gardens* voted the "best-designed small house of 1940." That design became popular after World War II for families throughout the nation. In 1961 he established a firm with Mayol H. Linscott.

ADRIANCE VAN BRUNT

Born in Englewood, New Jersey, Adriance van Brunt (1836–1913) came to Kansas City in 1878, and very soon began work with his brother, John, designing impressive residences—many of which no longer remain—for wealthy entrepreneurs like J. W. Merrill, R. M. Goodlett, and Edward Dickinson. Van Brunt's firm designed commercial buildings as well, including those for B. Adler & Company and Harvey Dutton Dry Goods (both 1903) on Broadway and bandstands and park buildings like the entrance to Swope Park (1904). The sensitivity to landscape in Van Brunt's designs demonstrated to the citizens of Kansas City the importance of planning and green space. He helped establish Kansas City's world-class parks and boulevard system and was a member and vital supporter of its parks board. Van Brunt (no relation to Henry Van Brunt) thought, too, in the practical terms of land use: he suggested zoning the city's West Bottoms for warehouses after a major flood in 1908.

In his honor, one of Kansas City's major thoroughfares became Van Brunt Boulevard just after his death. Van Brunt's contributions to Kansas City represent in a sense the broader City Beautiful movement and its transformation of urban spaces across the country.

VAN BRUNT & HOWE

The nationally renowned partnership of Henry Van Brunt (1832–1903) and Frank Maynard Howe (1849–1909) formed in Boston in 1883, although the two had worked together since 1868. Howe moved to Kansas City in 1885 to set up a local office for the firm; Van Brunt joined him there two years later. In 1893 Van Brunt & Howe was selected to design the Electricity Building for the World's Columbian Exposition in Chicago. Over the years, Kansas City architects Ernest Farrar, John G. Braecklein, Harry Drake, Frank Jackson, and others worked for the highly respected firm. Although Van Brunt & Howe designed more than 50 residential, commercial, and warehouse buildings in Kansas City, no more than 12 remained by the year 2000. Some of those no longer extant include the Emery, Bird, & Thayer Building; the Kansas City Club; and the Gibraltar Building. Surviving properties include the August Meyer and Coates residences and the Emery, Bird & Thayer Warehouse. Elected president of the American Institute of Architects in 1899, Van Brunt contributed frequently to the *Atlantic Monthly.* Howe was a senior partner in the successor firms of Howe, Hoit & Cutler and later, Howe & Hoit.

HOWARD VAN DOREN SHAW

Admired (and disliked) for his eclecticism and the individuality he applied to European vernaculars, Howard van Doren Shaw is perhaps best recognized for his many country houses in the Midwest, particularly around Lake Forest and Chicago, Illinois, and in Wisconsin. In Missouri, Hannibal and St. Louis County have a number of Shaw houses of the same genre; there are five in Brentmoor Park and Ladue. Several of these houses feature a reverse facade treatment, orienting garden facades toward the street; at Brentwood Park, planner Henry Wright referred to this as the "English forecourt plan."

Born in Chicago, Howard van Doren Shaw (1869–1926) graduated from Yale University and MIT. He worked for William LeBaron Jenny in Chicago beginning in 1891, as architects were grappling with questions concerning modern style in tall buildings, innovative construction methods, materials, and systems, and the interface of style and function. Shaw's training under Jenny was essential in designing the array of commercial, industrial, educational, and religious building types on which he worked throughout his career. Shaw worked for some of Chicago's most prominent families, and he worked on the Art Institute of Chicago; at the same time, he planned warehouses, worker housing, and the model steel town, Indiana Harbor, in East Chicago. Elected a fellow of the American Institute of Architects in 1907 and awarded a gold medal for achievement just prior to his death, Shaw died in Baltimore. He is buried in Chicago's historic Graceland Cemetery.

WILDER & WIGHT AND WIGHT & WIGHT

Thomas's brother, William Drewin Wight (1882–1947), literally followed in his footsteps: in 1900, William Wight began working for McKim, Mead & White (Thomas worked there from 1892–1904). Ten years later Wight moved to Kansas City to join his brother in practice. Wilder retired in 1912, but the office did not officially change its name until 1916, when it became Wight & Wight. The firm won some of the metropolitan area's major commissions, including the Nelson-Atkins Museum of Art (1930–1933), the Kansas City Life Insurance Company building (1923–1924), the Jackson County Courthouse (1934), and the Kansas City City Hall (1935–1936). Wight & Wight also designed the Wyandotte County Courthouse in Kansas City, Kansas (1925–1927). The firm remained active until William died in 1947; his brother, Thomas, died less than two years later.

HENRY WRIGHT

Born in Lawrence, Kansas, Henry Wright (1878–1936) trained under architects Walter Root and George Siemens in Kansas City and at the University of Pennsylvania. He began his career in the office of landscape architect George Kessler, working on St. Louis projects, including the Louisiana Purchase Exposition (the 1904 World's Fair) on what is now Washington University and Forest Park. After leaving Kessler's firm, Wright designed the elite suburban neighborhoods Brentmoor, Forest Ridge, and Brentmoor Park in Clayton (in St. Louis County) circa 1910–1913. The strengths of these plans—privacy, parklike common areas, and street patterns that limited traffic—were soon interpreted for the middle-class neighborhood of Delmar Garden in St. Louis; they became the basis of Wright's work after 1923 in collaboration with Clarence S. Stein, in projects like Sunnyside Gardens, New York, and Radburn, New Jersey. During the 1930s, Wright served as consultant for the housing division of the Public Works Administration, as city planning consultant to the New York State Commission on Housing and Regional Planning, and one year before his death, as head of the Columbia University School of Architecture. A man of wide-ranging abilities, Wright regarded himself as architect, landscape architect, landscape gardener, and engineer, reflecting the holistic thinking and integrated approach he brought to community planning.

Bibliography

Books, Periodicals, and Printed Matter

Alkire, Arthur N. *Men of Affairs in Greater Kansas City, 1912*. Kansas City: Kansas City Press Club, 1912.

American Architect and Building News, Boston & New York, 1884–1904.

American Historical Society. *Missouri: Special Limited Supplement*. Chicago: American Historical Society, 1930.

American Homes and Gardens, New York 1905–1915.

American Society of Landscape Architects. "Guide to Landscape Architecture of the St. Louis Region." 59 No. 3 (April 1969).

American Illustrating Company. *Pen and Sunlight Sketches of Greater Kansas City*. Kansas City: American Illustrating Company, 1914.

"An English Country Place Re-created." *The Kansas City Star Magazine*, January 10, 1926.

Annual Architectural Exhibition of the St. Louis Architectural Club, 1900.

Architectural Forum, New York, 1917–1941.

Architectural Record, New York, 1891–1932.

Aslet, Clive. *The American Country House*. New Haven, CT: Yale University Press, 1990.

Atlas of Kansas City, U.S.A. and Vicinity. Kansas City: Tuttle and Pike, 1900.

Bartley, Mary. *St. Louis Lost*. St. Louis, Missouri: Virginia Publishing, 1994.

Birnbaum, Charles A., and Robin Karson, eds. *Pioneers of American Landscape Design*. New York: McGraw-Hill, 2000.

Bone, D. M. *Annual Review of Greater Kansas City, 1908*.

Boswell, Harry James. *Kansas Citians with Records: City Builders, Representative Missourians*. Kansas City, 1912.

"Brick by Brick" exhibition. Samuel Cupples House, Saint Louis University, April–July 2004.

Brickbuilder, Boston, 1895–1916.

Bryan, John Albury, ed. *Missouri's Contribution to American Architecture*. St. Louis, Missouri: St. Louis Architectural Club, 1928.

Bush-Brown, Albert, and John Burchard. *The Architecture of America: A Social and Cultural History*. Boston: Little, Brown and Company, 1961.

Case, Theodore S. *The History of Kansas City, Missouri*. Syracuse, NY: D. Mason, 1888.

"C. C. Peters." *The Kansas City Star*, April 2, 1916.

Christensen, Lawrence O., et.al., eds. *Dictionary of Missouri Biography*. Columbia, Missouri: University of Missouri Press, 1999.

Cigliano, Jan, and Sarah Bradford Landau, eds. *The Grand American Avenue, 1850–1920*. San Francisco: Pomegranate Art Books, 1994.

Country Life in America, New York, 1900–1942.

Creel, George, and John Slavens. *Men Who Are Making Kansas City*. Kansas City: Hudson-Kimberly Publishing Co., 1902.

Coles, William A., ed. *Architecture and Society: Selected Essays by Henry Van Brunt*. Cambridge, MA: Belknap Press, 1969.

Comee, Fred T. "Louis Curtiss of Kansas City," *Progressive Architecture*, August 1963.

Corbett, Katharine T., and Howard S. Miller. *St. Louis in the Gilded Age*. St. Louis, Missouri: Missouri Historical Society Press, 1993.

"Country Estate of William J. Lemp to Be Sold Tomorrow." *St. Louis Globe-Democrat*, May 24, 1925.

Croly, Herbert D., and C. Matlack Price. "The Recent Work of Howard Shaw: Country Houses of the Middle West."

Architectural Record 33 No. 4 (April 1913).

Coyle, Elinor M. *St. Louis Homes 1866–1916: The Golden Age*. St. Louis, Missouri: Folkstone Press, 1971.

Czech, Tony. "Bothwell State Park." *Missouri Resource Review* 8 (3): 28–30.

"Daniel B. Dyer." *The Kansas City Star,* October 8, 1911.

———. *The Kansas City Times,* June 10, 1896; October 21, 1904; July 20, 1906; June 4, 1915.

De Botton, Alain. *The Architecture of Happiness*. New York: Pantheon Books, 2000.

Degener, Patricia. "Buildings of Elegant Rightness." *St. Louis Post-Dispatch*, February 13, 1983.

"Development of St. Louis Brickwork." *The Western Architect* 23, no. 6 (1916).

Downing, A. J. *The Architecture of Country Houses*. 1850. (Da Capo Press series in architecture and decorative art). New York: Da Capo Press, 1968.

"Dream of Baronial Grandeur." *Kansas City Journal,* November 23, 1906.

Duffy, Robert W. "It's All Over Now. Samuel Marx's May House: A Modernist Landmark Bites the Dust." *Modernism* 8 no. 4 (Winter 2005–2006): 114–121.

"Edwin W. Shields." *The Kansas City Star,* June 1, 1913.

Eidlitz, Leopold. *The Nature and Function of Art*. New York: A. C. Armstrong & Son, 1881.

Ehrlich, George. *Kansas City, Missouri: An Architectural History, 1826–1990*. Columbia, Missouri: University of Missouri, 1992.

Encyclopedia of the Representative Men of the West: Kansas City Edition. Kansas City: The Press Syndicate of America, 1907.

Examples of the Recent Work of Barnett, Haynes & Barnett. St. Louis, 1896.

Fitzgerald, Gerry. *Maritz and Young, Inc., a monograph of their work*. 2 vols. St. Louis, Missouri: Blackwell-Wielandy, 1929–1930.

Forsee, George H. "In Memoriam: William Rockhill Nelson." *Kansas Citian* 4 no. 8 (April 20, 1915).

Fowler, Richard B. *Leaders in Our Town*. Kansas City: Burd and Fletcher, 1952.

Fox, Tim, ed. *Where We Live: A Guide to St. Louis Communities*. St. Louis, Missouri: Missouri Historical Society Press, 1995.

Francis, David R. *The Universal Exposition of 1904*. St. Louis, Missouri: Louisiana Purchase Exposition Company, 1913.

Fuller and Wheeler Papers, Albany [New York] Institute of History and Art.

Gass, Mary Henderson, Jean Fahey Eberle and Judith Phelps Little. *Parkview: A Saint Louis Urban Oasis, 1905–2005*. St. Louis, Missouri: Virginia Publishing Company, 2005.

General History of Macon County. Chicago: Henry Taylor and Co., 1910.

"George I. Barnett Special Edition." *The Western Architect* 18, no. 2 (February 1912).

Hamilton, Esley. "A Note on Howard Van Doren Shaw." *Missouri Valley Chapter of the Society of Architectural Historians Newsletter* 7 no. 1 (Spring 2001).

———. "Warren Manning's Missouri Clients." *Missouri Valley Chapter of the Society of Architectural Historians Newsletter* 9 no. 2 (Summer 2003).

"Ha Ha Tonka." *St. Louis Globe-Democrat,* September 20, 1908.

Ha Ha Tonka Collection. Western Historical Manuscript Collection-Kansas City. University of Missouri–Kansas City.

Handlin, David P. *The American Home: Architecture and Society, 1815–1915*. Boston: Little, Brown and Company, 1979.

Hayden, Dolores. *Building Suburbia: Green Fields and Urban Growth, 1828–2000*. New York: Pantheon Books, 2003.

"H. C. Pierce Home Costing $800,000 Going to Be Razed." *St. Louis Globe-Democrat,* November 26, 1936.

Hegedorn, Hermann. *Brookings: A Biography*. New York: Macmillan, 1936.

Hill, Frederick E. Letter to Judge Edward L. Scarritt, Kansas City, Missouri. April 17, 1897.

Historic American Buildings Survey/Historic American Engineering Record. Administered by the Heritage Documentation Programs, part of the National Park Service, U.S. Department of the Interior.

Historic Kansas City News, Kansas City, 1979–1982. Architects Series.

History of Howard and Cooper Counties, Missouri. St. Louis, Missouri: National Historical Co., 1883.

Hook, Mary Rockwell. *This and That: Biography of Mary Rockwell Hook 1877–1978*. Kansas City, 1970.

"Horace La Pierre." *The Kansas City Star,* February 10, 1946.

Hunter, Julius. *Westmoreland and Portland Places: The History and Architecture of America's Premier Private Streets, 1888–1988*. Columbia: University of Missouri Press, 1988.

Hyde, William, and Howard L. Conard. *Encyclopedia of the History of St. Louis.* St. Louis, Missouri: Southern Publishing Company, 1889.

Inland Architect and News Record, Chicago, 1889–1908.

"J. W. Thompson House." *The Western Architect*, May 1910; February 1912.

" 'Kennet's Castle' Restored: A Famous Mississippi Landmark Comes to Life Again." *St. Louis Post-Dispatch*, July 21, 1940.

"Kennet's Castle Swept by Fire; Only Walls Left." *St. Louis Post-Dispatch*, March 13, 1939.

LaCoss, Louise. "In the Old Pierce Mansion, Unoccupied for 17 Years, the Grandfather's Clock Still Ticks Time Away." *St. Louis Globe-Democrat Magazine*, November 27, 1927.

Landmarks Commission. "John McKecknie." Kansas City: Landmarks Commission, 1981.

Lawrence Lowic Collection. Western Historical Manuscripts Collection-St. Louis, Missouri.

Lindeberg, H. T. *Domestic Architecture of H. T. Lindeberg.* Acanthus Press Reprint Series. 20th Century, Landmarks in Design, v. 6. New York: Acanthus Press, 1996.

Lowic, Lawrence. *The Architectural Heritage of St. Louis 1803–1891: From the Louisiana Purchase to the Wainwright Building.* St. Louis, Missouri: Washington University Gallery of Art, 1982.

Lubschez, Ben J. "First annual review of the architectural exhibit conducted by Kansas City Chapter A.I.A." *The Southern Architect*, September 1912.

Maher, George W. "Originality in American Architecture." *Inland Architect and News Record* 4, 1887.

"Maison D'Or," *The Kansas City Times*, November 27, 1881.

"Maritz, Young & Dusard." *Architecture and Design* 3, no. 13 (November 1939).

McCue, George. *The Building Art in St. Louis: Two Centuries.* 3rd ed. St. Louis, Missouri: St. Louis Chapter of the American Institute of Architects Foundation, 1981.

"Memorial Address Delivered at the Brookings Institution, May 19, 1933." Washington, D.C.: Brookings Institution, 1933.

Millstein, Cydney. "A Brief History of Epperson House." *Missouri Valley Chapter of the Society of Architectural Historians Newsletter* 1, No.1 (Winter 1994).

Mitchell, Giles Carroll. *There Is No Limit: Architecture and Sculpture in Kansas City.* Kansas City: Brown-White Co., 1934.

Muehl, Siegmar. "Greystone: Nineteenth-Century Gothic Revival Gem in Pevely." Missouri Historical Society *Gateway* (Summer 2005).

Myers, Robert A. "Harvey Ellis in St. Joseph, Missouri." *Missouri Valley Chapter of the Society of Architectural Historians Newsletter* 10, No. 4A (Winter 2004).

Neale, Alice E. Letter to Mrs. W. L. Scarritt, Kansas City, Missouri. June 2, 1899.

Newton, Norman T. *Design on the Land: The Development of Landscape Architecture.* Cambridge, MA: Belknap Press, 1971.

Nathaniel Leonard Papers. Western Historical Manuscripts Collection-Columbia.

Ostermeier, Eileen. "Brentmoor Park and Delmar Garden: Henry Wright in St. Louis." *Missouri Valley Chapter of the Society of Architectural Historians Newsletter* 9 no. 4 (Winter 2003).

Overby, Osmund. *William Adair Bernoudy, architect: bringing the Legacy of Frank Lloyd Wright to St. Louis.* Columbia, Missouri: University of Missouri Press, 1999.

"Pen and Sunlight Sketches of St. Louis: The Commercial Gateway to the South." Chicago: Phoenix Publishing Co., 1898.

Pickens, Bufford, and Margaretta J. Darnell. *Washington University in St. Louis: Its Design and Architecture.* St. Louis, Missouri: Washington University Gallery of Art, 1978.

Piland, Sherry. "Henry Van Brunt of the Architectural Firm of Van Brunt and Howe: The Kansas City Years." MA thesis, University of Missouri-Kansas City, 1976.

———. "Early Kansas City Architects: Adriance and John Van Brunt." *Historic Kansas City Foundation News*, April/May 1979.

"Potter House." *The Spectator*, January 6, 1883: 387–88.

Prawl, Toni M. "Historic Architects of St. Joseph, Missouri," City of St. Joseph, Missouri. June 15, 1989.

Primm, James Neal. *Lion of the Valley, St. Louis, Missouri, 1764–1980*, 3rd ed. St. Louis, Missouri: Missouri Historical Society Press, 1998.

"R. A. Long." *The Kansas City Star*, July 31, 1924; May 3, 1926; April 9, 1927; November 3, 1929; October 23,

1932; March 16, 1934; May 27, 1934; September 2, 1934.

Reps, John W. *Cities of the Mississippi: Nineteenth-Century Images of Urban Development*. Columbia: University of Missouri Press, 1994.

"Residence: Charles A. Braley." *The Kansas City Star,* July 3, 1927.

"Residences." *The Kansas City Star Magazine,* July 12, 1925; January 10, 1926.

———. *The Kansas City Star,* October 1911–May 1949.

———. *The Kansas City Times,* November 1881–May 1960.

Royster, Berenice Swinney Scarritt. "The House on the Edge of the Bluff." *Jackson County Historical Society Journal* 4 no.11 (July 1963).

Rutt, Chris L., ed. *History of Buchanan County and the City of St. Joseph and Representative Citizens, 1826–1904*. Chicago: Biographical Publishing Company, 1904.

Sandweiss, Eric. *St. Louis: The Evolution of an American Urban Landscape.* Philadelphia: Temple University, 2001.

Sandy, Wilda. *Here Lies Kansas City: A collection of our city's notables and their final resting places*. Kansas City: Bennett Schneider, 1984.

Savage, Charles C. *Architecture of the Private Streets of St. Louis: The Architects and the Houses They Designed*. Columbia: University of Missouri Press, 1987.

Schauffler, Edward R. "Seth E. Ward House." *The Kansas City Star*, May 2, 1949.

Scully, Vincent. "American Villas: Inventiveness in American Suburbs from Downing to Wright." *Architectural Review* 687 (1954).

Shoemaker, Floyd Calvin. *Missouri and Missourians*. Chicago: Lewis Publishing Co., 1943.

Simmons, David J. "The Architectural Career of Herbert C. Chivers in St. Louis." *Missouri Valley Chapter of the Society of Architectural Historians Newsletter* 10, No. 3B (Fall 2004).

Stilgoe, John R. *Borderland: Origins of the American Suburb, 1820–1939*. New Haven, CT: Yale University Press, 1988.

"St. Louis Suburban Homes, Past and Present." *St. Louis Star,* October 25, 1928.

Snyder Jr., Robert. *Ha Ha Tonka in the Ozarks*. Personal Journal. 1931.

"Sojourning in Old England Gave U. S. Epperson an Inspiration in Home-Building." *The Kansas City Star Magazine,* July 12, 1925.

Tarn, David E. "Co-operative Group Planning: A Suburban Development." *Architectural Record* 34 no. 5 (November 1913): 467–475.

"The History of Stoneyridge 'Castle.'" *The Sedalia Democrat*, May 14, 1961.

The Past in Our Presence: Historic Buildings in St. Louis County. St. Louis, Missouri: St. Louis County Department of Parks and Recreation, 1996.

"The Suburban Ideal: How It Is Improving and Beautifying the City." *St. Louis Globe-Democrat*, January 1889.

Toft, Carolyn Hewes, and Jane Molloy Porter. *Compton Heights: A History and Architectural Guide*. St. Louis, Missouri: Landmarks Association of St. Louis, 1984.

Toft, Carolyn Hewes, and Lynn Josse. *St. Louis: Landmarks and Historic Districts*. St. Louis, Missouri: Landmarks Association of St. Louis, 2002.

Tracy, Walter P. *Kansas City and Its One Hundred Foremost Men*. Kansas City, 1925.

"Vaile Mansion." *Jackson County Historical Society Journal*, April–June 1983.

Van Nada, M. L. *The Book of Missourians: The Achievements and Personnel of Notable Living Men and Women of Missouri in the Opening Decade of the Twentieth Century.* Chicago: T. J. Steele, 1906.

Van Ravenswaay Papers. Western Historical Manuscripts Collection-Columbia.

Vickery Jr., Robert L. *Anthrophysical Form: Two Families and their Neighborhood Environments*. Charlottesville, VA: University Press of Virginia, 1972.

"Walter S. Dickey." *The Kansas City Journal*, December 13, 1907.

"Walter S. Dickey Home Bought for University." *The Kansas City Journal-Post*, January 22, 1931.

"Walter S. Dickey." *Missouri Historical Review* 25 no. 3 (April 1931).

Weber, Kem. "Modern Art Movement, 1929." Lecture. University Art Museum, Santa Barbara, California.

"West Cabanne Place." *Spectator,* October 15, 1887.

Western Architect, Minneapolis, 1901–1931.

Williamson, Daniel C. "Howard Van Doren Shaw at 715 South Price Road." *Missouri Valley Chapter of the Society of Architectural Historians Newsletter* 7, No. 1 (Spring 2001).

Wilson, William H. *The City Beautiful Movement in Kansas City*. 2nd ed. Kansas City: Lowell Press, Inc., 1990.

Withey, Henry F. *Biographical Dictionary of American Architects (Deceased)*. Los Angeles, 1976.

Wolferman, Kristie C. *The Nelson-Atkins Museum of Art: Culture Comes to Kansas City*. Columbia, Missouri: University of Missouri Press, 1993.

Worley, William S. *J. C. Nichols and the Shaping of Kansas City: Innovation in Planned Residential Communities*. Columbia, Missouri: University of Missouri Press, 1990.

Wright, Henry. "The Autobiography of Another Idea." *Western Architect* 39, No. 9 (September 1930).

Writers' Program of the Works Projects Administration in the State of Missouri. *Missouri: the WPA Guide to the "Show Me" State.* 2nd ed. St. Louis, Missouri: Missouri Historical Society Press, 1998.

OBITUARIES

"Bernard Corrigan Dead." *The Kansas City Times*, January 7, 1914.

"Beverly T. Nelson, Former Architect Here, Dies in London." *St. Louis Globe-Democrat*, March 30, 1954.

"Charles S. Keith." *The Kansas City Times.* October 10, 1945.

"Colonel Daniel B. Dyer." *The Kansas City Times*, December 23, 1912.

"E. W. Tanner, Plaza Architect, Dies." *The Kansas City Star*, April 26, 1974.

"Frederick E. Hill." *Technology Review*, January 1930.

"H. M. Vaile." *The Kansas City Star*, June 5, 1894.

"James F. Halpin." *The Kansas City Star*, February 11, 1943.

"R. A. Long." *The Kansas City Times*, March 16, 1934; March 22, 1934; May 14, 1934.

NATIONAL REGISTER OF HISTORIC PLACES NOMINATIONS

Bass, V. J. "Parkview Historic District," St. Louis, Missouri, April 9, 1985.

Baxter, Karen Bode. "Pasadena Hills Historic District," St. Louis County, Missouri, September 10, 2004.

Becker, Linda, and Edward J. Miszczuk. "Quality Hill, Kansas City, Missouri," April 20, 1977.

Bradley, Lenore K. "R. A. Long Residence," Kansas City, Missouri, May 22, 1980.

Hamilton, Esley. "Brentmoor Park, Brentmoor and Forest Ridge," St. Louis County, Missouri, December 1980.

———. "Theodore Link Historic District," St. Louis County, Missouri, January 1980.

———. "Carrswold Historic District," St. Louis County, Missouri, September 1981.

———. "Alswel," St. Louis County, Missouri, March 31, 1988.

———. "Wydown-Forsyth District," St. Louis County, Missouri, March 1988.

———. "Vouziers, Joseph Desloge Estate," Lewis and Clark Township, Missouri, June 1988.

Holmes, M. Patricia. "Greystone," Pevely, Missouri, October 18, 1974.

Karel, Victoria and Edward J. Miszczuk. "Jansen Place," Kansas City, Missouri. September 1, 1975.

Michalak, Joan. "Hyde Park Historic District," Kansas City, Missouri. November 21, 1980.

Millstein, Cydney. "Charles S. Keith Residence," Kansas City, Missouri, August 26, 1999.

Miszczuk, Edward J. "Walter E. Bixby Residence," Kansas City, Missouri, June 25, 1977.

Piland, Sherry. "August Meyer House," Kansas City, Missouri, June 30, 1980.

Piland, Sherry, and Elaine Ryder. "Residential Structures in Kansas City by Mary Rockwell Hook," Kansas City, Missouri, June 28, 1983.

Porter, Jane. "West Cabanne Place Historic District," St. Louis, Missouri, July 3, 1980.

Restoration Design Class, University of Missouri–Columbia. "Ravenswood," Bunceton, Missouri, July 30, 1973.

Ryder, Elaine. "Bernard Corrigan Residence," Kansas City, Missouri, April 15, 1975.

———. "Seth Ward Homestead," Kansas City, Missouri, March 15, 1977.

Schwenk, Sally F. "George E. Nicholson House, Kansas City, Missouri, May 8, 2005.

Soren, Noelle. "Chatol, E. Gano Chance Guest House," Centralia, Missouri, 1979

Uguccioni, Ellen J., and Sherry Piland. "Longview Farm," Lee's Summit, Missouri, June 28, 1985.

WEB SITES

"Edward Gardner Lewis and University City." University City Public Library. *http://www.history.ucpl.lib.mo.us*

"Designing the Moderne: Kem Weber's Bixby House." Exhibition at the University Art Museum, University of California, Santa Barbara. November 29, 2000–February 11, 2001. *http://www.uam.ucsb.edu/Pages/weber.html*

"Greystone, Pevely Vicinity, Jefferson County, Missouri: HABS No. Missouri-1133." Historic American Buildings Survey/Historic American Engineering Record. Library of Congress. *http://www.loc.gov/index.html*

"Longview Farm, Longview Road, Lee's Summit, Jackson County, Missouri: HABS No. Missouri-1222." Historic American Buildings Survey/Historic American Engineering Record. Library of Congress. *http://www.loc.gov/index.html*

"Selma Hall, Crystal City Vicinity, Jefferson County, Missouri: HABS No. Missouri-1493."

Index

Photography Credits

Alswel National Register Nomination Form, State Historic Preservation Office Historic Nomination Files, Missouri State Archives, 152, 153, 154

Alvin Hansen File, St. Louis County Houses, State Historical Society of Missouri, 236, 237, 238, 239, 240

The American Architect, Linda Hall Library, Kansas City, MO, 60

The Architectural Record, 126, 128, 129 bottom, 130

Barry Cervantes Collection, 164, 165

Bothwell Lodge State Historic Site, Division of State Parks, Missouri Department of Natural Resources, 61, 62, 63, 64,

Brentmoor Park, Brentmoor and Forest Ridge National Register Nomination Form, State Historic Preservation Office Historic Nomination Files, Missouri State Archives, 129 top

Bryan, *Missouri's Contribution to American Architecture*, 163, 195, 200, 250 bottom right, 252 bottom left and center right,

The Brickbuilder, 106, 117 top and bottom, 120 top and center

Charles Van Ravenswaay Papers, Western Historical Manuscripts-Columbia, 38

Chatol National Register Nomination Form, State Historic Preservation Office Historic Nomination Files, Missouri State Archives, 224, 225, 226, 227, 228, 229

"The City that 'Jack' Built," Missouri Digital Heritage Initiative, 251 center right, 252 center left

Country Life (in America), 215, 216, 217

Cydney Millstein Collection, Kansas City, MO, 22, 139, 142

Dr. Kenneth J. LaBudde Department of Special Collections, Miller-Nichols Library, University of Missouri-Kansas City, 185, 186, 187

Dwight Weaver Collection, 81 top and bottom

Fohn, Len, photographer, 67, 68 top and bottom, 210, 211, 212 top

Franke, Billy, photographer, 255 top right

Ha Ha Tonka Collection, Native Sons Archives, Western Historical Manuscript Collection-Kansas City, 79, 80 top and bottom, 82

Hedrick-Blessing Collection, Chicago History Museum, 241, 242, 243, 244 top and bottom, 245, 246, 247

Henry Clay Pierce Scrapbook, Missouri Historical Society, 46, 47, 48, 49

Historic American Building Survey, United States Department of the Interior, 14, 28, 29, 30 top and bottom, 31, 32, 39, 40, 41 top and bottom, 42, 44, 45 top

The Inland Architect and News Record, Washington University Art and Architecture Library, St. Louis, 50, 57

Jackson County Probate, Independence, MO, 43

Jeanette Juden Collection, 253 bottom right

John and Robin Porta Collection 162

Kansas City Architect and Builder, Missouri Valley Special Collections, Kansas City Public Library, Kansas City, MO, 253 upper left

The Kansas City Times, Missouri Valley Special Collections, Kansas City Public Library, Kansas City, MO, 86

The Kessler Collection, Missouri Historical Society, St. Louis, 58, 59 top and bottom

Landmarks Commission, City of Kansas City, Missouri, 34 top, 35, 36

Lewis Photo Collection, The Archives of the University City Public Library, 75, 76 top and bottom, 77 top and bottom, 78, 254 top left, 254 top right

Lindeberg, *Domestic Architecture of H. T. Lindeberg*, 196, 197, 198 top and bottom, 199

Maritz and Young Collection, Washington University Archives, 201, 203 top and bottom

Maritz and Young, Inc., a monograph of their work, 202, 256 top left, 256 bottom left and top right

Mesco Pictures, A New Triumph for Missouri, The Kansas City Star, 84, 85 top and bottom

Millstein, Cydney, photographer, 255 center right

Missouri Historical Society, 16, 17

Missouri State Archives, Jefferson City, MO, 136

Missouri Valley Special Collections, Kansas City Public Library, Kansas City, MO, 20, 33, 34 bottom, 51 top and bottom, 52, 53 top and bottom, 54, 55, 56, 65, 66, 101, 132, 137, 150 top, 190, 191, 250 upper left, upper right, lower left, 251 upper left, center left, lower left, lower right, 252 lower right, 253 lower left, 255 lower left

Mrs. O. B. Hirsch Collection, 92, 93, 94, 95, 96

Pettus, Robert, photographer, 161

Sherry Piland Collection, Springfield, MO, 212 bottom, 213

Rick Rose, Rockcliffe Mansion Collection, 70, 71 top and bottom, 72, 73, 74,

River Bluff Architects, St. Joseph, MO, 179, 180, 181, 183 top and bottom, 251 upper right

Robert Brookings Personal Papers, Washington University Archives, 116, 118 top and bottom, 119, 120 top

The Royster Family Collection, Kansas City, MO, 69

Shelley Donaho Collection, 87, 88, 89 top and bottom, 90, 91

Southern Architect, Missouri Valley Special Collections, Kansas City Public Library, Kansas City, MO, 83

St. Louis County Department of Parks and Recreation, 194, 214, 223 top and bottom, 249, 254 bottom left, 254 bottom right, 255 top left and top right,

State Historic Preservation Office, Division of State Parks, Missouri Department of Natural Resources, Jefferson City, MO, 252 upper left, upper right, 253 upper right, center left, center right, 256 lower right

The Past in our Presence: Historic Buildings in St. Louis County, 256 center left, 256 center right

Trefts Collection, State Historical Society of Missouri, 218, 219, 220, 221, 222,

Union Station/Kansas City Museum, Kansas City, MO, 110, 111 top and bottom, 112, 113 top and bottom, 114 top and bottom, 156 bottom

University of Missouri-Kansas City; Campus Facilities Management, 122, 125, 188

Western Architect, 97, 98, 99, 100, 105, 107, 108, 127,

Western Historical Manuscript Collection-Kansas City, Alfred Edward Barnes, Jr. Collection (KC0004), 109, 144, 145, 146 top and bottom 147, 148, 149, 150 bottom, 151, 155, 156 top, 157, 158 top and bottom, 159 top, 160, 166, 167, 168, 169, 174, 175 top and bottom, 176, 177 top and bottom, 178

Hare and Hare Collection (KC0206), 159 bottom, 234

J. C. Nichols' Scrapbook (KC0054), 21, 24, 102 bottom, 140, 141 top and bottom, 184

J. C. Nichols' Company Records (KC106), 131, 134, 135, 235, 254 center left and center right, 255 center left

Missouri Valley Chapter-Society of Architectural Historians Architectural Collection (KC0006): 138 top and bottom

Ralph E. Kiene, Jr., Architectural Records (0777kc), 115

University of Missouri-Kansas City University Archives (KC1-151-000), 121, 123, 124

Wight and Wight Architectural Records (KC0445), 173 top and bottom, 193

Wilborn & Associates, Kansas City, MO, 204, 205, 206, 207 top and bottom, 208, 230, 231 top and bottom, 232, 233 top and bottom

Wight and Wight, Architects, Spencer Art Reference Library, Nelson-Atkins Museum of Art, 102 (top), 103 top and bottom, 104, 170, 171 top and bottom, 172, 189, 192

Wyeth Family Collection, St. Joseph, MO, 182